Consumerism, Waste, and Re-Use
in Twentieth-Century Fiction

A Brief Chronology of Chinese History

	夏 Xia Dynasty		About 2100 – 1600 BC
	商 Shang Dynasty		About 1600 – 1100 BC
周 Zhou Dynasty	西周 Western Zhou Dynasty		About 1100 – 771 BC
	東周 Eastern Zhou Dynasty		770 – 256 BC
	春秋 Spring and Autumn Period		770 – 476 BC
	戰國 Warring States		475 – 221 BC
	秦 Qin Dynasty		221 – 207 BC
漢 Han Dynasty	西漢 Western Han		206 BC – AD 24
	東漢 Eastern Han		25 – 220
三國 Three Kingdoms	魏 Wei		220 – 265
	蜀漢 Shu Han		221 – 263
	吳 Wu		222 – 280
	西晉 Western Jin Dynasty		265 – 316
	東晉 Eastern Jin Dynasty		317 – 420
南北朝 Northern and Southern Dynasties	南朝 Southern Dynasties	宋 Song	420 – 479
		齊 Qi	479 – 502
		梁 Liang	502 – 557
		陳 Chen	557 – 589
	北朝 Northern Dynasties	北魏 Northern Wei	386 – 534
		東魏 Eastern Wei	534 – 550
		北齊 Northern Qi	550 – 577
		西魏 Western Wei	535 – 556
		北周 Northern Zhou	557 – 581
	隋 Sui Dynasty		581 – 618
	唐 Tang Dynasty		618 – 907
五代 Five Dynasties	後梁 Later Liang		907 – 923
	後唐 Later Tang		923 – 936
	後晉 Later Jin		936 – 946
	後漢 Later Han		947 – 950
	後周 Later Zhou		951 – 960
宋 Song Dynasty	北宋 Northern Song Dynasty		960 – 1127
	南宋 Southern Song Dynasty		1127 – 1279
	遼 Liao Dynasty		916 – 1125
	金 Jin Dynasty		1115 – 1234
	元 Yuan Dynasty		1271 – 1368
	明 Ming Dynasty		1368 – 1644
	清 Qing Dynasty		1644 – 1911
	中華民國 Republic of China		1912 – 1949
	中華人民共和國 People's Republic of China		1949 –

Rachele Dini

Consumerism, Waste, and Re-Use in Twentieth-Century Fiction

Legacies of the Avant-Garde

Rachele Dini
Wandsworth, United Kingdom

ISBN 978-1-137-59061-9   ISBN 978-1-137-58165-5   (eBook)
DOI 10.1057/978-1-137-58165-5

Library of Congress Control Number: 2016955717

Cover image: "Petits Dechets Bourgeois" by Arman © Joel Saget / AFP/Staff

Printed on acid-free paper

This Palgrave Macmillan imprint is published by Springer Nature
The registered company is Nature America Inc.
The registered company address is: 1 New York Plaza, New York, NY 10004, U.S.A.

*To Nonno Sergio, who brought things home off the street
and to Nonna Nina, who made him throw them away*

ACKNOWLEDGEMENTS

This book owes its genesis to many people. My most sincere thanks go to Michael Sayeau for taking me on as a student in the English Department at UCL and to Matthew Beaumont for his advice and support in the last six months of my PhD project, and as I broached writing this manuscript. Thanks as well go to Max Saunders, Mark Turner, Jo McDonagh, and Lara Feigel in the English Department at King's College London, for their guidance and inspiration during my first foray back into academia; to Ardis Butterfield for her encouragement in the first year of my PhD; and to John Mullan and Neil Rennie for their guidance as the project drew to a close. And, of course, I am grateful to Morag Shiach and Esther Leslie for a stimulating doctoral examination process that greatly improved the quality of my final project.

Of the many wonderful people I met as a student at King's College London and UCL, both in the departments and beyond, I owe special thanks to Luke Davies, Heather Scott, Karina Jakubowicz, Adam Whybray, Alex Pavey, and Chisomo Kalinga for their friendship, unwavering support, and eagle-eyed copy-editing skills. Thanks as well to all those who suggested titles of novels and short stories relevant to the project's topic. Of these, Michael Sayeau, Matthew Beaumont, Gregory Dart, Mark Ford, Alan Marshall, David Dalyrmple-Pryde, Benjamin George, Theo Savvas, Arianna Dini, Alexandra Parsons, and Caroline Calder deserve special mention. A very, very special thanks goes to Will Viney for reading my first draft, and for the inspiration provided by his own writings on waste, and to Rick McGrath and David Pringle for their input on Ballard.

I am equally thankful to those who enabled me financially to pursue this project. Among those who gave me paid employment special thanks go to Michelle Strutton at Mintel, Mike Dash and John M. Gómez at Macat, Tom Mott at the Institute of Practitioners in Advertising, and Julie Andreshak-Berman, Zehra Sonkaynar, and Hannah Feakes at the Foundation for International Education. I have likewise benefited from UCL's Faculty Institute of Graduate Studies scholarship, which allowed me to take time off from paid work to focus on my research. And of course, this project would not have been possible without the team at Palgrave, particularly Peter Cary, Ryan Jenkins, and Paloma Yannakakis.

Finally, I owe thanks to all the friends, relatives, colleagues, and in some instances strangers who in the last four years have expressed interest in the project and offered their own perspective on it. Thank you in particular to Arianna Dini, Giovanni Dini, Peter Poland, Zia Pita, Julia George, Theodora Tsimpouki, Sheila George, Alessandra Dini, Lauren Hewitt, Damian Lord, Jenny Naish, Nicola Chelotti, Julia Fritz, and finally little Phoebe Fritz and Oscar George, whose love of garbage trucks makes me very proud indeed. But above all, my deepest gratitude goes to Chiara Briganti, whose unwavering faith in my abilities and whose willingness to read drafts of my work are unparalleled; to Paolo Dini, for letting me shift any conversation back to my work; and, of course, to Benjamin George, who married me despite, and perhaps even because of, my waste obsession. I look forward to a lifetime together of charity-shop hunting and dumpster-diving.

CONTENTS

LIST OF FIGURES

CHAPTER 1

Introduction

"There is nothing like a good rummage through someone's rubbish before nightfall," asserts the anonymous narrator of Ellis Sharp's novella, *The Dump* (1998).[1] Sharp's narrator claims to have woken up one morning in an immense landfill on the fringes of his native Walthamstow, North London, joining a "rickety population" of several thousand scavengers (*TD*, 15). The Dump, as the landfill is called, is a vast and inexplicable "place of the rejected, the worthless" (*TD*, 19), whose incoherence is reflected in the narrator's own disjointed speech. But in among the asynchronous babble there appear brief moments of insight during which the narrator cogently distils The Dump's broader meaning: this is a place for "all that is superfluous. [...] Built-in obsolescence, the very marrow of every gleaming product" (*TD*, 51). Describing himself as "the mundane distilled into human form," Sharp's narrator recognises that these surroundings agree with him: "untroubled (bliss!) by capitalism or troublesome sex," he can instead learn from the "bits and pieces" in which he is immersed (*TD*, 29; 58; 57). Indeed,

> The only other place where you learn about the truth of things is down in the city sewers, in among the shit and the gin bottles and the thousand-and-one things that guilty shamefaced folk flush down the loo when no one else is about. (*TD*, 57)

© The Editor(s) (if applicable) and The Author(s) 2016
R. Dini, *Consumerism, Waste, and Re-Use in Twentieth-Century Fiction*,
DOI 10.1057/978-1-137-58165-5_1

1

The Dump offers a unique perspective on the world: "You get a real sense of life's rich variety and mystery. [...] In fact you probably end up knowing more about life [in the real world] than [its inhabitants] do themselves" (*TD*, 57). Further, in its inchoate, disordered state, The Dump raises questions about the logic underpinning the workings of mainstream society: "one of the intriguing and interesting things about life on The Dump is the strange things that get thrown away for no apparent reason, not to mention the strange juxtaposition of things which don't belong together at all" (*TD*, 57). Our discards not only reveal the irrationality underlying our attributions of value: re-contextualised in The Dump, they take on new and absurd meanings.

Sharp's narrator is not alone in his fascination with what he calls "the tease of enigmatic scraps" (*TD*, 60). Rather, his ideas are but an extension of a centuries-long enquiry into the narrative and philosophical value of our domestic and industrial discards, and, relatedly, into the value of human beings themselves. Since the Industrial Revolution and the rise of commodity culture, writers have condemned the things we throw out for their hygienic, moral, and ecological toll, and they have seen in the disposal of such items a metaphor for capitalism's marginalisation of the poor or unemployed. At the same time, others have acknowledged the aesthetic, ontological, and even historiographical value of our discards. Like Sharp's narrator, they have identified in the world of waste the means to echo and parody mainstream society and throw its peculiarities into relief.

This book examines the representation of manufactured waste and remaindered humans—humans cast out of the job market, or who actively resist being put to use—in literary critiques of capitalism by twentieth-century writers associated with the historical avant-garde and their descendants. From an initial exploration of waste and re-use in three Surrealist texts—Giorgio de Chirico's *Hebdomeros* (1929), André Breton's *Nadja* (1928), and Mina Loy's unfinished novel *Insel* (1930–1961)—I trace the conceptualisation of waste in the prose Samuel Beckett published between 1950 and 1964, Donald Barthelme's *Snow White* (1967), J.G. Ballard's 1970s urban disaster trilogy (*High-Rise, Concrete Island, Crash*), William Gaddis' *J.R.* (1975), and a selection of novels by Don DeLillo written between 1971 and 1997, before considering waste's role in three post-millennial novels. All of the texts discussed stand out in their use of waste to interrogate capitalist ascriptions of value and test the novel form in ways that echo and extend the practices of the historical avant-garde. In examining the relationship between waste, capitalism, and literary experimentation, this book looks to demonstrate the extent to which the legacy of the historical avant-garde is bound up with an enduring faith in the radical potential of waste—its potential, in other words, to represent active resistance to commodification.

The Commodity

This project takes waste to be intimately tied with commodities. But what *is* a commodity? From a strictly historical materialist perspective, a commodity is an object characterised by its use-value and reducible to being considered a "congelation of homogeneous human labour."[2] In the last few decades, however, new ways of thinking about the value of objects have complicated Marx's definition. This development is partly attributable to a broader shift in the humanities and social sciences from a language- and linguistics-based theoretic approach to literature and culture, to one grounded in materiality—often referred to as the "thingly turn."[3] The emergence of "Thing Theory" and the fields of material culture studies, New Materialism, and discard studies have opened the entire lifespan of objects to scrutiny. Scholars in these fields recognise commodities to be more than the end result of a manufacturing process and to exceed strict dichotomies such as useful/useless. In their foundational essays on the subject, Arjun Appadurai and Igor Kopytoff argue that Marx's analysis of commodity fetishism misses the non-economic dimension of commodities—that is, the cultural value they are ascribed *after* they are produced and which fundamentally shapes their inclusion or preclusion from exchange.[4] Appadurai calls for a modification of two of Marx's assumptions: that "commodities either exist or do not exist, and [that] they are *products* of a particular sort" (Appadurai, 9). Instead, he posits that commodities are:

> things in a certain situation, a situation that can characterize many different kinds of thing, at different points in their social lives. This means looking at the commodity potential of all things rather than searching fruitlessly for the magic distinction between commodities and other sorts of things. It also means breaking significantly with the production-dominated Marxian view of the commodity and focusing on its *total* trajectory from production, through exchange/distribution, to consumption. (Appadurai, 13)

Appadurai proposes we abstain from defining objects as commodities or not-commodities and consider them instead as moving *in* and *out* of the commodity stage, as their marketability, utility, and status as "innovative" or *démodé* changes (Appadurai, 13). Likewise, Kopytoff argues that commodification itself "is best looked at as a process of becoming than as an all-or-none state of being" (Kopytoff, 73). More recently, New Materialists such as Jane Bennett, Maurizia Boscagli, and Susan Signe Morrison have sought to attend to what Bennett terms matter's "vitality" and what Boscagli terms its "unruly" potential—to recognise the "plasticity possible at the moment of subject-object interaction."[5] Matter exists in the culture of commodities, but its status as a commodity should not be presupposed.

These different articulations call attention to the malleability of the commodity as a concept and in turn suggest the fruitfulness of conceptualising waste, too, as a phase in an object's life. Expanding Marx's original definition allows us to consider not only the processes by which products appear on the shelf but also their complex trajectories from shop to home, from home to garbage bin or landfill, and from garbage bin/landfill to someone else's home. Relatedly, we might consider how such ascriptions of value extend to human beings (of which I will have more to say in the sections below).

WASTE AND RECUPERATION

Based on the ideas just discussed, I propose that in the texts examined in this study, commodities and waste exist on a Möbius strip; that they are shown to be dialectically inseparable from one another; and that under capitalist exchange relations, each is revealed capable of being alchemised into the other. This definition—to which I return later in this section—departs from the vast majority of waste scholarship, which in the last few decades has largely taken its cue from Mary Douglas' structural analysis of dirt and cleanliness in tribal law, *Purity and Danger*.[6] Douglas' work conceptualises dirt, after William James, as "matter out of place," arguing that social groups use the concept of dirt to maintain social order.[7] The dichotomies of purity/impurity, cleanliness/dirt, and use/useless are a means of upholding hierarchical structures and re-instating moral values. They also reflect spatially contingent social boundaries, such as body/world, self/other, and private/public. Dirt's presence thus suggests both uncleanliness and a challenge to the system that has accorded things their specific place and has mandated that things *be* clean. Ambiguity and otherness amplify dirt's fear-inducing qualities: as well as matter out of place, dirt is matter *without* place, matter that crosses boundaries indiscriminately, hovering without agreeing to "settle."

Problems arise, however, when we attempt to apply Douglas' analysis of dirt to the category of waste. Yes, there are affinities between dirt's profane associations among primitive cultures and our repulsion at the sight or smell of certain typologies of waste such as bodily emissions. There are likewise affinities in dirt and waste's respective disruption of our sense of aesthetic order and the efforts we make to circumscribe them within particular boundaries (the garden, the trash bin). But beyond this the analogy fails, and applying it meaningfully becomes difficult. For waste's existence in the world, contrary to dirt, is distinguished by narrative, origin, and time. Douglas ascribes dirt's discomfiting qualities to its dislocation: not the process by which it became dislocated, but the very fact of its being dislocated. By contrast, I argue that the strong feelings aroused by organic waste matter (faeces, urine, semen) and inorganic waste matter (the consumer and industrial remnants that form the topic of this book) are ascribable to the fact that they are material remnants of an event. Put differently, waste is the product of a process: it signals the aftermath of an occurrence, be that occurrence a dog defecating, the explosion at a nuclear plant, or the end of a fashion trend. This temporal dimension endows waste with narrative qualities: with its very presence a waste object signals that something has come before. Where dirt is matter out of place, waste is matter out of time.

An earlier theorist, Michael Thompson, can help shed light on this temporal and narrative dimension of waste.[8] For Thompson, all objects can be classified as "transient," "durable," or "rubbish," depending on whether they depreciate in value over time (Thompson, 7). Transient objects "decrease in value over time and have finite life-spans"; durable objects such as antique furniture "increase in value over time and have (ideally) infinite life-spans"; and, finally, objects "of zero and unchanging value [that] do not fall into either of these two categories" are defined as "rubbish" (Thompson, 7). Crucially, all three categories are understood to be fluid—an object might start out as "transient," fall into disuse and lose all value (becoming "rubbish"), and then be re-discovered at a later moment and given new meaning, thus moving into the category of "durable" (Thompson, 9). The shift from "rubbish" to "durable" entails an attribution of value: for the object to be no longer considered waste, it must be of use. Like Appadurai and Kopytoff's elaborations of Marx's definition of the commodity, Thompson's conceptualisation hinges on the recognition that new meanings can be assigned to old things. The sawdust off a carpenter's table is waste insofar as it evidences a process and has no use;

but the moment it is sold for re-use, it becomes a commodity once more. Where Douglas would see waste as illegitimate matter, a temporal reading sees waste as matter that has served its purpose—for the time being.

This study thus defines waste as a stage in the lifecycle of a thing, which is also to say, a stage that can pass. In contrast to Thompson's assertion that certain objects remain impervious to decay or obsolescence, I argue that *any* object has the potential to become waste. Following Appadurai, I read the depictions of waste objects in the texts under review as snapshots of one phase of these objects' lives. The full story of these lives encompasses far more than their sojourn in a tip or landfill—which each of the novels discussed makes clear. I extend this definition to consider how the waste-potential of commodities under capitalism relates to the waste-potential of people.

The implications of the waste-potential of commodities—and the commodity-potential of waste—become apparent when we consider them as vital components of capitalism itself. At heart, capitalism is driven by two very different visions of waste. Manufacturers and retailers are at pains to minimise the waste involved in production and distribution, and to put by-products and expired merchandise to use (a logic that extends to minimising the labour-time necessary to produce the goods, and, in turn, minimising the number of workers to employ in that process[9]). Ford conceived the assembly line to streamline production and dispense with superfluous tasks. In the century since, waste reduction has remained at the heart of manufacturing, as perhaps exemplified by Japanese automobile manufacturer Toyota's reliance on "Lean Six Sigma," a methodology that seeks to eliminate waste ("muda"), which it divides into eight different categories: Time, Inventory, Motion, Waiting, Over-Production, Over-Processing, Defects, and Skills ("TIMWOODS").[10] And yet the hope of manufacturers like Toyota is that their customers will use their products *inefficiently*, and dispose of them soon, so that they might purchase a newer version of them. Capitalism is thus contingent upon extreme efficiency on the side of production and extreme inefficiency on the side of consumption. It is predicated on the finite lifespan of objects and the creation of new needs and desires (what the industry refers to as planned, or built-in, obsolescence, which, as Harry Braverman notes, is an "attempt to gear consumer needs to the needs of production instead of the other way around").[11] The accumulation of detritus is inherent to modernisation, which "produces obsolescence as part of its continual demand for the new."[12]

Built-in obsolescence in the form of product upgrades, new fashions, and expired warranties ensures the perpetual becoming-waste of commodities, which in turn ensures the purchase of replacements.

David Foster Wallace conveys this beautifully in his encyclopaedic novel, *Infinite Jest* (1996), which follows the search for a film cartridge (the titular *Infinite Jest*) so entertaining it renders its viewers uninterested in anything beyond viewing it. Eventually, these catatonic viewers die of malnutrition or dehydration. The myth surrounding the "purportedly lethal" film is

> nothing more than a classic illustration of the antinomically schizoid function of the post-industrial capitalist mechanism, whose logic presented commodity as the escape-from-anxieties-of-mortality-which-escape-is-itself-psychologically-fatal, as detailed in perspicuous detail in M. Gilles Deleuze's posthumous Incest and the Life of Death in Capitalist Entertainment. (*IJ*, 792)

The analysis is of course ironic, and the text ascribed to Deleuze—who was in fact still alive when Wallace published the novel—is fictitious.[13] But the character's point is eerily accurate: the perfect commodity is not that which renders all other commodities unnecessary, sustaining its owner until their death. Such a commodity would have severe "implications for any industrialized, market-driven, high-discretionary-spending society," taking away individuals' motivation to earn money to purchase other products (*IJ*, 473). The perfect commodity provides *finite* jest, without taking away its owner's capacity to do work, before quietly losing its lustre and allowing itself to be thrown away.

The works I discuss question this system, examining the story behind the discard, the process by which it lost its value, and its geophysical trajectory from rubbish bin to landfill (or, in some cases, the story of a vagrant's travels from one dump or landfill to another, and the many ways a person might resist being put to use). They also assume, in different ways, that discards can not only shed light on capitalism but also serve as a bizarre equaliser, shedding light on humankind as a whole. All humans excrete, regardless of class, race, or creed, and all humans produce rubbish. Once in the landfill, our leavings mingle with everyone else's. Status symbols utilised to distinguish their owners from other people are reduced to putrid, foul-smelling relics. Marguerite Duras articulates this view in "Madame Dodin" (1954), in which the narrator recounts the everyday tribulations of her building's concierge—the titular Madame—and her deep resentment of her tenants' rubbish, which she must dispose of daily.[14] As the story unspools, Madame Dodin's incessant complaints about the dustbins alert the reader to both the ubiquity of waste and its opacity. On the one hand, this is a story about class differences: Madame Dodin's resentment stems from the fact that her job "exists only because of the refuse people leave in their wake without even seeming to notice, like dogs" (*MD*, 100). The livelihood of an entire class of people is contingent upon the inability—or refusal—of the bourgeois to clean up their own mess. But it is also about the peculiar sense of superiority that comes from disposing of others' leavings—from seeing that even the wealthy excrete, and that their excretions look no different from those of their servants. Hence the awe that inflects the narrator's realisation that the sound of "the grinding of the rubbish truck" as it moves, "each morning, each and every day of the year" through the city is as ingrained and indispensable as "one's own heartbeat" (*MD*, 103). The dump truck sings the "great chant of human rumination," she realises:

> It sings the song—like it or not—of the irrefutable organic community of man in our age. Ah! Before the dumptruck there are no more strangers or enemies. All are equal before the enormous, magnificent mouth of the dumptruck, all stomach in the face of eternity. For to the fine fat throat of the dumptruck all differences cease to exist. And in the last analysis, no tenant of [Building] #4 who wishes me such ill, even as our dust, one day, will be mixed together in the earth, so does the bone of my Sunday joint mix unceremoniously with yours in the original belly, the final belly of Mother Dumptruck. (*MD*, 104)

A bittersweet eulogy to the entity that enables the city's inhabitants to go on consuming at will and that sees those inhabitants as ultimately undifferentiated, the passage endows the dump truck with a god-like, or perhaps more accurately, Madonna-like, status. A conduit of modernity's excretions, the thing that allows the city to keep on being what it is, the dumptruck levels difference, making a community of our leavings.

Duras' story bears another important affinity to the texts discussed in this study: it attends less to the physical form of specific waste matter than to the story waste tells. While physical form in these works is important (insofar as it is part of an object's story), the texts are ultimately less concerned with the material composition of waste objects than with their role in the composition of narrative, and with the role that narrative has in "composing" them. Thus, narrative, and the meaning attached to the object, ultimately overpowers form. This is especially the case in instances *disposal of specificity*

where the waste object discussed is a metaphor or analogy for some-thing else, such as the perceived worthlessness of a person or an idea. Thus, although I embrace the New Materialist recognition of matter's "thingly power" (exemplified by Bruno Latour's conceptualisation of "actants" and "quasi-objects"), my focus throughout this book is on the relationship between disposed objects and the human stories that resulted in their disposal.[15] My contention is that through commodification, objects inevitably become signs that refer back to the people who made, used, cast them away, or re-purposed them. The material qualities that render a commodity desir-able—appearance, texture, scent—are inextricable from the social value we ascribe them, and to which we have fixed a price. Neither truly "alive" nor "dead," waste exists somewhere in between these two states, reminding us of what Julian Stallabrass terms the "broken utopian promise of the commod-ity" but also seeking, at every turn, to be made a commodity once more.[16]

The different forms that this return from the garbage grave can take—and what happens when it does not lead all the way back into the market-place, but stalls somewhere along the way—is one of the central focuses of this study. Thus, by recuperation I not only intend actual re-use (such as the inclusion of waste objects in collage) or re-purposing (the mending of a broken object). Rather, I extend the idea to encompass any recognition or attribution of meaning, based on the premise that to investigate the story of an object's manufacture, its owner, or the culture from which it emerged is to recognise its historiographical and ontological value (not to mention its potential ongoing use-value). To ponder why an object ended up in the trash or to imagine the life of its owner is to re-introduce it into a signify-ing system: in this case, a narrative system as opposed to a commercial one. The novels under review show us that recuperation is not confined to recy-cling plastic, or to turning bicycle handlebars into bulls' heads (as Picasso famously did, to make his 1942 sculpture, "Bull's Head"). Recuperation is at work in any instance in which an item is recognised as having other values beyond that which it has purportedly lost. It is to identify the histori-cal significance of an old cereal box or the psychological significance of a basement full of old wigs. And, also, it is to recognise that the lifespan of objects—which is to say, their capacity to serve their original function—is far longer than the consumer economy would have us believe.

In their very different ways, the novels under review are but a reflec-tion of a dialogue that has been taking place over the last century in homes, shops, factories, offices, museums, libraries, and junkyards across the developed world. They invite us to think about what it means to be deemed irrelevant, démodé, or beyond repair. They remind us that there are many ways to not want, many reasons to discard, and many ways to recuperate—and they encourage us to dwell on those instances when the imperative is not heroic, and when the salvaging act itself is pathological, or spectacularly unethical (as perhaps exemplified by Marx's description in *Capital* of nineteenth-century bakers' practice of adulterating bread with ashes and chalk to cut production costs (*C*, 238), or the Nazis' salvaging practices, which Esther Leslie notes borrowed "in gruesomely parodic form some of the tactics of the avant-garde that was its nemesis"[17]).

This emphasis on the material in turn leads us to recognise the capacity of texts themselves to be taken apart and repurposed—as articulated in Leopold Bloom's recognition, in *Ulysses* (1922), of the life an old newspaper might lead after it has been read: "what becomes of it after? O, wrap up meat, parcels: various uses, thousand and one things."[18] The authors we discuss draw attention to the fact that their texts are physical entities composed of matter that might be used for kindling or wrapping paper. In attending to the waste-potential of things and the potential to recuperate waste, these texts also attend to their own transience—they self-consciously gesture to both the likelihood they will be pulped and the possibility that those copies that endure might be re-imbued, many years hence, with new meanings.

HUMAN WASTE

As this is a study of the literary depiction of waste deployed in the critique of capitalist ideology, the focus throughout is on manufactured, visible waste—waste that is very obviously caught up in, and part of, the processes of production and consumption, and that the authors in question seek to put to radical use, either by observing and describing it, or by turning it into something else. However, it is also true that a number of the texts discussed make frequent reference to bodily emissions, and that in some cases manufactured and bodily waste serve as metaphors to underwrite the perceived worthlessness or marginalisation of a person rather than an object. In Sharp's novella, the narrator invites us to observe those inhabitants of The Dump who wake up every day at quarter past six "as if still in salaried employment." He tells us that their morning routine is indicative of a "biological clock throbbing in tune to capitalism's awesome requirements" despite there being no office to go to and no work to do (*TD*, 9). Like the food wrappers, pools of urine and dismantled furniture items through which the narrator guides us, The Dump's human inhabitants have no purpose, and that lack of purpose becomes their defining feature.

This conceptualisation of landfill scavengers as entities cast out of society due to their perceived lack of use-value is closely connected to a broader exploration of value manifest in all of the texts discussed. To this end, I adopt Zygmunt Bauman's term "human waste," which Bauman uses to discuss the marginalisation of those deemed supernumerary, and which he argues is an "inevitable outcome of modernisation, and an inseparable accompaniment of modernity."[19] Bauman argues that

> To be declared redundant means to have been disposed of *because of being disposable*—just like the empty and non-refundable plastic bottle or once-used syringe, an unattractive commodity with no buyers, or a substandard or stained product without use thrown off the assembly line by the quality inspectors. 'Redundancy' shares its semantic space with [...] *waste*. The destination of the *un*employed, of the 'reserve army of labour,' was to be called back into active service. The destination of waste is the waste-yard, the rubbish heap. (Bauman, 12)[20]

In a context in which human subjects are assumed to be replaceable—indeed, interchangeable—"appendage[s] of the machine," as Marx termed the division of labour, those unnecessary to the "machine" are seen as disposable.[21] Joyce's Leopold Bloom aptly articulates this, in passing, while observing a pointsman operating the wheel of a tramway interchange: "Couldn't they invent something automatic so that the wheel itself much handier? Well but that fellow would lose his job then? Well but then another fellow would get a job making the new invention?" (*U*, 114). Once a more efficient model of production requiring fewer hands has been found, the worker-object becomes waste, although, as Bloom notes, the creation of new technologies itself is a form of labour creation. The capitalist machine produces new workers in the same breath as it spits others out, resembling nothing so much as an immense and insatiable metabolism.

The treatment of the unemployed as obstructions to the "smooth functioning of economy" is in turn an extension of capitalism's ordering practices (Bauman, 39). From the perspective of production, the unemployed are human waste since goods can be produced "more swiftly, profitably and 'economically'" without them (Bauman, 39). Lack of income in turn makes the unemployed "flawed consumers": the consumer market deems them human waste since they cannot purchase goods and since industry cannot profit from the demands that they create (i.e., their need for state welfare). Deemed irrelevant by society, such "flawed consumers" may as well be invisible—a notion conveyed most vividly in the depiction of landfill scavengers in children's literature in the latter half of the twentieth century. Reflecting the anxieties of the post-war era and a growing environmental awareness, Mary Norton's *The Borrowers* series (1952–1982), Clive King's *Stig of the Dump* (1963), and Elisabeth Beresford's novel *The Wombles* (1968) also examine the experience of those "flawed consumers" whom society ignores. Norton's tiny scavengers live under the floorboards of a Victorian house unbeknownst to its owners. King's dump-dwelling caveman is only visible to a little boy, whose parents assume he is making him up. And ordinary people never see Beresford's "Wombles," who recycle cast-offs in the dump outside London's Wimbledon Common. These tales about diminished humans, anachronistic cavemen, and imaginary creatures who repurpose waste without anyone noticing are very much in the Surrealist spirit. They assume that magic and the marginalised go hand in hand—that the people who sift through rubbish for hidden meaning are likely to be deemed deranged, and, likewise, that it is the people whom society has cast out who are most likely to go scavenging. Echoing Breton's incitement to the reader, in the *Surrealist Manifesto*, to once more "turn back toward his childhood," we might argue that a childlike imagination is the best placed to truly "see" waste and those who scavenge it—to recognise both the objects and the people whom society invites us to ignore.[22]

Throughout this study I thus use the term "human waste" to refer to both waste manufactured *by* humans and to humans who are treated *as* waste in order to draw attention to an explicit and intentional slippage between these two typologies in many of the texts reviewed. My contention is that these texts deploy waste through realist detail and metaphor to say interesting things about not only the valuation of objects under capitalism but about the valuation of human beings and about the relationship between the two.

Moreover, although we might assume such slippage between the figuration of objects as "lively" and the figuration of people as "thingly" to be merely a literary device, my contention is that the overlap between the figuration of surplus humans and rubbish is actually born out of the capitalist system and is specifically tied to a conceptualisation of unemployment that emerged at the end of the nineteenth century, as a result of the first global depression.[23] As Michael Sayeau notes in his study of unemployment in Conrad, the effects of the crisis of 1873 lingered well into the 1890s and resulted in the first attempts, in the fields of economics and social policy, to actually define and assess unemployment.[24] Following the first inquiry into the problem of joblessness, in 1895, there emerged a new understanding of unemployment not as "an accidental effect [or] a manifestation of the lack of personal industry or gumption on the part of the jobless individual" but as a "*normal* category of economic life, a structural effect of the wage system and modern industrial competition itself" (Sayeau, 155). This view of the unemployed had as palpable an effect on those in work as those out of it. The implementation of F.W. Taylor's *Principles of Scientific Management* (1911), which included the intensification of the individual worker's efforts and the deskilling of work (as exemplified by the introduction of the assembly line) "would have been impossible without a permanent well of unemployed workers—Marx's 'industrial reserve army'—from which to draw" (Sayeau, 156). One of the long-term effects of the first global depression was thus the creation of a class of remaindered people whose superfluity was deemed a natural, and in some ways useful, component of the capitalist system. To Bauman's assessment of capitalism's view of human waste as an inevitable product—or, as he puts it, "collateral casualt[y]"—of economic progress (Bauman, 39–41), we can add the populace of those "disposed of" in periods of crisis and whose disposal serves to dissuade those in work from demanding better working conditions. This understanding of the unemployed forms an integral, if not always explicit, strand of the story the texts reviewed tell.

It is likewise noteworthy that Igor Kopytoff's conceptualisation of commodification as a "process of becoming" as opposed to an "all-or-none state of being," to which I alluded in my discussion of the commodity, is in fact based on his study of commoditised people in the slave trade in Africa, and in particular on the fluidity of slaves' identity over the course of their careers (Kopytoff, 73; 64). Indeed, as Bill Brown notes in his reading of Kopytoff's essay, "the spectral completion of commodity fetishism (where things appear to have lives of their own) is human reification (where people appear to be no more than things)."[25] In other words, "the commodity form itself depends on 'the conversion of things into persons and the conversion of persons into things'" (Brown, 178).

The semantic slippage between superfluous or marginalised humans and manufactured waste is rendered explicit in Michel Tournier's *Gemini* (1975), in which one of the central characters, a homosexual landfill manager called Alexandre, notes the affinities between his job, his abode, and his status as a gay man.[26] The cheap lodging in which he lives, "a rendezvous for all the town's misfits, the nomadic or semi-nomadic laborers, seasonal workers, tramps, and, in particular, all those engaged in any way in the world of waste and salvage," mirrors the "much-abused stuff in which [he] work[s]" so that his "life is besieged by refuse on all sides" (85). This "refuse" includes the unemployed and the socially marginalised: the garbage workers are soon to be made redundant by the introduction of large incineration plants, while gay men such as himself, it is rumoured, are being "arrested wholesale" and eliminated by the Nazis (87). Indeed, by framing the issue of incineration as a "strange, prophetic analogy!" for the eradication of gays, Alexandre draws all of these different categories—garbage; garbage men; garbage men made redundant by new technologies; and the persecuted—under the broader category of human waste. Through his narrative, they are shown to be inextricably intertwined.

I will have more to say about the slippage between these categories in the chapters themselves; for now, what is most important is to recognise the points of connection between manufactured waste under capitalism and remaindered (unemployed, unemployable) humans, and that the literary depiction of these different forms of superfluity, as well as the depiction of their rehabilitation, frequently overlaps.

Symbols of Transience and Change

Waste in the texts under review reveals the ephemeral nature of the ideas we hold dear by demonstrating how quickly the recent past in capitalist modernity becomes irrelevant. Simultaneously endearing and off-putting, these figurations exemplify Sigmund Freud's definition of the uncanny— the "familiar made strange" and that which "ought to have remained secret and hidden but has come to light."[27] It is, in other words, a thing that elicits at once a keen sense of recognition and wary diffidence. The uncanny nature of manufactured waste is perhaps most evident in the works of the French Surrealists (alluded to earlier, and the subject of the next chapter), who were greatly influenced by Freud and profoundly interested in the life of the unconscious. But it remains a prevalent theme throughout the latter half of the century as well: for to resist rational understanding or linear explication is also to resist commercial valuation. The texts in the upcoming two chapters sully the bourgeois logic of capitalist discourse by juxtaposing the past with the present in non-linear narratives that make no attempt at creating order out of experience. The things the capitalist system throws out are re-integrated within the system of the novel in a different process of putting-to-use: the repressed rears its head and moves to the narrative's centre. In this way, the novel form itself provides an alternative history (although, to be sure, the novel's own participation in the marketplace makes this putting-to-use a form of commodification, as well).

The uncanny however only partially explains the significance of the last century's literary engagements with waste, and thus it is only part of the story this book tells. The other part has to do with human beings' long-standing tendency to ascribe meaning to bodily emissions and spoils. Societies throughout the ages have codified what to do with excrement, carcasses, broken tools, weapons, and architectural ruins. And in most cases these rituals of avoidance or disposal had both religious and pragmatic functions: to abide by them was to practice good hygiene, but also good citizenship. The Ancient Greeks from the Homeric period onward not only had sophisticated waste management and disposal practices, and a semantic system based on notions of impurity; they operated recycling infrastructures that allowed the re-use and re-processing of building materials and statues. These processes had both practical and symbolic value, allowing for the conspicuous re-contextualisation of the past as a reminder or celebration of charged historical events.[28] There is likewise a strong correlation between the concepts of sanitation and cleanliness, and the concept of good rule: the evolution of sanitation management in medieval Britain, for example, occurred in tandem with the evolution of city rule.[29] Basic necessities common to any kind of collective living situation (disease prevention, avoidance of unpleasant smells) are connected to broader ideological constructs relating to history, the dead, otherness, and the volition of a superior being. It is the correlation between waste's long-standing instigation of fear, awe, and dread and its estranging effect in consumer culture that makes it such a compelling subject in the last century's literature. In these works we see up close the affinities and overlap between an almost ingrained, primordial dread of animal and human bodily emissions and a systematised, quantified, regulated abhorrence towards the by-products of production and the relics of consumption— and the extent to which radicalism, and a radical art praxis, involves a resistance to both of these.

My reading of the radical potential of waste collection and scavenging is partly informed by recent studies by queer theorists on the politics of hoarding, which show how cultural understandings of waste collection and scavenging have changed and been shaped by heteronormative, capitalist interests. Hoarding as a pathology is a remarkably recent concept,

formally diagnosed only in the early 1990s as "the acquisition of, and failure to discard, possessions which appear to be useless or of limited value"
(and only included in the fifth edition of the *Diagnostic and Statistical
Manual of Mental Disorders*, published in 2013).[30] Scott Herring and
Martin F. Manalansan compellingly suggest how the "wayward relationship to material objects" might be seen as both radical and queer: in
Herring's words, hoarding upsets "normative social boundaries."[31] From
this perspective, our codification of hoarding as a "disease," like our codification of other waste disposal practices, is ideologically inflected. For
instance, although there are instances of hoarding practices in nineteenth-
century literature (Nikolai Gogol's miser in *Dead Souls* is also an obsessive
collector of trash; Krook, the rag and bottle merchant in Dickens' *Bleak
House*, never actually sells off the scraps he collects[32]), the practice gained
prominence and notoriety only in the 1930s, due to the much-publicised
story of Homer and Langley Collyer.[33] These were two wealthy brothers
who filled their mansion in Harlem with trash and eventually died under
the mountains of debris they had accrued. Herring argues that the brothers' story is very specifically modern, born out of, and at the same time
opposing, a new relationship to material goods. By tracing the shifts in the
public and academe's perception of the Collyer case over the course of the
last century, Herring questions our tendency to pathologise those who
deviate from participating in the cycle of purchase and disposal (Herring,
179). E.L. Doctorow's historical novel about the Collyer brothers, *Homer
and Langley* (2009), makes this radicalism explicit, depicting Langley as a
countercultural figure, a deranged artist, and an archivist of the American
century (among the items he collects are a Model T Ford, numerous
typewriters, and 70 years' worth of daily newspapers).[34] Langley refers to
himself as both "sui generis" and "prophetic" (*HL*, 176), while the only
characters in the novel who are not disgusted by the brothers' house are
a group of young hippies, who in fact spend an entire summer helping
Langley build tunnels through his mounds of stuff. Likewise, Homer (the
narrator) recalls:

> [Langley] did not limit himself to oil paints for his composition, but attached
> to the canvas any matter of things as the spirit moved him. Found objects, he
> called them, and to find them he needed only to look around, our house being
> the source of the birdfeather [*sic*], string, bolts of cloth, small toys, scraps of
> wood, newspaper headlines, and everything else that inspired him. (*HL*, 133)

Doctorow's reference to "found objects"—a term for scavenged waste first used by the Surrealists—suggests the parallels between Langley's pathology and the practices of the historical avant-garde. By framing the Collyer house as both a repository for America's recent past and a space in which to examine that past critically (*HL*, 176), Doctorow, like Herring, suggests the radical—perhaps even illuminating—potential of hoarding.

The depictions of waste by Western writers over the last century play on the contrasts between social norms and ideologies dating back to early modernity, and new modes of relating to the material world under capitalism. The artist picking up street-side bric-a-brac; the vagrant wading through a municipal landfill; the solitary individual contemplating the vast expanse of a recycling centre at dusk are compelling not only in their exemplification of a radical socio-cultural shift in the ascription of value to objects and people. They are also reflections of a much longer-standing, perhaps immemorial, concern with our relationship to time, to each other, and to the earth.[35]

THE CASE FOR THE NOVEL AND FOR DESCENDANTS OF THE AVANT-GARDE

This study contends that the novelists under discussion use waste to say interesting things about capitalism and to do interesting things to the novel form. It also contends that these two endeavours—the critique of capitalism and the subversion of realism—are related and that both endeavours are profoundly indebted to the Surrealist tradition's challenging of bourgeois norms. To highlight the aesthetic value of waste objects, in these texts, is also to dismantle the logic of the bourgeois novel, and the complicity of realism in maintaining the status quo.

Realism is concerned with the recovery of the multifarious infinitesimally small details that make up human experience. Details such as an overflowing trash bin or a crumpled paper napkin lend themselves to the realist task because *they have no other function*. As readers, we implicitly recognise the objects in a narrative that are important to the plot and those that are just there to create a sense of authenticity—what Roland Barthes, in *The Rustle of Language* (1967), terms the "reality effect," as exemplified by the role of the barometer in Flaubert's *Madame Bovary*.[36] The logic driving the novel form is analogous to the logic of capitalism: everything must be put to use—a concept that Franco Moretti suggests, as well, in *The Novel: Vol I* (2006), where he dates the emergence of "mediating" or "catalytic" events (events of no import beyond that of driving the plot forward), to the early nineteenth century, and ascribes their pervasiveness, by the early twentieth century, to the rationalising tendencies of bourgeois society.[37] There is an important difference, of course, since for Barthes the function of objects in narrative is inherent: they are useful to the narrative by virtue of their existence (and, specifically, by virtue of their uselessness). Capitalism, by contrast, has to first *find ways* to put things to use. The realist detail is like a plastic bottle that sells itself, as opposed to a recycled plastic bottle being marketed by society for profit. For our purposes, however, it is sufficient to recognise that the *impulse* driving the two systems is the same.

This brings us to the difference between the narrative value of objects and that of waste objects. In a realist novel, ordinary objects are put to use by the characters while waste objects aid the story, setting the tone, suggesting broader themes, and even instantiating their own narrative. A lengthy description of waste objects draws attention to itself. Rather than simply assimilating the details into our sense of the narrative as a whole, we wonder whether their meaning adds up to more than the sum of their parts and whether events (a proliferating disease, the discovery of a clue) will transpire as a result. Thus, waste is the result of a narrative process but can also be its instigator. Dickens' oft-quoted opening in *Bleak House* (1852–1853) perhaps exemplifies this concept and the degree to which waste narratives extend from modernity back to the beginning of time.[38] "There is as so much mud in the streets," the omniscient narrator tells us, "as if the waters had but newly retired from the face of the earth, and it would not be wonderful to meet a Megalosaurus, forty feet long or so, waddling like an elephantine lizard up Holborn Hill" (*BH*, 18). The reference to the Megalosaurus explicitly relates the modern urban *milieu* to the pre-human: the city may have sprung up in the meantime, and commuters' passage may have "add[ed] new deposits to the crust upon crust of mud, sticking at those points tenaciously to the pavement, and accumulating at compound interest," but these are only recent phenomena. Dickens counters capitalism's notion of time with a reminder of the epochal time scale that preceded it. As well as a humorous account of the unhygienic conditions of London's streets, the text relates the life therein to the pre-historic, reminding us that all life begins in the mulch, from the original story of God's creation of mankind from mud, to his own narrative. Waste functions as both a realist device and a mythical trope, relating the novel's modern concerns to long-standing ones.

Relatedly, literary depictions of waste amplify the novel's concern with subjectivity. All reading involves looking at the world through another's eyes, but reading about waste reminds us of the (often extreme) dissonance between that perspective and our own. If in real life we shudder at the sight of garbage, or ignore it altogether, as readers we know to look ⌒ closer. Literature primes us, like children, to look for the meaning within things—to anticipate that the sticky sludge pooling out from under the sink is toxic and assume the bric-a-brac found in a flea market or car boot sale serves a revelatory purpose. Crucially, the imaginative leap required to understand a character's fascination with an object of waste is greater than that required to understand their desire for money or material goods: it involves a logical inversion, thus reminding us of the idiosyncrasies of lived experience itself. In reading the narrative of a landfill dweller or a dumpster diver, we are reminded of the distance between self and other and invited to seek out the affinities between the two.

It is only fitting that the novel form, traditionally invested in the life of people, should also be alive to the imaginative import of humanity's discards, particularly when the process by which those discards came to be is a systemic one. The novel form is concerned with origins, endings, and the transformation of individuals and societies, be these over the course of a day or a lifetime. The novelist sees, in our discards, a material record. In perhaps not so dissimilar a way from primitive cultures' purifying rites, the novel seeks to create order and form out of experience. The experimental movements that have followed since the form's inception may challenge this, asserting that experience is fundamentally neither unified nor ordered, but they have not disavowed the imaginative import of the elements that make up experience, and the fact that whether we pay attention to those elements or not has largely to do with how much narrative value we attribute to them. Waste is at the centre of this discourse. It draws attention to itself by resisting to or complying with our efforts to organise or monetise it; by suggesting that there is more to its presence than simple description; and by inviting questions about its origins, what its enduring presence might signify, and whether leaving it there will have consequences. A material form with undeniable physical attributes (stench, unseemly appearance, toxic fumes), waste lends itself to narratives that investigate both process and the repercussions of process. Thus, I echo Véronique Bragard who, building on Dana Phillips and Heather Sullivan's concept of "storied bodies," contends that "literature, with is faculty to portray discarded objects as 'storied bodies' perhaps manages to rejoin what we perceive as refuse with the productive capacity inherent in matter, thus rendering it beautiful and/or sensuous to human perception."[39]

As the twentieth century unfolds, the acknowledgement of waste's literary merit is coupled with a sense of urgency, a sense that this is not only stuff *worth* telling but in *need* of telling. Such urgency, of course, is not solely confined to narratives that interrogate capitalist excess: rather, it is manifest in numerous post-war novels addressing the ramifications of totalitarian regimes, genocide, and nuclear holocaust, in which waste is figured as all that which any hegemonic system deems of no value. These are not critiques of capitalism, but they are critiques of a particular system of oppression in which one social strata or race is valued above another. They are narratives in which the marginalised or oppressed are treated as waste—relegated, in other words, to the status of human waste—and in which writing provides a means to speak out against that treatment. The most extreme and literal example of this can be found in narratives about the Jewish Holocaust, as exemplified by Primo Levi's *If This Is a Man* (1947), in which we find detailed descriptions of piled up corpses and accounts of internment camp dwellers being made to dig graves for fellow inmates who have died.[40] Levi's book subverts the notion of a superior race and of an inferior one that belongs to the scrapheap to the extent that the scraps in the heap are allowed to speak. As a recuperative act, the Holocaust survivor's recorded experience is the antithesis of the Nazis' own recycling practices: to the horrific process of annihilating a race and then using its remainders to make lampshades, the author finds (some) redemption in the articulation of the experience, in making those horrors known.

This brings us to the final reason for focussing on the novel form: the idea underlying all of the novels I discuss is that language and narrative have a unique capacity to reclaim meaning out of waste, even when that waste resists logical interpretation. Narrative provides a means to glean understanding from the "unexpected but more meaningful" combinations in which waste is often cast. For instance, the anonymous narrator of Ivan Klíma's *Love and Garbage* (1986) identifies an inherent affinity between writing and collecting waste.[41] A former member of the Czechoslovak Communist Party, the narrator has abandoned a half-finished manuscript on Kafka to instead clean the streets of his native Prague. He has chosen "this unattractive occupation" to gain an "unexpected view of the world," for "unless you look at the world and at people from a new angle your mind will get blunted" (*LG*, 2). Waste collection provides that fresh angle, allowing him to meditate on the fact that:

> No matter ever vanishes. It can, at most, change its form. Rubbish is immortal, it pervades the air, swells up in water, dissolves, rots, disinte-

grates, changes into gas, into smoke, into soot, it travels across the world and gradually engulfs it. (*LG*, 6)

The narrator's own career trajectory from writer to garbage collector marks a reverence for this enduring but ultimately unknowable matter. Klíma's novel suggests the deep affinities between street sweeper and writer: to deal in discards is to move out of step with society and to pay heed to all of the things society no longer notices. Like the novelist, the street sweeper is acutely attuned to the passage of time. Each item he sweeps up is a reminder of events past, which it enjoins us to explain. The central conceit of *Love and Garbage*—that the novel might be a site for negotiating different kinds of value—is premised on what Peter Boxall terms the novel form's "particular gift" for demonstrating "how art is always becoming matter, and how matter is always becoming art," and its knack for putting "the relationship between art and matter, between words and the world, into a kind of motion."[42] Klíma's novel about a man at pains to describe matter as he removes it literalises Boxall's definition of the form as "work[ing] at the disappearing threshold between the world that exists and that which does not" (Boxall, 13).

Of course, this book is not a definitive account of waste in literature (or, for that matter, of literary critiques of capitalism or avant-gardist approaches to either of the above). As Susan Signe Morrison cogently argues in her recent contribution to waste studies, "virtually every piece of literature contains waste, depending on one's definition": waste is "so pervasive a theme, topic, metaphor, and element" in literature that an exhaustive study of it would amount to an account of the entire Western canon (Morrison, 5). Even texts in which objects are not represented can be seen to deal *in* waste, insofar as all literature echoes and reprises that which has been said or done before. Thus, while the prominence of waste in canonical twentieth-century novels such as James Joyce's *Ulysses* is undisputed, I bypass these to focus specifically on waste's role in testing the limits of realism and the tenets of capitalism, and the intersection between these ideas and Surrealism. A study of waste in Virginia Woolf's essays and short stories would be fruitful indeed: one thinks of her famous articulation of overlooked or irrelevant narratives, in "How Should One Read a Book," as part of the "rubbish heap" of literature—those "rings and scissors and broken noses buried in the huge past" that perhaps warrant examination.[43] But it would be a very different project. Likewise, the rich scholarship that has developed around the outhouse scene in *Ulysses* and the shoring up of

ruins in T.S. Eliot's *The Waste Land*—which many view to be the quintessential work of literary recycling—while fascinating in and of itself, is not
directly relevant to the questions addressed here.[44]

FROM SCAVENGING TO WINDOW-SHOPPING

To fully understand the radical nature of the different literary figurations
of waste discussed in this study, it is necessary to understand their origins. Although the periodisation of the origins of commodity culture itself
remains contested—scholars such J.H. Plumb date it back to the end of
the sixteenth century; Rosalind Williams and Thomas Richards place it
in the nineteenth—the mid-nineteenth century is generally recognised as
the beginning of mass culture in England, the USA, and France, resulting, in part, from the transformation of the advertising industries in these
countries.[45] In the last decade, a rich discourse has arisen around the narrative underlying the object culture of the nineteenth century, combining
material culture studies and Marxist criticism to consider the origins of
these objects and what they say about industrialisation, Imperial rule, and
military oppression. For example, David Trotter has shown the symbolic
charge of specific material surfaces, textures, and sheens as indicators of
anxieties about social mobility.[46] These anxieties are at the heart of Charles
Dickens' *Our Mutual Friend* (1864–1865), in which the main source of
wealth is an immense mountain of dust, and in which the upwardly mobile
classes are represented by the aptly named Mr and Mrs Veneering. The
Veneerings' house is full of "things [...] in a state of high varnish and
polish," and "what was observable in the furniture, was observable in the
Veneerings—the surface smelt a little too much of the workshop and was a
trifle sticky."[47] Profligate spenders and ostentatious in their choice of home
décor, the couple endow wealth with a sticky, sickly quality—provoking
disgust rather than awe.[48] For Trotter, "The Veneerings have come a long
way and in a short time and the stickiness which coats their new identity,
and which hangs about it, suggests that they have not yet settled fully into
position" (Trotter, 184). These *nouveau riche* are dressed-up trash.

At the other end of the social scale, working class Victorians practised
the process we refer to as recycling long before we gave it a name and a
logo: they separated food waste for composting, and either re-used old
textiles or gave them to door-to-door rag pickers for collection.[49] Industry
itself relied on the "stewardship of objects": rag-picking and waste separation were essential to both manufacturing and agriculture, and households

regularly repurposed old clothes, broken furniture and food scraps.[50] The impulse driving such recuperation was both financial and moral—as exemplified by the moral compass of *Our Mutual Friend*, the crippled dressmaker Jenny Wren, who makes her living sewing doll dresses from rags brought to her by an orphaned foundling called Sloppy. Her creative and moral acts of reclamation counter the corrupt accrual of wealth by those seeking to commercialise even dust.[51] The form of the novel, with its many narrative strands and sub-plots, is testament to the kind of skilful, and arresting, work that can result from such patchwork. Dickens exemplifies the novelist as dressmaker, patching together the stories of Londoners from all classes and backgrounds to create a multi-textured portrait of the present.

The evolution of waste's role from necessity to hindrance can be traced to the development of sanitation engineering, which emerged in the 1890s out of the science of bacteriology. One result of this new scientific field was a shift in concerns over public health: worries surrounding poverty and questions of moral degeneracy were in large part supplanted by new ones regarding the effects of urban filth. The sanitation engineer was thus elevated to the status of a scientist, in a similar way to the nineteenth-century detective and the forensic expert of today, and by the 1930s had become a powerful figure in his own right (Rogers, 70). In turn, the sanitation engineering industry's emphasis on the diseases and infections carried by waste altered the public's view of recuperation: once a mark of good citizenship, re-use was cast as unhygienic. This new lexicon of sanitation was aimed at stamping out disease, but also at encouraging consumption. Industrialised agriculture had no need for households' waste scraps, while the future of retail was contingent upon the purchase of new clothes rather than the mending of rags. While periods of economic stagnation such as the Great Depression of the 1930s and the Second World War saw a return to previous frugal methods of re-use, "the growth of markets for new products came to depend in part on the continuous disposal of old things" (Strasser, 15). While these ideas did not gain traction until the 1920s, the seeds were already being sown at the end of the nineteenth century. Consumption's compulsive attraction is at the heart of Emile Zola's *Ladies' Paradise* (1883), which depicts the department store—born in Paris in the 1850s—as an erotic space.[52] In the novel, goods on display arouse the desire of the female shoppers who gaze upon them, catalysing violent and frenzied impulses to purchase. In turn, the objects the women already possess lose their appeal: as in love, familiarity breeds *ennui*.[53]

While commodity culture has its roots in the mid-nineteenth century, consumerism as we know it today did not truly emerge until the early 1900s, with the growth of mass production and mass marketing.[54] The idea that capitalism depends on the finite lifespan of objects was first articulated in the 1920s, by the advertising consultant Christine Frederick. For Frederick, encouraging purchase was contingent upon the supplanting of existing products with newer models: she termed this process "progressive obsolescence."[55] To re-use in such a context would be anathema: the whole point was to encourage customers to be thinking about replacing the object they have yet to purchase. The circulation of goods relied on fetishising novelty and making the objects of the recent past appear archaic. The logic driving this was desire, as articulated by Joyce's advertising canvasser, Bloom: "everything is dear if you don't want it. That's what good [sic] salesman is. Makes you buy what he wants to sell" (U, 375). The objective of advertising, from this period onwards, is to make the unnecessary appear essential and one's current possessions appear inadequate.

I take this period of transition as my starting point, while the garbage crisis of the late twentieth century marks the study's endpoint. Foster Wallace's *Infinite Jest* parodies the crisis in his depiction of an ingenious presidential campaign by celebrity-turned-politician Johnny Gentle (presumably based on Ronald Reagan, although eerily anticipating Donald Trump) and his "Clean U.S.A. Party" (C.U.S.P). In a period lacking "any real Foreign Menace" (IJ, 382), Gentle attracts both the "ultra-right jingoist[s]" and "far-left [...] ponytailed granola-crunchers" by promising to rid the country of the

> toxic effluvia choking our highways and littering our byways and grungeing up our sunsets and cruddying those harbours in which televised garbage-barges lay stacked up at anchor, clotted and impotent amid [...] those disgusting blue-bodied flies that live on shit (first U.S. President ever to say shit publicly, shuddering), rusty-hulled barges cruising up and down petroleated coastlines or laying up reeky and stacked and emitting CO as they await the opening of new landfills and toxic repositories the People demanded in every area but their own. (IJ, 383–384)

The passage humorously identifies the simultaneous shame elicited by waste and resentment towards anything that suggests we temper our excesses, our coterminous recognition of the need for landfills, and horror at the thought of living near one. Foster Wallace weaves these anxieties into a parable that relates American outsourcing to disgust for the "cohesion-renewing Other" (*IJ*, 384). For, once elected, Johnny Gentle gives a slice of the northeastern USA to Canada, while allowing US waste management companies to continue depositing garbage there via immense catapults. The solution to the garbage crisis thus fuels xenophobia: Canada is now America's dumping ground, the garbage therein evincing the same disgust as that provoked by the sight of one's own excrement. What to do about this anxiety-inducing end product, and what lessons it might still teach us, is at the centre of my fifth chapter.

CHAPTER OVERVIEWS

This study begins by examining the depiction of waste, recuperation, and superfluity in Giorgio de Chirico's *Hebdomeros* (1930), André Breton's *Nadja* (1928), and Mina Loy's unfinished novel, *Insel* (1929–). Each of these artist-novelists was closely associated with what Peter Bürger terms the "historical avant-garde"—those early twentieth-century experimental movements, including Cubism, Dada, and Surrealism, that sought to oppose the commodification of art under capitalism.[56] In each novel, waste and remaindered humans are deployed to advance a radical artistic praxis and advance alternative modes of valuation beyond the commercial.

Chapter 3 examines the representation of discarded objects and superfluous humans in Samuel Beckett's novels and prose between 1950 and 1964. Beckett re-works Surrealism and Dada's aesthetic of recuperation to oppose the export of Fordist rationalisation and (American) consumer culture. Waste in these texts extends Loy's preoccupation with remaindered humans and the valuation of human beings as use-values.

Chapter 4 explores waste in Donald Barthelme's *Snow White* (1967), J.G. Ballard's "urban disaster" trilogy—*Crash* (1973), *Concrete Island* (1974), and *High-Rise* (1975)—and William Gaddis' *JR* (1975). Like Beckett, each of these novelists is a descendant of the historical avant-garde and their fascination with waste carries on its legacy. Barthelme's recognition that his book is a product whose worth is dependent on audience "satisfaction," Ballard's dystopian depictions of the post-war economic boom, and Gaddis' comedic interpretation of the finance market as trading in rubbish extend the novel form in new ways.

Chapter 5 takes us to the late twentieth century, where we examine the depiction of waste and recuperation in the works of the Don DeLillo. Here, recycling is alternately cast as a form of historical reclamation; an

obsessive-compulsive effort to classify and order; a derivative attempt
to make art out of the nation's most humiliating secrets; and, in
Underworld's closing narrative about the recuperation of nuclear waste
outside Chernobyl, the most extreme form of unethical commercialisation
of a devastating event.

The conclusion looks forward to the twenty-first century, examining
waste in Thomas Pynchon's *Bleeding Edge* (2013), Jonathan Miles' *Want
Not* (2013), and Tom McCarthy's *Satin Island* (2014). Through their
attention to the speculative dimension of neoliberal ideology, the limits
of dumpster-diving, and the trash-like quality of online effluvia, Miles,
Pynchon, and McCarthy suggest the untenability of subverting the productivist paradigm. All three highlight the difficulty of conceiving a radical discourse through waste in a landscape that is suffused with it and in
a culture that is all too willing to put even the radical to commercial use.

The Case for Pursuing "This Unattractive Occupation"[57]

This project extends the parameters of waste theory to consider the economic dimension of waste, an area under-explored by scholars in the
discipline, and to indicate how literary criticism with an investment in
socio-economic contexts, in turn, might benefit from waste theory. I
intend to draw out the extent to which waste narratives indebted to the
historical avant-garde parody the economistic tendencies of Western capitalism—that is, its tendency to reduce all social phenomena to exchange
values and to view (human) life as merely a process of producing, selling,
and acquiring things. Where research on the intersections of art and waste
have tended to concentrate on the commodity as a static object, to be
read passively and symptomatically in relation to systems of exchange, my
intent is to explore how commodities are materially implicated in processes of use and disuse, even in their abandonment.

This book also provides unique contributions to the critical discourse
around the specific writers examined, highlighting areas where scholarship is virtually absent. My focus on waste's use by writers indebted to the
avant-garde seeks to illustrate waste's enduring amenability to different
kinds of narratives of dissent. The texts examined reveal the aesthetics
of waste to be a fluid, changing thing—not a fixed category, but a discourse that evolves in line with the culture to which it responds—that has
however been indelibly shaped by the historical avant-garde. To Donald

Barthelme's oft-quoted dictum that "The principle of collage is the central principle of all art in the twentieth century in all media" we might add that waste is, if not the central trope of all twentieth-century fiction, the central trope of countercultural fiction intent upon resisting capitalism's enveloping of language and art.

The texts I have chosen not only provide compelling examples of how Surrealism has shaped the writing of waste but also help us to reflect upon the tensions between financial, aesthetic, and moral value, and how these tensions have changed over the course of the last century. Each of the texts discussed is a meditation on the meaning of value—itself a charged term with a multitude of associations. Together, they help tell the story of capitalist commodity culture's relationship with manufactured waste and remaindered humans, and provide compelling examples of how that story has evolved. Each demonstrates literature's role in resisting the norm and bringing about social change, as well as showing how that task can help transform the rhetorical and formal devices of literature itself.

NOTES

1. Ellis Sharp, *The Dump* (London: Zoilus Press, 1998), 60. Henceforth *TD*.
2. Karl Marx, *Capital*, transl. Samuel Moore and Edward Aveling (Oxford: Oxford University Press, 2008 [1867–1883]), 350.
3. As far as I am aware, the phrase "thingly term" was first used by Steve Connor in "Thinking Things," a plenary for the 2008 ESSE conference subsequently published on his website, http://www.stevenconnor.com/thinkingthings/. The expression was a reference to Bill Brown's "thing theory," which in turn builds on ideas first developed by Modernists such as William Carlos Williams and T.S. Eliot. For an account of these developments, see *What Things Do: Philosophical Reflections on Technology, Agency, and Design* (Penn State University Press, 2005). For a sense of their application in literary studies, see Douglas Mao, *Solid Objects: Modernism and the Test of Production* (Princeton University Press, 1998); Bill Brown, *A Sense of Things* (University of Chicago Press, 2004); Elaine Freedgood, *The Ideas in Things: Fugitive Meaning in the Victorian Novel* (University of Chicago Press, 2009); and Peter Boxall, *The Value of the Novel* (Cambridge University Press, 2015).
4. Arjun Appadurai, "Commodities and the politics of value" and Igor Kopytoff, "The Cultural Biography of Things" in *The Social Life of Things: Commodities in Cultural Perspective*, ed. Arjun Appaduai (Cambridge University Press, 1986), 3–63; 64–91.

5. Jane Bennett, *Vibrant Matter: A Political Ecology of Things* (Durham, NC: Duke University Press, 2010); Susan Signe Morrison, *The Literature of Waste: Material Ecopoetics and Ethical Matter* (London: Palgrave Macmillan, 2015); Maurizia Boscagli, *Stuff Theory: Everyday Objects, Radical Materialism* (London: Bloomsbury, 2014), 3.

6. For readings characteristic of this approach see Sophie Gee, *Making Waste: Leftovers and the 18th-Century Imagination* (Princeton, New Jersey: Princeton University Press, 2009) and Morrison, *The Literature of Waste*. For a refreshing counter to it, see Will Viney's temporal analysis, *Waste: A Philosophy of Things* (London: Bloomsbury, 2013).

7. Mary Douglas, *Purity and Danger: An Analysis of Concepts of Pollution and Taboo* (London: Routledge, 2002 [1966]).

8. Michael Thompson, *Rubbish Theory: The Creation and Destruction of Value* (Oxford: Oxford University Press, 1979).

9. For an account of the relationship between modernisation and the reduction of labour costs, see John Burnett, *Idle Hands: The Experience of Unemployment, 1790–1990* (London: Routledge, 1994). Harry Braverman's *Labor and Monopoly Capital: The Degradation of Work in the Twentieth Century* (New York: Monthly Review Press, 1974) provides a salient overview of the dynamics underlying the transfer of power from worker to owner/manager, and the treatment of the unemployed as surplus entities.

10. Steven Spear and Kent H. Bowen. "Decoding the DNA of the Toyota Production System." *Harvard Business Review* (September/October 1999).

11. Braverman, *Labor and Monopoly Capital*, 185. See also Susan Strasser, *Waste and Want: A Social History of Trash* (New York: Metropolitan Books, 1999) and Jennifer Seymour Whitaker, *Salvaging the Land of Plenty: Garbage and the American dream* (New York: Harper Collins, 1994).

12. Ben Highmore, "Benjamin's Trash Aesthetics" in *Everyday Life and Cultural Theory: An Introduction* (London: Routledge, 2002), 60–75. Citation on 61.

13. The allusion to Deleuze, and the description of the cartridge's "schizoid" function, is an evident reference to Volume I of *Capitalism and Schizophrenia* and can be seen to imply that the cartridge embodies the schizophrenic impulse of capitalism, which for Deleuze and Guattari is also the key to its subversion. I explore this concept in more detail in Chap. 3, in relation to Beckett's *Trilogy*.

14. Marguerite Duras, "Madame Dodin," in *Whole Days in the Trees and Other Stories*, transl. Anita Barrows (London: John Calder, 1984 [1954]), 83–126. Henceforth *MD*.

15. Bruno Latour, *We Have Never Been Modern*, transl. Catherine Porter (Cambridge, MA: Harvard University Press, 1993), 55. For insight into more recent readings of the agential potential of waste, see "The Material

Politics of Solid Waste: Decentralization and Integrated Systems," in *Objects and Materials: A Routledge Companion,* ed. Penny Harvey (London: Routledge, 2014), 61–70; and Bennett, vii–viii; 4–6.

16. Julian Stallabrass, *Gargantua: Manufactured Mass Culture* (London: Verso, 1996), 175.

17. Esther Leslie, "Recycling," *Restless Cities* (London: Verso, 2010), 243. For a more thorough account of Nazi salvaging practices, see Anne Berg, "The Nazi Rag-Pickers and their Wine: The Politics of Waste and Recycling in Nazi Germany," *Social History* 40.4 (November 2015): 446–472.

18. James Joyce. *Ulysses* (London: Penguin, 2000 [1922]), 152. Henceforth, *U.*

19. Zygmunt Bauman, *Wasted Lives: Modernity and its Outcasts* (Cambridge: Polity Press, 2004), 5.

20. Morrison's insightful development of Bauman's concept in *The Literature of Waste* complements my approach. See in particular Chapter Eight: "The Toxic Metaphor of Wasted Humans: Those Filthy Cleaners Who Scrub US Spotless" (97–117).

21. Karl Marx and Friedrich Engels, *The Communist Manifesto* (London: Penguin Classics, 2015 [1848], 5.

22. André Breton, "Surrealist Manifesto of 1924," *Manifestoes of Surrealism,* transl. Richard Seaver and Helen R. Lane (Ann Arbor: University of Michigan Press, 1969), 3; 222.

23. For an overview of unemployment following the depression of 1873, see Charles P. Kindleberger and Robert Z. Aliber, *Manias, Panics and Crashes: A History of Financial Crises* (London: Palgrave Macmillan, 2005 [fifth edition]), 61.

24. Michael Sayeau, *Against the Event* (Oxford: Oxford University Press, 2013), 155.

25. Bill Brown, "Reification, Reanimation and the American Uncanny" in *Critical Inquiry 32* (Winter 2006): 175–207; citation on 178.

26. Michel Tournier, *Gemini,* transl. Ann Carter (Baltimore, MD: Johns Hopkins University Press, 1983 [1975]).

27. Sigmund Freud, "The 'Uncanny'" (1919), in *The Standard Edition of the Complete Psychological Works of Sigmund Freud: Vol. XVII,* ed. James Strachey (Hogarth Press: London, 1955), 228–256.

28. Astrid Lindenlauf. *Waste Management in Ancient Greece, from the Homeric to the Classical Period: Concepts and Practices of Waste, Dirt, Disposal and Recycling* (2000), 160. http://discovery.ucl.ac.uk/1317693/1/271246_Vol_1.pdf. Accessed 14 May 2013.

29. Dolly Jorgensen, "'All good rule of the Citee': Sanitation and civic government in England, 1400–1600," *Journal of Urban History* 36.3 (2010), 300–315.

30. Randy O. Frost and Rachel C. Gross, "The hoarding of possessions," *Behaviour Research and Therapy*. 31. 4 (May 1993): 367–382. Citation on 367.

31. Scott Herring, "Material Deviance: Theorizing Queer Objecthood," *Postmodern Culture* 21. 2 (2011): 45; Scott Herring, *The Hoarders: Material Deviance in Modern American Culture* (Chicago: University of Chicago Press, 2014); Martin F Manalansan IV, "The 'Stuff' of Archives: Mess, Migration and Queer Lives," *Radical History Review* 120 (Fall 2014): 94–107.

32. Fred Penzel, "Hoarding in History" in *The Oxford Handbook of Hoarding and Acquiring*, ed. Randy O. Frost and Gail Steketee (Oxford: Oxford University Press, 2015), 1–13. Citations on 5 and 6.

33. Scott Herring, "Collyer Curiosa: A Brief History of Hoarding," *Criticisms* 53. 2 (2011): 159–188.

34. E.L. Doctorow. *Homer and Langley* (London: Abacus, 2009). Henceforth, *HL*.

35. The long-standing twinning of cleanliness and morality and the harrowing history of "cleansing" society of entire ethnicities or subcultures are both outside the scope of this study. However, it should be acknowledged that the concept of impurity as a justification to eradicate otherness is a central tenet in twentieth-century literary representations of waste, and the lexicon of cleanliness and purity remains an overwhelmingly prevalent tool in propaganda today. See, for instance, Tricia Starks, *The Body Soviet* (Madison: University of Wisconsin Press, 2009) and Kristin Ross, *Fast Cars, Clean Bodies* (Cambridge, MA: MIT Press, 1995).

36. Roland Barthes, "The Reality Effect" (1967) in *The Rustle of Language*, transl. Richard Howard (Oxford: Blackwell, 1986), 141–148. I provide a more thorough analysis of Barthes' theory in Chap. 3.

37. Franco Moretti, "Serious Century" in *The Novel, Volume I: History, Geography and Culture*, ed. Franco Moretti et al. (Princeton and Oxford: Princeton University Press, 2006), 364–399.

38. Charles Dickens, *Bleak House* (Oxford University Classics, 1996 [1852–1853]), 17, Henceforth, *BH*.

39. Véronique Bragard, "Introduction: Languages of Waste: Matter and Form in our Garbage," *Interdisciplinary Studies in Literature and the Environment* (*ISLE*) 20. 3 (2013): 459–463. Bragard is citing Dana Phillips and Heather Sullivan, "Material ecocriticism: Dirt, waste, bodies, food, and other matter," *ISLE* 19. 3 (2013): 445–447.

40. Primo Levi, *Se questo é un uomo* (Einaudi: Torino, 2012 [1947]).

41. Ivan Klíma, *Love and Garbage* (London: Picador, 1990 [1986]), 2. Henceforth, *LG*.

42. Peter Boxall, *The Value of the Novel* (Cambridge: Cambridge University Press, 2016), 13.

43. Virginia Woolf. *The Common Reader, Second Series* (London: Vintage, 2003 [1926]), 380.
44. For insight into the vast scholarship on waste and recycling in these texts, see in particular: Maude Ellmann, "Ulysses: The Epic of the Human Body," in *A Companion to James Joyce,* ed. Richard Brown (Oxford: Blackwell, 2008), 54–70; Martin O'Brien, "Rubbish Literatures" in *A Crisis of Waste?: Understanding the Rubbish Society* (London and New York: Routledge, 2008), 35–56; Will Viney, "The Poetic Economies of T.S. Eliot" and "Reading Joycean Disjecta" in *Waste: A Philosophy of Things,* 79–99 and 100–123; Tim Armstrong, "The Regulation of Energies" in *Modernism, Technology and the Body: A Cultural Study* (Cambridge: Cambridge University Press, 1998), and Susan Signe Morrison, *The Literature of Waste.* Of these, Armstrong and Viney's studies are particularly worth mentioning. Viney demonstrates the extent to which the language of literary narrative structures Bloom's waste-making, while references to waste signal the indeterminate limits or borders of the novel itself (Viney, 102–103). For Armstrong, Eliot's poem displays a "simultaneous fascination with, and revulsion from, waste," which he defines as "both the abject and a valuable surplus which enables culture to continue, creating its own moment as it orders its abjection. There can be no production without waste" (Armstrong, 70–71).
45. J.H. Plumb, *The Birth of a Consumer Society* (Bloomington: Indiana University Press, 1982); Rosalind Williams, *Dream Worlds: Mass Consumption in Late Nineteenth-Century France* (Berkeley and LA: University of California Press, 1982); Thomas Richards, *The Commodity Culture of Victorian England: Advertising and Spectacle, 1851–1914* (Stanford University Press: 1991); See also Peter N. Stearns, "Stages of Consumerism: Recent Work on the Issue of Periodization." *Journal of Modern History* 69 (Spring 1997): 102–117.
46. David Trotter, *Cooking With Mud: The Idea of Mess in Nineteenth-Century Art and Fiction* (Oxford: Oxford University Press, 2000), 184.
47. Charles Dickens, *Our Mutual Friend* (Oxford: Oxford World Classics, [1864–1865]), 17.
48. See, for instance, Ellen Handy, "Dust Piles and Damp Pavements: Excrement, Repression and the Victorian City in Photography and Literature," *Essays in Criticism* 2.3 (1973): 206–212; Michelle Elizabeth Allen, *Cleansing the City: Sanitary Geographies in Victorian London* (Athens, OH: Ohio University Press, 2008), 190.
49. Heather Rogers. *Gone Tomorrow: The Hidden Life of Garbage* (New York: The New Press, 2005) and Susan Strasser, *Waste and Want.*
50. Strasser, *Waste and Want,* 24–27.
51. For a nuanced analysis of this, see Nancy Metz, "The Artistic Reclamation of Waste in *Our Mutual Friend,*" *Nineteenth-century Fiction* 34 (1979): 68.

52. Emile Zola, *Ladies' Paradise* (Oxford: Oxford World Classics, 2008 [1883]).
53. Rachel Bowlby provides an exceptional analysis of this eroticism in *Just Looking: Consumer Culture in Dreiser, Gissing and Zola* (New York: Methuen, 1985).
54. Cross notes that discretionary spending in the USA increased from 20 % to 35 % in the first three decades of the twentieth century thanks to industry growth. Bauer and Greyser note that national advertising campaigns became ubiquitous in the 1910s, growing between $500m to $1.3bn between 1900 and 1915. Gary Cross, *An All-Consuming Century* (New York: Columbia University Press, 2000); Raymond A. Bauer and Stephen A. Greyser, *Advertising in America* (Boston: Harvard University Press, 1968).
55. Christine Frederick, *Selling Mrs. Consumer* (New York: Business Bourse, 1929), 246; 250–251, as cited in Strasser, 16.
56. Peter Bürger, *Theory of the Avant-Garde,* transl. Michael Shaw (Minneapolis: University of Minnesota Press, 1984 [1974]). For an in-depth exploration of the European literary counterculture's resistance to commodification, see Walter L. Adamson, *Embattled Avant-Gardes* (Berkeley and Los Angeles: University of California Press, 2007), 38.
57. Klíma, *Love and Garbage,* 2.

CHAPTER 2

In Search of an Epiphany: Waste and the Historical Avant-Garde

Waste and its recuperation were central to the formal experimentations of artists at the beginning of the twentieth century, many of whom saw cast-off materials as a means to break with the strictures of tradition and re-imbue art with political purpose. Such a view is embodied in the Surrealist writer André Breton's concept of the *objet trouvé*—a discard that the artist identifies as aesthetically valuable in its capacity to seduce and estrange.[1] In his seminal study, *Theory of the Avant-Garde* (1974), Peter Bürger reads Surrealism and its precursors, Cubism and Dada, as historical phenomena that went beyond modernism's assault on traditional techniques or form to challenge art's autonomous role in bourgeois society and its complicity with bourgeois ideals.[2] The historical avant-garde built on nineteenth-century aestheticism's opposition to bourgeois rationalism (as exemplified by the Art for Art's Sake movement's non-utilitarian ethos), which was itself a product of art's emancipation from religious worship and its growth as an industry. However, it opposed aestheticism's end result, which was an art divested of social use—an art aimed at satisfying needs repressed in everyday life, and therefore complicit in maintaining the status quo (Bürger, 28). Artists such as Kurt Schwitters and Marcel Duchamp sought to develop a radical artistic praxis that would redefine the very idea of representation and allow art to irrupt into the everyday.

In this context, the scavenging and re-use of waste functioned as part of a broader, politically charged aesthetic, exemplified by two emergent forms: collage and montage.[3] First developed by Georges Braque and Pablo Picasso,

R. Dini, *Consumerism, Waste, and Re-Use in Twentieth-Century Fiction*, DOI 10.1057/978-1-137-58165-5_2 a collage is any work of formal art composed of different forms or media. Braque and Picasso layered new materials on the canvas in order to introduce volume into the pictorial plane.[4] Later practitioners including Hans Arp and Kurt Schwitters used found materials to destabilise the unity of their work and, in Arp's case, to reveal the "transience [...] brevity [and] withering [...] of our existence" and to rage "against the mechanisation of the world."[5] The use of materials not of the artist's making—what Bürger terms "reality fragments"— blurred the boundary between representation and reality, allowing art to intrude into, and alter, the everyday (Bürger, 72; 49). This subversive intent was at the heart of Tristan Tzara's identification of resistance and active protest (against the devastations of the First World War, as well as the commodification on everyday life) as Dada's defining traits: "the new artist protests, he no longer paints."[6] The techniques of montage, collage's literary equivalent, can be found in the novels of Breton and his contemporaries, which are marked by discontinuity and rupture, and whose individual narrative strands do not form a coherent whole. By punctuating their tales with aesthetic and ontological reflections and incidents apparently unrelated to each other—which, as Bürger notes, one might easily remove from the narrative proper without affecting it—Breton and his fellow avant-gardists undermined the principle of aesthetic unity, suggesting that art could be illogical, and that its parts could add up to something different than their whole (Bürger, 80).

While the influence of the historical avant-garde on literature can be found in explicit references to collage (the first being in 1918, in Wyndham Lewis' *Tarr*[7]) and in the development of forms such as Max Ernst's "collage novels," what is more interesting for our purposes is the influence that the movement's scavenging practices had on the literary representation of objects and their value.[8] This chapter examines the extent to which recuperation of the démodé came to be used in experimental writing to challenge both aesthetic ideals under capitalism and the form of the novel itself. My reading, here, is based on Franco Moretti's elaboration of Roland Barthes' seminal study of realism, to which I alluded in the previous chapter. In "The Reality Effect," Barthes distinguishes between narrative episodes with a cardinal function ("nuclei") and the unimportant things that occur between them ("catalysers").[9] Moretti argues that over the course of the nineteenth century, description in the novel increasingly came to attend to both "nuclei" (which he calls "turning points") and "catalysers" (which he re-names "fillers").[10] The narrative filler's role is to help convey time's passage and amplify the narrative's realism without actually modifying it, thus offering up a circumscribed sense of uncertainty that effectively channels what Max Weber termed the bourgeois logic of rationalisation under capitalism.[11] Fillers enable the author to "*rationalis[e] the novelistic universe*: turning it in to a world of few surprises, fewer adventures, and no miracles at all" (Weber 154, emphasis added by Moretti).[12]

Extending Moretti and Barthes' analyses, I argue that the historical avant-garde challenges realist conventions to focus, instead, on non-events and useless objects that underscore reality's resistance to rationalisation. Where the nineteenth-century novel circumscribes chance within the order of logic, the novelists under review deploy chance to shatter logic altogether. Chance events and inexplicable objects work together to convey the enigmatic and ultimately unknowable qualities of everyday experience. Attending to these provides us—as readers of these texts—with a glimpse of a world outside the confines of capitalist commodity culture. In this sense, then, the historical avant-garde novel's filler can be seen as a narrative equivalent to the Surrealist found object: it is a cast-off worthy of more attention than the narrative interrupted by its discovery, similarly seeking to challenge "the reign of logic" and "absolute rationalism" the movement viewed as limiting human thought.[13]

The writers in this chapter examine both the possibilities and limits of recuperation within the novel form. The first of these, Giorgio de Chirico, served as a key reference point for the historical avant-garde and Surrealism in particular (although the novel of his that we examine, *Hebdomeros*, was in fact published a year after Breton's *Nadja*). The young de Chirico visited Appollinaire's salons, where he exchanged ideas with artists including Picasso and Breton[14]; these, in turn, made frequent reference in their work to de Chirico themes (enigma, melancholy), tropes (mannequins, empty squares), and even specific paintings.[15] Similarly, as the Paris representative between 1931 and 1936 for Julien Levy's New York gallery, which represented de Chirico as well as an impressive roster of Surrealists, it is likely that Loy's own references to the artist were based on an actual meeting between the two.[16] The following sections attend to both the affinities and differences between the three artists' engagement with human waste, both in terms of the kinds of waste they examine and in their articulation of its aesthetic merits.

"THE ENIGMATIC SIDE OF BEINGS AND THINGS"[17]: DE CHIRICO'S *HEBDOMEROS*

A slim, odd little narrative, written in French rather than in de Chirico's native Italian, and long after he had broken with the Surrealist movement, *Hebdomeros: The Metaphysician* (1929) is difficult to classify. It is even more difficult to square within the artist's broader oeuvre: at the time of its publication, Max Ernst commented on the paradox of it having been conceived when de Chirico himself had returned to realist painting.[18] It is precisely the novel's strangeness, however, that makes it such a compelling subject. This is an experiment in form, but also an experiment in thinking about form—and one that the Surrealists themselves praised for its embodiment of metaphysical ideals and superimposition of historical past, personal memory, and narrated present, often in the same sentence. Largely plotless, *Hebdomeros* traces its eponymous protagonist's slow progression across a nameless country. The contemplation of rotting foods, broken machines, and archaic objects provides a focal point for an otherwise aimless journey. Human waste directs the uncertain nomad's gaze, organising his thoughts and patterning his experience. "Instinctively attracted by the enigmatic side of beings and things," the novel's protagonist invites us, too, to look at the effluvia of the material world from a different angle (*H*, 14). Waste in his narrative thus becomes less a material for making than a material for thinking.

While scholars have acknowledged the relationship between de Chirico's visual works and prose, the affinities between the waste objects in *Hebdomeros* and those in his paintings have been largely ignored, and *Hebdomeros* itself has received very little critical attention.[19] The following section seeks to rectify this neglect, and to demonstrate how the depictions of remaindered humans and waste objects in the novel serve to reveal the metaphysical, hidden dimensions of modernity.

Giorgio de Chirico's early paintings sought to transcend representation, evoking the likeness of the object while fostering a sense "of something new, of something that, previously [the viewers] *have not known.*"[20] His yawning spaces, reduction of humans to mannequin-headed assemblages, and transformation of inanimate things into toy-like entities reveal the dehumanising effects of capitalist modes of production and critique the changing shape of labour under industrialization. As Keala Jewell notes, the hybrid mannequin of these paintings resembles a mindless robot, a modern monster borne out of an alienating industrialised modernity.[21] De Chirico's concept of the metaphysical juxtaposes this industrialised modernity and the otherworldly, the everyday and that which transcends it. The metaphysical waste in his works expresses anxieties about Italy's rapid urbanisation in the 1930s and human reification under capitalism.[22]

In turn, de Chirico's depiction of cast-offs in *Hebdomeros* is an extension of his prior efforts to articulate Scuola Metafisica (Metaphysical Painting). de Chirico identified the importance of the marginal, or "insignificant," in his work as early as 1911, when he articulated Scuola Metafisica as a matter of seeking out the enigmatic in the everyday:

> One must [...] understand the enigma of things generally considered insignificant. [...] To live in the world as if in an immense museum of strangeness, full of curious many-coloured toys which change their appearance, which, like little children we sometimes break to see how they are made on the inside, and, disappointed, realise they are empty.[23]

The material world calls attention to itself, but its deconstruction reveals a void. The toy the child breaks in order to understand its origins, its *raison d'être*, reveals an enigma and the limits of rational thinking. The process depicted exemplifies Derek Winnicott's concept, in *Playing and Reality*, of the "transitional object"—a toy the child invests with "excess" meaning, and which gains a unique hold on him/her. As an entity the child recognises as simultaneously separate from him/herself and manipulable (i.e., to be stroked, chewed, or broken), the transitional object nurtures illusion. But as the child gradually loses interest the toy loses its value and becomes an object of disillusion: it becomes a "resting place" between fantasy/desire and the real world. The transitional object is a space between dream and reality, infancy and adulthood, the spiritual and the material, the rational and the irrational.[24] Metaphysical representation captures the world as seen in that interstitial state, but goes further, representing *broken*, fragmented objects caught between fantasy and reality, things that to the "developed" self—to an adult modernity—are divested of logical meaning, function, or commercial value. The approach amplifies the transitional aspect of Winnicott's concept, making broken, partial objects—objects that are already transitional in their quality as waste—the site of imaginative play.

This interplay of reality and play, vibrant matter and inert, is pivotal to *The Great Metaphysician*, a de Chirico painting to whose central figure, the titular "Metaphysician," Hebdomeros, has often been likened (see Fig. 2.1).

The construction of a human from wooden planks, empty picture frames, and a featureless mannequin head is common in de Chirico's paintings. However, the re-situation of these elements against a backdrop of skewed perspectival lines and anonymous building façades sets it apart from his earlier work and anticipates the representation of effluvia in *Hebdomeros*. While

Fig. 2.1   Giorgio de Chirico, "The Great Metaphysician" (1917). Oil on canvas: 110 × 80 cm, BPK, Berlin (Nationalgalerie, Staatliche Museen, Berlin, Germany)/ Joerg P. Anders/Art Resource, New York and ARSNY

de Chirico's earlier paintings represent heaped objects indoors, this is the first to bring them into the open—as if there were no more space, inside, to house them. Traditionally a site for commemorating religious and literary figures or national heroes, the piazza is transformed into a home for a disquieting pile of assembled rubbish that, however, also resembles an official monument. The title meanwhile suggests the pile's other-worldliness. This is metaphysical waste—waste that transcends the material and the everyday—and *meta-waste*: waste conscious that it is an interloper, merely imitating a human or god-like form. James Thrall Thoby likewise notes the evolution of this figure during the course of the next eight years, from a composition of "relatively simple, mostly angular forms" to an increasingly "complicated heap of strange bric-a-brac" (Thoby, 132).

The ideas present in *The Great Metaphysician* prefigure those explored in *Hebdomeros*. The novel opens with a childhood memory triggered by the visit to a strange building reminiscent of a "German consulate in Melbourne" in a space redolent with the "atmosphere which pervades Anglo-Saxon towns on Sundays" (*H*, 10). Following this vision of disjointed geospatial impressions, Hebdomeros recalls how, as a child, he broke a vase that had sat on the family's living room mantelpiece for 90 years (*H*, 14). Rather than scolding him, the little boy's family members stare, transfixed, at the fragments on the floor:

> They spoke of sticking the pieces together again. [...] Some of them alleged that they knew specialist craftsmen who carried out this kind of work so perfectly that afterwards the break was invisible. [His] brother made out that it was the way in which the pieces of the vase were scattered over the floor which was largely responsible for fascinating the [family] in this way. The pieces in fact were arranged in the form of a trapezium, like a well-known constellation, and the idea that the sky was turned upside-down fascinated to the point of immobilisation [these people] who, after all, apart from the fact that instead of looking up were looking down, [resembled] those first Chaldean or Babylonian astronomers who through the fine summer nights kept watch, lying on terraces, their heads turned towards the stars. (*H*, 15)

It is a disorientating passage, reminiscent of Jean Arp's account of his and the Dadaists' collage processes, which were similarly characterised by the examination of constellations of fragments strewn on the floor. It is as if de Chirico were commenting directly on the historical avant-garde's recuperative efforts and yet slyly poking fun at such naïveté: the child who has broken the vase wonders at the fact that no one has laid any blame upon him for his participation in the fall of the gods (the vase is from Rhodes) and marvels at the assertion that that which has been broken can be put back together. In this he resembles a disillusioned avant-gardist, critiquing his contemporaries for not mourning the ruins of tradition and merely observing them like "curious archaeologists" (*H*, 15). Indeed, the "scene had been for Hebdomeros the cause of a disappointment followed immediately by a feeling of shame" (*H*, 16)—an echo of the artist's own disenchantment with Surrealism and attempts to distance himself from its practices. It is ironic that the movement should have heralded a work that in fact critiqued its practice through mimicry.

One manifestation of this mimicry is in Hebdomeros' canny predilection for punning, which parodies the punning games of the Surrealists (as exemplified, perhaps, by Ernst's *La femme sans/100 tête*). To the cries of "The acropolis, the acropolis!" Hebdomeros replies, that:

> cette fois-ci, ni *d'accroc*, ni de *Paul* et bien qu'il y ait meme un Périclés, ce n'est pas celui auquel vous tous instinctivement pensez, celui [...] qui fuit le tendre ami des peintres, des sculpteurs, des architects et des poétes.[25]
>
> [No, there is no question this time either of *a crow* or of *Pollis*. And although there is a Pericles, it is not the one of whom you are all instinctively thinking [...] he who was the loving friend of painters, sculptors, architects and poets.] (*H*, 66)

The reference to the "acropolis" and the word game that follows (a pun on *accroc*—French for snag—and the name Paul) results in a triple subversion—a *détournement* of classical mythology and Christianity, a deployment of the methods of the historical avant-garde, and, at the same time, a *détournement* of those methods. The use of classical mythology and Christian theology (the allusion to Pericles and Paul) in the punning game breaks the rule-breaking rules of Surrealist practice: it amounts to a re-introduction of that which the historical avant-garde sought to brush aside. The myth of Pericles is debunked; the apostle Paul is referenced as an absence; and the reference to the loss of the subject for "painters, sculptures, architects and poets" gives utterance to the modern crisis of representation. The garbling of the mythical hero's name signals a consciousness of the inevitable wasting of body and text—an awareness that the corporeal is caught up in processes of waste and that artistic production both generates waste and will one day end up as/in waste.

A preoccupation with waste, disease, and artistic creativity runs throughout *Hebdomeros*, partly influenced by Nietzschean thought, a fact de Chirico openly acknowledged.[26] Like the "revelation" Nietzsche delineates in *Ecce Homo* (1888/1908), de Chirico claimed that his metaphysical aesthetic was conceived while he was in a suspended state, emerging from a long gastrointestinal illness akin to that which Nietzsche experienced intermittently throughout his life.[27] However, *Hebdomeros* does not feature scenes of recovery so much as of physical decay and intestinal disorder, in which gastrointestinal ailments serve as a metaphor for civic dysfunction: glimpses into the boarding house rooms of characters rendered invalid by their malfunctioning livers and intestines (*H*, 84–85; 93) are juxtaposed with different attempts at urban renewal, in which the city itself is presented as a body in disarray (*H*, 111). For instance, Hebdomeros stays in a hotel next door to a "famous invalid" whose impending death is explicitly related to a malfunctioning urinary tract:

> He suffered from a pernicious disease which demanded that his body should always lie in the chair at a fixed angle for otherwise he was liable to a sudden death due to the bad turn that the stagnant urine in his body might have played on him; for he could only expel it with great difficulty (he often remained whole days without passing water). (*H*, 32)

Shortly thereafter, Hebdomeros ends up in the room of a different hotel, in a city unsettled by revolution, where financial uncertainty is fomented by "greedy bankers who ai[m] to cause a fall in prices and speculate afterwards on the rise which w[ill] follow" (*H*, 92). Here, he observes a sick man lying in bed surrounded by bandages and medications, wearing a short nightshirt and no underwear, his flaccid genitals exposed as he "smok[es] his pipe and gaz[es] dreamily at the mouldings on the ceiling" (*H*, 93). Both passages depict man as an assemblage of malfunctioning bodily processes that eerily parallel the dysfunctions of the body politic. Conduits for stagnant urine, immobile fixtures that neither see nor think, the bodies of the two invalids stand for a stalled, malfunctioning modernity, incapable of entirely disposing of—or excreting—the past. The passage brings to mind de Chirico's 1927 painting, *Two Figures*, in which indeterminate brown matter and fragments of ancient buildings appear caught in the intestinal tracts of the two human forms (see Fig. 2.2).

As well as focusing on those afflicted by degenerative disease, *Hebdomeros* dwells on human beings that appear inanimate and waste objects that appear almost alive. A signal of incipient transformation and change, these hybrid, de-contextualised entities elicit thoughts of a metaphysical modernity—what, in his early writings on representation, de Chirico termed the capacity for "the things of this world [to] speak" and for "modern times [to] appea[r] strange and distant."[28] The fact that the images themselves are ones recycled from his paintings and the technique a veritable textual translation of his visual practice can be seen as one more de-contextualisation. One such transposition is apparent in a depiction of a city of men who construct trophies for a living:

Fig. 2.2 Giorgio de Chirico, "Two Figures" (1927). Oil on canvas. Art Resource, New York and ARSNY

curious scaffolding, simultaneously severe and amusing, rose in the middle of the bedrooms and drawing-rooms, the delight and enjoyment of guests and children. Constructions which assumed the shape of mountains, for like mountains they were born from the action of internal fire and, once the upset of creation was over, they proved through their tormented equilibrium the ardent urge which had led to their appearance [...] they were immortal, for they knew neither dawns nor sunsets, but eternal noon. The rooms which sheltered them were like those islands which are found outside the great shipping routes, where the inhabitants sometimes wait for whole seasons for an oil-tanker [...] to toss them some cases of damaged canned food. (*H*, 47)

Beginning as a description of constructed objects, the sentence ends with an attribution of immortality that is difficult to gauge: does it refer to

Fig. 2.3 Giorgio de Chirico, "Silenzioso Maestoso" (1927). Oil on canvas. Art Resource, New York and ARSNY

the constructions or their creators? The ambiguity extends to the following lines—to whom, or to what, does the sheltering effect of the room refer? And is it the trophies, or the men, which are being likened to marooned beings subsisting on others' waste? The housed constructions recall the subjects of de Chirico's still-life interiors: assemblages of precariously piled detritus mainly composed of wooden frames and wood planks, the whole resembling a strange hybridisation of building scaffolding, de-constructed easel, and human form (see Fig. 2.3).

The link between body and built environment is made even more explicit in the novel's strange depiction of a series of gigantic stone men sitting on the park benches surrounding a group of villas. Without ever moving from their perch, these living statues converse until the day they suddenly "sp[eak] no longer" and summoned specialists determine that "the small amount of life which had animated them until now ha[s] vanished" (*H*, 78). The city decides that the carcasses of the stone men must go, so that they "no longer uselessly encumber the little gardens of the villas"—and thus, de Chirico tells us, "one after another the great stone men [are] broken up and the pieces thrown into a valley which soon look[s] like a battlefield after combat" (*H*, 78). This startling account of not-quite-living beings and their subsequent death and disposal brings together de Chirico's fascination with fragmentation and the relationship between objects and space, as well as underscoring a preoccupation with the processes of urban renewal and reconstruction. The living statues, who spent their days discussing their hunting exploits in forests long since gone, extend the artist's concern with urban alienation—the city, in this context, has turned its inhabitants into stone, and its central concern with those bodies is to dispose of them efficiently once they have ceased to be of use.

Elsewhere, Hebdomeros travels through a landscape recently trans-formed by the convulsions of modernity, where "gradually, huge build-ings had risen up on all sides [and] there were new faces to be seen in the streets" (*H*, 24). Hebdomeros "fle[es]" the district and its "strangely accelerated rhythm of life" only to find himself in a forest infected by industrial progress. A "strange epidemic rage[s]" among the trees, mani-fest in a "giant spiral staircase of untreated wood which ended in a kind of platform" that "strangles" each tree trunk (*H*, 24). On one such plat-form lies a "strange" inert man—resembling neither human nor statue, he recalls, rather, the

> petrified [...] corpses discovered at Pompeii. Lying on the platform made him in the end become one with it, he became platformised; he began to resemble a large piece of wood with unsquared corners nailed in place hastily in order to protect the floor from a shock which would never occur. This is why, when he was on the look-out, the platform appeared upside-down for any reinforce-ment of the planks could only be imagined as nailed *underneath*. (*H*, 25)

It is a collision of things: the self merges with the built environment, nature is "strangled" by modernity, and the text is infiltrated by the materials that characterise de Chirico's visual practice. "No longer human," evoking death, and foreshadowing that "which will never occur," the image of the "platformised" man recalls the mannequins in *The Disquieting Muses* series (1917 to c. 1947) and the *Great Metaphysician* series (1917 to c. 1925). Recalling the pivotal role wood plays in these paintings and throughout de Chirico's pictorial views, and already significant for its involvement in catalysing the subject's "de-animation" (if not itself the catalyst), the plank, here, shudders to life. The city has infected the tree, but the wood has infected the self. In this way, the "platformised" individual gains the metaphysical aura of the objects intrinsic to the artist's visual *oeuvre*.

Obstructions such as those described above are less a reflection of language's limits than testament to de Chirico's fascination with their narrative value—the role they might play in conjuring images in the reader's imagination as forceful and disquieting as his paintings. Thus, for instance, de Chirico attends to the "rubbish of all types" scattered in an empty piazza at the end of a market day in a town where people flock to be treated for their venereal diseases (*H*, 49). The description of the ailing patients is juxtaposed with the haphazard assortment of "orange-peels and crushed cigarette ends" they leave behind at day's end, conveying a *malaise* in a manner acutely reminiscent of the motifs of his paintings, in which remainders are as—if not more—important than whole entities. Waste here is all too aware of its quality *as* waste and eerily capable of expressing itself as such. The metaphysics of De Chirico's prose lies precisely in this: language's absorption (consumption, *exhaustion*) in the description of rubbish, in attending to what de Chirico himself termed the need to *débarasser* (clean up) art from logical thought or realist concerns.[29] The subtext or underlying signification evoked by the disquieting object remains subtextual, embedded in the object described, eluding coherent explanation. The ambiguity of the objects' meaning in turn leads us to appreciate them for themselves, and for their sheer absurdity and inexplicability, often in a humorous, quasi-Dadaist fashion. Consider:

> Among the drums of broken columns where big horses suffering from dysentery come each evening when the square is deserted and crop avidly the tender camomile plants flourishing in the shadow of the glorious ruins, everyone was in his place. (*H*, 66)

The scatological reference and the notions of ruin and decay are juxtaposed with the suggestion of regeneration. The medicinal plants sprouting from the cracks of the city's ruins suggest that the urban space has become a place for pasture; there is a place for everything in this strange landscape, and everything—humans, animals, forgotten buildings, and flora—is in its place. The incessant motion of modernity triggers an inclination towards inertia. It is a tactic that hinges on appropriating the inanimate qualities of the detritus excreted by the urban and whose decomposition the act of narration seeks to stall.

That things are going precisely nowhere, that human waste is both means and end, is further evidenced in the figuration of the wandering "madman" who "without being a gastronome" perambulates the city streets, asking passers-by for an account of their last meal and "pok[ing] about in cases full of rubbish which he f[inds] outside the main doors," telling whoever will listen that "he [is] very fond of sausage and rice"

(*H*, 41). A mere imitator of a "true" culinary *connoisseur*, the parasitic vagrant who feeds on second-hand accounts—cast-off stories, cast-off comestibles—speaks of an aesthetic entirely preoccupied with absorbing, pastiching, or satirising the practices of its contemporaries.

This impasse is exemplified by the devolution of Hebdomeros' *flânerie*, in the novel's conclusion, into the senseless wandering of a homeless man among unsignifying signifiers. de Chirico sets the scene up carefully, situating his protagonist among walls and billboards covered with political manifestoes and urban renewal plans in order to satirise the bureaucratic processes of modernity as well as the idealisation of progress (*H*, 110). The political manifesto reproduced in the text is absurdly ornate, rife with obscure turns of phrase whose opacity is highlighted by the narrator's footnote: "Hebdomeros never succeeded in understanding the meaning of these [...] words" (*H*, 110). The municipal plan is similarly set up as an absurdity, promising a "prophylactic clinic for combating venereal diseases [,] the installation of a collective rubbish dump [and] a lighted bowling-alley [for] lovers" (*H*, 111). In both cases, the text shrilly calls attention to the failings of modernity, while suggesting the role that language can play in conveying them.

"What is the meaning of this dream [of] trenches dug in haste," Hebdomeros eventually asks—of "tiny hospitals [...] where even the [...] poor wounded zebras, are cared for with skill and tenderness, and emerge bandaged, sewn up again, repaired, disinfected, patched up, renewed again, in fact. Is life no more than a vast lie?" (*H*, 91). The question self-consciously gestures to the form of the novel itself, with its endless digressions, repetitions, and allusions to de Chirico's previous work. To the very end, *Hebdomeros* enacts de Chirico's own version of the historical avant-garde's recuperative practices. As well as testing the limits of translating its author's visual recuperations into prose, the novel suggests that the true value of metaphysical waste is its ambiguity and resistance to interpretation.

"QUITE UNEXPECTED, QUITE IMPROBABLE"[30]: ANDRÉ BRETON'S *NADJA*

Like de Chirico's, the Surrealist André Breton's artistic vision was based on a melding of life and art, and his practice was governed by the principles of juxtaposition and re-use of discards. According to Mark Polizzotti, Breton appropriated the collage technique as a regenerative means.[31] This idea was indebted to Comte de Lautréamont's earlier articulation, in the *Poésies*, that "Plagiarism is necessary. Progress implies it": a new aesthetic holds within it echoes of those that have come before. This recycling of methods and materials went beyond Breton's artistic practice, infiltrating his life and relationships: Polizzotti notes that "Letters to close friends became cut-and-paste assemblages of newspaper clippings, labels, scraps of cigarette packages, medical reports and pieces of others' letters" (Polizzotti, 77–78). Breton himself became increasingly concerned with collecting both valuable primitive objects and everyday ephemera. One journalist described the ageing artist's living room as a "junkyard,"[32] while in his posthumous (1970) account of Breton, James Lord recalled:

> an extraordinary interior [...] filled literally as full as can be, with an aston-ishing profusion of heteroclite objects, paintings, sculptures, constructions, and whatnot. I have never seen so many crowded into such a limited space. And yet it does uncannily make a whole, which is the strangest thing of all.[33]

Assembled together, the discards and valuables contained in Breton's home constituted a tenuous living assemblage in which each item was saved from the scrapheap by virtue of its categorization (for the moment) as sentimentally or aesthetically valuable.

Such recuperation forms a central tenet of Breton's arguably most well-known novel, *Nadja* (1928). The antithesis of Moretti's description, after Max Weber, of a narrative sustained by the logic of bourgeois rationalism (Moretti, 381), Breton's narrative is set against a *milieu* entirely exposed to coincidence and chance—"quite unexpected, quite improbable" occurrences that he holds up as evidence of an irrational, otherworldly alternative to bour-geois existence (*N*, 52). From the very first page, Breton conceives of identity as both arbitrary and fluid, as exemplified by the novel's famous opening, "Who am I?" and the narrator's view that the verb "to haunt," when used in relation to place, calls attention to the previous ("ghostly") selves one sloughs off over the course of one's life (*N*, 11). In this way, *Nadja* self-consciously claims to exemplify a new, revolutionary, form that challenges both literary realism and the works of Breton's avant-garde forerunners. Of these, the fig-ure of Giorgio de Chirico looms most prominently. de Chirico's metaphysical painting style is an important reference point for the narrator, and the analysis of his aesthetic approach provides a clue to the way the text itself should be read. It is to de Chirico's eye for the aesthetic possibilities inherent in the ordinary and the cast aside that the entire novel gestures:

> Chirico acknowledged at the time that he could paint only when *surprised* [...] by certain arrangements of objects [...] the entire enigma of revelation

consisted for him in this word: surprise [...] the resulting work [...] resembled [its source of inspiration] only 'in the strange way two brothers resemble each other, or rather as a dream about someone resembles that person in reality. It is, and at the same time is not, the same is not, the same person; a slight and mysterious transfiguration is apparent in the features.' (*N*, 15)

Surrealism itself looked to seize upon surprising encounters and material finds. The found object, or *objet trouvé*, already alluded to at the outset of this chapter, is a challenge to the art-work-as-commodity, but it is also a challenge to aesthetic norms: to find the object is to be astonished by something outside of the pictorial frame. In *Mad Love* (1937), Breton states that it must "dra[w one] as something [one] ha[s] *never seen*."[34] More specifically:

> What is delightful here is the dissimilarity itself, which exists between the object wished for and *the object found*. This *trouvaille*, whether it be artistic, scientific, philosophic, or as useless as anything, is enough to undo the beauty of everything beside it. [...] It alone can enlarge the universe, causing it to relinquish some of its opacity, letting us discover its extraordinary capacities for reserve, proportionate to the innumerable needs of the spirit. Daily life abounds, moreover, in just this sort of small discovery, where there is frequently an element of apparent gratuitousness, very probably a function of our provisional incomprehension, discoveries that seem to me not in the least unimportant. (*ML*, 15)

The found object, like chance events, has the capacity to interrupt the everyday, catalyse reverie, and shed light on that which bourgeois society eschews or intentionally obscures. The found object inhabits the waste phase and recuperative phase, because although it no longer serves its original purpose and is "as useless as anything," it is imbued with an aesthetic and spiritual purpose by the artist. "The finding of an object serves here exactly the same purpose as the dream [:] it frees the individual from paralysing affective scruples" (*ML*, 32). Of course, the implication that the incorporation of the waste object into an aesthetic work renders it immune to the "paralysing affective scruples" of everyday life is somewhat disingenuous. After all, the found object's recuperation will contribute to the creation of a sellable artwork that participates in the commodity pathway regardless of how much it shocks or unnerves. But Breton circumvents this issue through narrative. The novel provides an arena in which to test the limits of the "finding" process and imagine how Bürger's "life praxis [based] in art" might play

out (Bürger, 49). *Nadja* is thus a fiction-qua-manifesto that deploys waste
objects and waste on a metaphorical level to make its points. We see this
from the outset, as Breton discusses de Chirico's search for the enigma of
objects in order to then stipulate his own view of contingency and chance:

> We have said nothing about Chirico until we take into account his most per-
> sonal views about the artichoke, the glove, the cookie, or the spool. [...] As
> far as I am concerned, a mind's arrangement with regard to certain objects
> is even more important than its regard for certain arrangements of objects,
> these two kinds of arrangement controlling between them all forms of sen-
> sibility. (*N*, 16)

By shifting our attention away from the objects themselves—including their quotidian unimportance and the divesting of their former function—and towards the "arrangement" of the mind that observes them and
identifies their importance, Breton underscores the significance of their
mystical qualities and the irrelevance of their original purpose. The functional aspects of the glove or artichoke are unimportant, while their combination with other, similarly incongruous, objects undermines any realist
intent. Rather, we are made to notice their decontextualized state and the
likely irrationality of the mind that selected them. Contemplation of the
irrationality of that mind's arrangement adds to the dislocating effect of
the objects: the one enhances the other, creating a cyclical "sensibility"
rooted in peeling away our (flawed) perception of the material world as
ordered.

Breton's statement of intent in the novel's opening both substantiates
Moretti's thesis and re-affirms the Surrealist Manifesto, functioning as a veritable attack on art's role in bourgeois society. As Bürger articulates it, avant-
gardist literature wilfully undermines the concept of authorship through
references to actual events and theoretical elaborations, which result in a
work comprising juxtapositions of reality and artifice (Bürger, 22). Similarly,
Breton situates himself against the literary canon. Against, that is:

> those empiricists of the novel who claim to give us characters separate from
> themselves, to define them physically, morally—in their fashion!—in the ser-
> vice of some cause we should prefer to disregard! Out of one real character
> about whom they suppose they know something they make two characters
> in their story; out of two, they make one. (*N*, 16)

[handwritten annotation: waste and the found object catalyst and support an anti-realist endeavour — for anti-bourgeois ends]

The Surrealist non-novel as conceptualised by Breton centres on the infinitesimal detail divested of its moral value and of its relation to the grand narrative of a life governed by destiny or predetermination. It centres on that which the infinitesimal detail reveals, or presupposes to reveal, about the author-qua-biographical-subject. Where the Surrealist house is a glass edifice open to outside scrutiny, and whose "walls sta[y] where [they are] as if by magic" (*N*, 18), the Surrealist non-novel is a transparent narrative that appears more fictional than any fiction could claim to be, and which teases us with its blurring of art and reality. These infinitesimal details out of which it is constructed are precisely the materials the traditional novel sidelined: his work, in fact, undercuts the very notion of centre and side, text and margin:

> I intend to mention, in the margin of the narrative I have yet to relate, only the most decisive episodes of my life *as I can conceive it apart from its organic plan*, and only insofar as it is at the mercy of chance—the merest as well as the greatest—temporarily escaping my control, admitting me to an almost forbidden world of sudden parallels, petrifying coincidences. [...] I am concerned, I say, with facts [...] which on each occasion present all the appearances of a signal, without our being able to say precisely which signal, and of what. (*N*, 19, emphasis in the original)

"*Life as conceived apart from its organic plan*" suggests the margin of a narrative as yet to be narrated, and coincidences that render the lived life novelistic. Breton breaks with the formal guidelines of his predecessors: the rationalising, ordering functions of bourgeois logic give way to a programme designed to highlight the irrational, the chaotic. In rejecting the moral value of work (which underlies the Protestant work ethic), Breton re-draws the lines governing the *writer's* work ethic, effectively countering what Franco Moretti defines as the moral purpose of description: "And after this, let no one speak to me of work—I mean of the moral value of work," Breton says. "I am forced to accept the notion of work as a material necessity [...] life's grim obligations make it a necessity, but never [will] I [...] believe in its value, revere my own or that of other men" (*N*, 59–60). If the function of work (*travaille*) is no longer moral, then neither is the function of *the* work (*l'oeuvre*).

The aim of Breton's project is thus to discuss "things without pre-established order, and according to the mood of the moment which lets whatever survives survive" (*N*, 23)—an aesthetic plan that mirrors Breton's urban practices—and much of the narrative is dedicated to meditating upon chance encounters and chance objects, and determining how they might relate to each other. The novel's narrator—who may or may not be Breton himself, as he suggests at various points—can be seen to enact the historical avant-garde's commitment to an aesthetic that intrudes into the fabric of everyday life. This is evidenced not only by a meandering, largely plotless narrative that mimics the perambulations of its protagonist but by the minute attention given, throughout, to the mundane and worthless. For instance, Breton's narrator dedicates nearly two pages to describing his fascination with a woman's glove and his ensuing fear at the prospect she might give it to him: "I don't know what there can have been, at that moment, so terribly, so marvellously decisive for me in the thought of that glove leaving her hand forever" (N, 56). In keeping with Surrealism's championing of "not knowing," the reason underlying his fear is never disclosed: to resolve the mystery would undermine it.

Breton explores unkowability at length by observing cast-offs and effluvia that are unknowable by their very nature. The most compelling of these objects is depicted in the famous flea market scene:

> Again, quite unexpectedly, when Marcel Noll and I went one Sunday to the Saint-Ouen flea-market (I go there often, searching for objects that can be found nowhere else: old-fashioned, broken, useless, almost incomprehensible, even perverse—at least in the sense I give to the word and which I prefer—like, for example, that kind of irregular, white, shellacked half-cylinder covered with reliefs and depressions that are meaningless to me, streaked with horizontal and vertical reds and greens, preciously nestled in a case under a legend in Italian, which I brought home and which after careful examination I have finally identified as some kind of statistical device, operating three-dimensionally and recording the population of a city in such and such a year, though all this makes it no more comprehensible to me), our attention was simultaneously caught by a brand new copy of Rimbaud's *Oeuvres Complétes* lost in a tiny, wretched bin of rags, yellowed nineteenth-century photographs, worthless books, and iron spoons. (N, 52–53)

The delineation of the found object's significance erupts into the space of the text. It shatters it. Housed in parentheses is the very ethos of Surrealist exploration—the search for the surprising, the laying one's self open to surprise, and the ability to look at things, and thus the world, anew. The scene represented, the practice described, and the urban space in which it occurs are all liminal spaces in the body of the text. Their representation within parentheses exemplifies Surrealism' ethos of stealth and subversion. The fact that the first time we encounter the found object occurs within brackets is further testament to the object's liminal quality: like the world that treats waste as worthy only of rejection, the text itself expunges it. At the same time, the fact that the parenthetical statement ends up taking up so much space—growing to several paragraphs, spilling onto two pages—says something about the resistant, order-defying nature of detritus, and Surrealism's faith in its capacity to resist circumnavigation and evince change. Like the anecdote the protagonist told us, earlier, that he intends to "mention, in the margin of the narrative [he has] yet to relate," the parenthetical description of the found object is both one of the "most decisive episodes of [his] life" (*N*, 19) and one to be glossed over. The found object's mention is a clue for the reader to seize upon and recognise as deserving of attention in its parenthesised displacement in much the same spirit as the "mind's arrangement" that Breton urges us to consider when contemplating a de Chirico painting.

The novel's other central concern is to dismantle social assumptions about the moral value of work and commercial value, and to highlight the relationship between idleness and creativity—a key element of the Surrealist credo. Scavenging, the extraction of meaning from chance encounters, and idleness are inextricable from each other. To attend to the city's effluvia, one must be unencumbered by work; to imagine the meaning underlying said effluvia, one must be in an unencumbered state of mind. Thus, when Breton admonishes the reader, "let no one speak to me of work—I mean the moral value of work" (*N*, 59), he specifies that the difference between himself and Nadja, and those who work, is that the latter spend the train ride home "thinking about what they have left behind until tomorrow, only until tomorrow" (*N*, 68). Caught between the just-completed and as-yet-to-do, they neglect to notice their surroundings, let alone contemplate an alternative way of life. He adds: "People cannot be interesting insofar as they endure their work. [...] How can that raise them up if the spirit of revolt is not within them? Besides, at such moments you see them and they don't see you" (*N*, 68). The labourer's desire to do his duty impedes his imagination. It is the artist's role to illuminate all that goes unobserved, and in so doing to suggest alternative ways of seeing. The novel's efforts to delineate why doing one's duty is a form of self-imprisonment is in keeping with Surrealism's central tenets, while its disjointed narrative structure and meditative, inconclusive tone can be seen to offer an alternative to the blinkered vision of the working day. This idea is crystallised in the narrator's forceful assertion that:

> there is no use being alive if one must work. The event from which each of us is entitled to expect the revelation of his own life's meaning—that event which I may not yet have found, but on whose path I seek myself—*is not earned by work.* (N, 60, emphasis in the original)

Breton's novel is essentially driven, however fitfully and digressively, by its narrator's desire to find "that event [...] on whose path" he seeks himself; the process of sifting through flea market bins and wandering into deserted areas of the city are components of that search.

A similar faith in the epiphanic value of the everyday spurs the narrator's account of his and Nadja's accidental visit to the Place Dauphine. The episode is curious, for it is immediately followed by a long parenthetical explanation that, like the description of the flea market, elaborates on the unimportance of the place itself while drawing attention to its evident significance for a Surrealist mind:

> (The Place Dauphine is certainly one of the most profoundly secluded places I know of, one of the worst wastelands in Paris. Whenever I happen to be there, I feel the desire to go somewhere else gradually ebbing out of me, I have to struggle against myself to get free from a gentle, over-insistent, and, finally, crushing embrace. Besides, I lived for some time in a hotel near this square, the City Hotel, where the comings and goings at all hours, for anyone not satisfied with oversimplified solutions, are suspect). (N, 80)

The Place Dauphine is at once an unexceptional wasteland, and a magnetic space Breton is loath to abandon. The place is seedy—as implied by the "suspect" comings and goings "at all hours" at the nearby hotel—but it is also enigmatic. One is tempted to draw connections between Breton's attraction for the Place Dauphine and his attraction to Nadja (underscored by the triangular shape of the Place, which Breton described, in *La Clé des Champs*, as "le sexe de Paris," and which Dagmar Motycka Weston notes was "long associated, in the Surrealists' imagination, with the female pudendum"[35]). In both cases, what renders them attractive for Breton is their marginalisation from bourgeois society, the one existing near a hotel but having no use-value of its own, the other explicitly identified as poor and without a fixed home or source of income beyond prostitution and selling cocaine. Both entities exist outside the sphere of capitalist exchange and are plundered, by Breton's narrator (and, indeed, by Breton himself), for artistic inspiration—as manifest in their inclusion in the novel. Both the Place Dauphine and Nadja are, in other words, two further forms of waste that share characteristics with the found object of the flea market, but whose surplus status is directly related to their exclusion (or marginalisation), respectively, from the property market and the labour force. Indeed, Nadja too appears to see herself in precisely such interstitial terms. As she herself puts it, "I am the soul in limbo" (*N*, 71). Similarly, among the first parenthetical asides Breton makes regarding their first meeting is a qualifying statement about her very intentions: "(I say claimed because she later admitted she was going nowhere)" (*N*, 65). An articulation of her plans for that day, the statement contributes to the reader's over-arching sense of her lack of direction.

Breton's novel takes us through a perambulating, dream-like exploration of Surrealist practice, inviting us to gaze upon the city and its marginalia with the eyes of an artist open to otherness. His meditations on the nature of chance, madness, aesthetic beauty, and paid employment meld autobiography, fiction, literary theory, and social criticism, and throw into relief the central role that waste plays in these discussions. His faith in the aesthetic and metaphysical qualities of cast-offs and his meditations on idleness are also a search for an alternative to capitalist logic and its influence on everyday experience.

HUMAN WASTE AND THE AESTHETICS OF THE "ECONOMICALLY NUDE"[36]: MINA LOY'S *INSEL*

While Giorgio de Chirico is best remembered for his visual art and André Breton for his novels, Mina Loy (1882–1966) is most known for her poetry and for her personal and professional connections to the avant-garde movements in Paris and, later, New York.[37] As well as engaging with Italian Futurism in her poetry, Loy collaborated closely with the likes of Tristan Tzara and Francis Picabia. She had affairs with Futurism's leaders, Tommaso Marinetti, and Giovanni Papini, and later married the proto-Dadaist poet Arthur Craven, whom Breton cited as a key source of inspiration for Surrealism.[38] Her poetry and stories engage closely with the concerns of the historical avant-garde—perhaps most explicitly in her mock-manifestos, which undermine the central tenets of Futurism—while excrement, garbage, and human waste in the form of the homeless are prevalent in both her writing and visual art. One of her best-known poems, "Love Songs to Joannes" (1917), begins with a description of Cupid as a pig, "His rosy snout/Rooting erotic garbage"—a figuration that startlingly undermines the distinction between the spiritual and the earthly, conceiving of waste as an alternative to heavenly manna, and with its own peculiar erotic charge.[39] A similar preoccupation with manufactured waste and remaindered humans runs throughout Loy's work. Like de Chirico and Breton, Loy identifies, in waste, a radical potential and a means to break with past forms and traditions, as exemplified by the desire expressed in "Oh Hell" (1920), "To clear the drifts of spring/Of our forebear's excrements" and her description of the modern poet as "Choked with the tatters of tradition" (*LLB*, 271). Where she differs from Breton and de Chirico however—and from other fellow artists such as Duchamp—is in her deployment of waste as a metaphor for the socially excluded, the marginalised, and the financially vulnerable: what she terms, in the unfinished novel *Insel*, the "economically nude" (*I*, 23). For Loy, waste is both a means to overthrow tradition (material with which to create visual art), and a medium through which to explore marginality, including the marginality of unsuccessful (often starving) artists, the unemployed, and the homeless.

The materialist concern manifest in *Insel* and Loy's poetry can be partly ascribed to her own design practice. Throughout the 1920s, Loy designed hats, dresses, perfume bottles, and jewellery out of bric-a-brac from the flea market in Porte de Clignancourt, which she then sold to the Paris department stores (Burke, 338). She also owned a lamp and lighting shop funded by Peggy Guggenheim, where she sold lamps she herself had made out of Parisian flea market finds. This work brought its own challenges: fear of selling out (Peggy Guggenheim recalls Loy's fear that selling through department stores cheapened her creations[40]) and financial instability (Burke, 338). Caroline Burke notes that by the late 1920s Mina "was so confused about what she owed to whom that she not only threatened to sell the [lampshade] shop but told [her daughter] that her apartment was about to be seized" (Burke, 369). For Jessica Bernstein, Loy's engagement with design situates her in between the role of artist and producer. This "perennial awareness of the economy supporting [her] enterprise" underpins her work, and particularly her reflections on the making of art and the "play between firstness and reproducibility."[41] Loy's one attempt at the novel, the unfinished, posthumously published, *Insel*, provides a compelling insight into the historical avant-garde's recuperative efforts and the tension between a radical aesthetic and the more practical issue of making a living.

Loy started writing *Insel* while she was still living in Paris, inspired by her relationship with the German Surrealist painter Richard Oelze, whom she met while an agent for her son-in-law Julien Levy's New York gallery (Burke, 400). Her work on the novel continued intermittently after she moved to New York in 1936 but was largely superseded by her interest in the street bums of the Bowery, where she lived throughout the 1930s and 1940s, writing about their relationship to the city and making collages from junk she collected off the street.[42] Scholars have read this shift away from the international artistic circles in which she initially took part and her turn to the observation of homeless people as part of a wider rejection of the historical avant-garde's insularity.[43] The novel's concern with the negotiation of commercial work and art, its playful derision of the Paris art scene, and its parodying of avant-gardist values anticipates her later work, while its challenge to the Surrealist patriarchy, particularly in *Insel*, sheds light on the historical avant-garde as a whole.

Firstly, Loy's novel inverts the gender roles of Breton's *Nadja*: the first-person female narrator, Mrs Jones, an artist who supports herself by finding new works of art for a New York gallery, meets a homeless male Surrealist artist, Insel, who lives off the kindness of various (female) strangers who feed and house him in return for sexual favours. Mrs Jones' reference to Insel, throughout the novel, as her "pet *clochard*" (tramp, or bum), likewise bears affinities to Breton's depiction of Nadja. While it would be difficult to ascribe these similarities to an intentional effort to satirise Breton's novel, Loy's inversion of roles certainly challenges the Surrealist *Kunstlerroman*'s representation of gender and artistic creativity. Moreover, Loy's depiction of Insel complicates Breton's idealised vision of the wandering Nadja, suggesting the extent to which the commodification of artistic genius involves the glamorisation of poverty. In this way, she suggests both the impracticality and ethical dubiousness of living one's art in a Surrealist vein. Thus, Loy's novel is not so much about the recuperation of actual waste—there are in fact very few references to the scavenging Loy herself enjoyed—as about the narrator's failed efforts to rehabilitate her homeless, starving friend and turn him into an art-producing unit of value. The waste object here is Insel himself—a man who dwells on the outskirts of the market economy, neither labouring in the traditional sense nor producing art.

My reading of Insel as human waste chimes with recent studies by Sandeep Parmar and Sara Crangle, both of which address the relationship between poverty, waste, and avant-gardism in Loy's work. The Loy who emerges from Parmar's study of her unpublished prose is a writer concerned with both material rubbish and human beings treated as rubbish by society, and who, by 1930, has "lost faith in the avant-garde's ability to offer a directive to society."[44] Sara Crangle likewise reads the central homeless woman in Loy's late poem, "Chiffon Velours" (1942–1949), as "a waste product of a consumerist system devoted to a productivity she neither embodies nor engenders."[45]

Building on these ideas, my analysis of *Insel* reads Loy's ambiguous classification of waste objects as complicating Surrealist values, and Insel himself as caught between waste and use-value, continuously fluctuating between human waste and artist-producer. Insel is thus more than a focal point for the narrative: he is a use-value whose identity as a wastrel is in part a constructed persona designed to increase his appeal as an artist. Loy's interest in this starving artist anticipates her later concern with the Bowery bums, while her depiction of Insel as human waste anticipates her figuration of the homeless, in her later collages, out of trash. In these collages, huddled, prostrated figures made of rags are juxtaposed against a blank backdrop or layered over other waste items (see Fig. 2.4). While assuming the appearance of human beings, their immobility and dislocation render

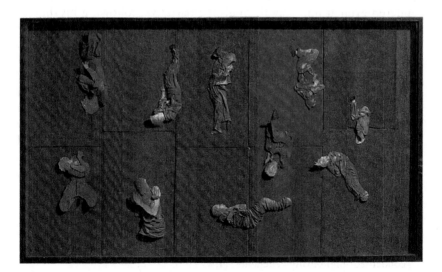

Fig. 2.4 Mina Loy, "Communal Cot" (1949). Collage of cardboard, paper and rags: 28.1 × 116.25 cm (27¼ × 46½ in), Elrick-Manley Fine Art, New York

them akin to found objects. Their resemblance to waste, and their composition out of waste, underscores their status as surplus entities.

Like the transient homeless of her junk collages, Insel stands for the uncommodifiable and unassimilable. However, as well as a surplus entity deemed useless by bourgeois society, he is also useless to the very avant-garde circles that claim to reject bourgeois norms. Loy broaches these ideas from the novel's outset, through references to Surrealism that subtly undercut its practices. Mrs Jones introduces Insel as "a madman, a more or less Surrealist painter,"[46] who lives off scraps (*I*, 25), finds shelter in the homes of the women he seduces and, failing that, sleeps under bridges (*I*, 86–87). He does not use scraps to make art, but for nutritional sustenance, while his vagrant antics are so extreme as to alarm even the Surrealists: "None of the[m] will have anything to do with me," he notes wistfully. "They know only too well, if they did, I should try to borrow money" (*I*, 129). Contrary to Breton's narrator, who looks for the epiphanic value of found objects, Loy's Mrs Jones is captivated by the potential to put Insel to some form of use (*I*, 64). This tension between the aesthetic and the commercial throws into relief the paradox of the *objet trouvé* itself, which, once turned into art, is once more a commodity. Insel's affinity with the objet trouvé is rendered explicit mid-way through the narrative, following his digressions with Mrs Jones among the bookstalls along the Seine. In a scene reminiscent of Breton's discovery of the Rimbaud in the flea market, the two happen upon the same book and the same passage: "in identical silence" they find "one significance in an early Greek fragment—I do not remember which" (*I*, 86). What sets their discovery apart from Breton's is that Mrs Jones later describes Insel himself as imbued with "the same eternal conviction of the Greek fragment" (*I*, 97). Where the first simultaneous discovery of the fragment recalls Breton's concept of the relationship between chance and the objet trouvé, Loy's comparison of Insel to the fragment suggests that he is the real enigmatic find. She underscores this by recalling, in the very next passage, how:

> Once at dark in the Maine woods, I had stumbled on a rotten log. The scabs of foetid bark flew off revealing a solid cellulose jewel. It glowed in the tremendous tepidity of phosphorescence from a store of moonlight similar to condensed sun in living vegetables. (*I*, 97)

The description, intended as a metaphor for Insel's hidden artistic genius, hinges on the resemblance between the rotten log's foetid bark and Insel's own disintegrating attire, as well as the enigmatic qualities she assumes they both hide. The passage's attention to the matter underneath the apparently "foetid" anticipates Loy's own scavenging practices in later life and her fascination with the overlooked. The rotten log is not human waste—that is, it is not a by-product of capitalist production or consumption, or a remaindered human—but it is biological waste, and Mrs Jones' recollection of its mysteriousness is intended to underscore her curiosity about the "solid cellulose jewel" within her "pet *clochard*" (*I*, 84).

Insel appears to share this view of himself as a "thing." In a characteristically humorous episode, Mrs Jones points to a coin on the floor and asks him: "Would you pick that up?" Insel assumes that she is pointing at him and, ignoring the coin, he "beg[ins] pulling himself together" (*I*, 86). The misunderstanding is telling. Although the item here is not a waste object but rather a coin, it is a discarded object to be collected, and the conflation of it with Insel is apt given the financial imperative governing Mrs Jones' stewardship of him. Left to his own devices, Insel would remain, like the coin on the floor, of no use to anyone; picked up and polished (and in his case also fed), he can potentially be put to use. Moreover, in contrast to Breton, who specifically searches for the magical qualities of Breton's *objet trouvé*, Mrs Jones is cognisant that she is not after the unexpected truths to which her human *objet trouvé* might expose her, but the art he might produce—rendering her relationship to him no different than those of the women who pay him for sex. This is made clear early in the novel, when Mrs Jones' meditation on the capacity of Insel's presence to imbue the most mundane objects with beauty is superseded by her recognition that "I [am] a tout for a friend's art gallery, feeding a cagey genius in the hope of production" (*I*, 74). This is not an epiphany about the human *objet trouvé*'s hidden magic but an anticlimactic recognition of Mrs Jones' own commercially driven intentions.

The financial imperative above-described is iterated repeatedly in Mrs Jones' incessant efforts to convince Insel to sell his paintings. But to her explanation "When you have money and can eat you paint a picture so as to have more money—when you haven't any more money" he counters, "It is more complicated than that," explaining that his painting is still wet, and thus not ready (*I*, 134). The retort is absurd—wet paint being a weak excuse to delay the sale of a painting—but the humour belies a more serious point. Insel highlights a disconnection between the world of artistic creation and the expectations of the art market, the slow pace of creativity, and the more rapid pace of production and consumption. Where Breton uses his novel as a platform for the Surrealist vision, Loy uses hers to indicate that the challenges facing art might require more than a manifesto or an eye for scavenging.

We see this very clearly in the novel, as Mrs Jones describes her first encounters with Insel, dwelling at length on the precariousness of his life-style. Her description of the job market as a "metal forest of coin bearing machinery" that is anathema to the "*révolté* [...] incapable of taking it as it is" highlights the extent to which Insel's artistic practice is born out of a particular economic condition and his radicalism limited by it (*I*, 24). She elaborates:

> A man who finds himself economically nude, should logically, in the thickset iron forest of our industrial structure, be banged to death from running into its fearfully rigid supports. He is again the primordial soft-machine without the protective overall of the daily job in which his fellows wend their way to some extent unbettered by this sphere of activity. For them, the atrocious jaws of the gigantic organism will open at fixed intervals and spit at them rations sufficient to sustain their coalescence with the screeching, booming, crashing dynamism of the universal "works." (*I*, 23–24)

It is a magnificent passage, both in its linguistic play and in its figuration of labour as an amorphous body that flows in and out of the jaws of industry. Loy conceives of the job market as a "thickset iron forest" against whose forbidding structure the "economically nude" unemployed thrust themselves, to no avail. At the same time, the emphasis on poverty and employment as a form of "nudity" complicates the figuration of industry as a dehumanising machine. As dispiriting as it may be to daily enter the "atrocious jaws" of the workplace and receive the "rations" it "spits" out, Mrs Jones recognises that exclusion from these jaws leaves one with no means to subsist, let alone make art. The idealised notion we might have of the starving artist is very different from the actual condition of starvation.

Loy further complicates our understanding of the plight of the *révolté* who abstains from—or is rejected by—the market by revealing how Insel leverages his image as a bum to endear himself to the wealthy women off whom he feeds. For example, his resistance to having his threadbare, dirt-encrusted suit mended stems from what Mrs Jones describes as a reluctance to "cut a slice from" his "beggar's capital" (*I*, 108). To Mrs Jones, the suit is waste—an item that should be either disposed of or re-purposed—and her efforts throughout the novel to wash and mend it become a source of comical contention. When Insel burns a hole in the trousers within hours of her finally patching it up, she interprets this as an effort to "replenis[h] his beggar's capital" (*I*, 129). To remain of interest to the women he seduces and to retain his image as a vagrant genius (and, one suspects, to continue eliciting sympathy from art buyers such as Mrs Jones), he must remain a *clochard*. To be a use-value he must, paradoxically, continue to appear a non-use-value: his livelihood depends on looking the part of the homeless scavenger he is. Thus, Mrs Jones notes, "It's marvellous [...] your knack of dying on doorsteps. [...] You might make a good thing out of it. Perhaps you do. Insel, I believe you put *lots* of money in the bank!" (*I*, 164).

Loy's depiction of Mrs Jones' working life—which effectively takes up any time she might otherwise spend making art—also sheds light on the life of the artist under capitalism: unless she is able to sell her art, she must confine that creative practice to the fringes of the working day. For Loy, the responsibility of running a business and the repeated threat of having her designs stolen from larger businesses encroached on the time she was meant to be writing: by the time the lamp shop finally closed down, Bernstein notes that it had become a "burden to the artist it had meant to liberate" (Bernstein, 188). In *Insel*, this confinement is expressed in Loy's attention to how Insel's rehabilitation (or recuperation) ultimately distracts Mrs Jones from making art. A contributing factor to this constant distraction might be what David Trotter has termed modernity's self-awareness of its own "messiness" and of the many kinds of mess to be negotiated: that is, the untidiness of the artistic process, the domestic mess to which the female artist is persistently recalled, and the mess of negotiating the making and selling of one's art—that is, of moving between the (however idealised) disorder of artistic creation as espoused at least for as long as Romanticism and the order and system required by business. If not Insel's, then certainly the narrator's and Loy's own artistic paralysis results from a sense of the myriad practical constraints on the modern artist. "So complex is the status of the [usually starving] artist, dining with affable millionaires every other night" (*I*, 25).[47] All the more so if the artist is female, which the narrator suggests towards the very beginning, in recounting her exasperated attempt to create order out of a room full of manuscripts to have the space in which to write:

I sat looking at that apartment obsessed with the necessity of disencumbering it of personalia. The onus of trying to make up one's mind where to begin overpowered me. The psychic effort of retracting oneself from the creative dimension […] while the present actuality is let to go hang […] was devastating. The contemplation of a bureau whose drawers must be emptied—the idea of some sort of classification of manuscript notes and miscellaneous papers […] the effort to concentrate on something in which one takes no interest, which is the major degradation of women, gives a pain so acute that, in magnifying a plausible task to an inextricable infinity of deadly detail, the mind disintegrates. The only thing to do is to rush out of the house and forget it all. (*I*, 40)

In solving the issue not by escaping but by sewing up the neck and sleeves of a pair of painter overalls to make a "corpse-like sack" in which to "stuff" all the "scribbles," the effluvia of everyday life is literally stuffed away, making space for art: once the overalls are cast out of sight, Mrs Jones feels "once more [her]self" (*I*, 40). What is more, the reference to "Something in [her] brain click[ing]" upon first discovering the overalls renders the overalls agents in unblocking her creative paralysis (*I*, 40). Loy thus takes Surrealist practice indoors, showing how the subversive practices of the urban might be practiced within the domestic space, not to make art but to make way for it.

The project of the historical avant-garde, Peter Bürger tells us, was destined to fail. "An art no longer distinct from the praxis of life but wholly absorbed in it will lose the capacity to criticize it, along with its distance" (Bürger, 50). Loy's narrative gestures towards that failure, her depiction of Mrs Jones' efforts to rehabilitate the *clochard* artist and to find time to make her own art, and the novel's complication of the concepts of waste, the *objet trouvé* and scavenging, suggest the limits of Surrealist practice. Through her depiction of Insel as human waste that resists both interpretation and being put to artistic use, Loy's novel playfully parodies Surrealist values, drawing attention to the contradictions inherent in attempting to both live a radical aesthetic and sell it.

de Chirico, Breton, and Loy demonstrate the extent to which the historical avant-garde's putting-to-use of waste sets it apart from both nineteenth-century realism and literary modernism. Their exploration of the marginal and the contingent sheds light on commodity culture's effect on our relationship to the objects and people around us. Within the consumer economy, today's purchase is tomorrow's rubbish, and the physical world itself is understood in terms of the markets it fuels. The historical avant-garde shows us the other side of this codified world, revealing the uncanny, metaphysical, or merely evocative aspects of the cast-off and the démodé, and exploring the imaginative and political dimensions of idleness. Failed prototypes, obsolete technologies, and remaindered humans have a mysterious allure of their own, attracting us with their unreadability and their patina of failure while continuously tempting us to make them commercially useful once more. The texts discussed play out the tension between waste's recuperative potential as art and the risk of co-option that recuperation entails.

NOTES

1. "Dada, Surrealism and Scuola Metafisica" in *Theories of Modern Art*, ed. Hershel B. Chipp (Berkeley: University of California Press, 1992), 366–455.
2. It would be remiss to suggest that Bürger's is a definitive assessment of avant-gardism, which is in fact a contested term. The most influential efforts to define avant-gardism aside from Bürger's are Clement Greenberg's "Avant-Garde and Kitsch" (1939); Max Renato Poggioli's eponymous *The Theory of the Avant-Garde* (1962); and Theodor Adorno's *Aesthetic Theory* (1970). For an analysis of the differences between modernism and the avant-garde and the controversies over the use of these terms, see Matei Calinescu, *The Five Faces of Modernity: Modernism, Avant-Garde, Decadence, Kitsch, Postmodernism* (Durham, NC: Duke University Press: 1987), 94–110 and Andreas Huyssen, "The Search for Tradition: Avant-garde and postmodernism in the 1970s" in *After the Great Divide* (Bloomington: Indiana University Press, 1986), 163.
3. Rona Cran provides an in-depth discussion of collage's ramifications for and application in artistic, musical and literary practices across the twentieth century in *Collage in Twentieth-Century Art, Literature and Culture* (London: Routledge, 2014). Cran succinctly defines collage as the "experimentation with and the linking of disparate phenomena: democratically, arbitrarily, and even unintentionally" but notes that its multi-medial nature render its origins both "deceptively simple and contentious" to locate (4).
4. Harriet Waldman, *Collage, Assemblage, and the Found Object* (London: Phaidon, 1992), 10.
5. Hans Arp, "Looking" in *Arp*, ed. James Thrall Soby (New York: Museum of Modern Art, 1958), 12–16, citations on 15–16 and 13.
6. "Dada Manifesto 1918" as cited in Gavin Grindon, "Surrealism, Dada, and the Refusal of Work: Autonomy, Activism, and Social Participation in

the Radical Avant-Garde," *Oxford Art Journal* 34. 1 (2011): 79–96. Citation on 89.

7. *Chambers Dictionary of Etymology*, ed. Robert K. Barnhart (New York and Edinburgh: Chambers Harrap, 1988). See Wyndham Lewis, *Tarr* (Oxford: Oxford University Press, 2010), 18.

8. Paul van Capelleveen et al., *Voices and Visions. The Koopman Collection and the Art of the French Book* (The Hague: Koninklijke Bibliotheek, 2009).

9. Roland Barthes, "Introduction to the Structural Analysis of Narratives" (1966) in *Barthes: Selected Writings*, ed. Susan Sontag (Glasgow: Fontana, 1983), 265–266, as cited in Moretti, 366.

10. Franco Moretti, "Serious Century," 364–399.

11. Max Weber (1922), *The Protestant Ethic and the Spirit of Capitalism* (New York: Scribners, 1958), 154, as cited in Moretti, 381.

12. Of course, it is also the case that the evolution of realism, and literary description, can be read in an entirely different way: Peter Boxall for example argues that "the history of realism itself is the history of an ongoing struggle between word and world, in which the capacity of the word to represent has always been fundamentally shaped by the resistance of the world to its mimetic power"—the experimentation of literary modernism, according to this reading, "does not mark the abandonment of the realist project, but rather the intensification of it." Although this is a valid argument, it is difficult to reconcile with the views of the specific authors discussed in this chapter—and, indeed, the views of Beckett or the authors in Chap. 4—who adamantly sought to distance themselves from a form they viewed (however incorrectly, or shortsightedly) to be constricting and unsuited to the needs of their time. One might in fact view this as one further way in which the historical avant-gardists stood apart from their fellow modernists. See Peter Boxall, "Is This Really Realism?" in *The Value of the Novel* (Cambridge: Cambridge University Press, 2015), 39–68. Citations on 67.

13. Breton, "Surrealist Manifesto of 1924," *Manifestoes of Surrealism*, 10.

14. James Thrall Thoby, *Giorgio de Chirico* (New York: Museum of Modern Art and Arno Press, 1955), 249.

15. Giovanni Lista, *De Chirico et l'Avant-Garde* (Lausanne: L'Age d'Homme, 1983), 35.

16. Caroline Burke, *Becoming Modern: The Life of Mina Loy* (Berkeley: University of California Press, 1996), 377.

17. Giorgio de Chirico, *Hebdomeros*, transl. Margaret Crossland (London: Peter Owen, 1992 [1929]), 14. Henceforth *H*.

18. Michael R. Taylor and Guigone Rolland, *Giorgio de Chirico and the Myth of Ariadne* (London: Merrell in association with the Philadelphia Museum of Art, 2002), 173.

19. Among the few studies of *Hebdomeros* is Renée Riese Hubert, "The Fabulous Fiction of Two Surrealist Artists," *New Literary History*, 4. 1 (Autumn, 1972): 151–166).

20. de Chirico, as cited in Thoby, Appendix A, 244, emphasis in the original.

21. Keala Jewell, *The Art of Enigma* (Penn State University Press, 2004), 40.

22. Wieland Schmied, "L'histoire d'une influence: 'Pittura Metafisica' et 'nouvelle Objectivité'" in *Les Realismes* (Paris: Centre Pompidou, 1980), 20.

23. de Chirico, as cited in Thoby, Appendix A, 246.

24. Derek Winnicott. *Playing and Reality* (London: Tavistock, 1971), 1–5.

25. Giorgio de Chirico, *Hebdomeros* (Paris: Flammarion, 1964 [1929]), 71. I have included the original French version to highlight the wordplay.

26. Giorgio de Chirico, *Memorie della Mia Vita* (Bologna: Bompiani, 2008 [1962]), 61; Michael R. Taylor, "Between Modernism and Mythology: Giorgio de Chirico and the Ariadne Series" in *Giorgio de Chirico and the Myth of Ariadne*, 33.

27. Giorgio de Chirico, "Meditations of a Painter," in Chipp, *Theories of Modern Art*, 397–401. Matthew Beaumont provides a compelling reading of this moment in his analysis of the aesthetics of urban convalescence in *Restless Cities*, ed. Matthew Beaumont and Gregory Dart (London: Verso, 2010), 59–78.

28. Giorgio de Chirico, "Manuscript from the Collection of Paul Eluard," 1911–1915, as cited in Thoby, Appendix A, 246.

29. Giorgio de Chirico, *De Chirico par de Chirico* (Paris: Jacques Damase, 1978), 35.

30. André Breton, *Nadja* (1928), transl. Richard Howard (New York: Grove Weidenfeld, 1960), 52. Henceforth, *N*.

31. Mark Polizzotti, *Revolution of the Mind: The Life of André Breton* (London: Bloomsbury, 1995), 76.

32. Anon, "Un Parisien Solitaire," *Combat* (29 September 1966), 7, as cited in Polizzotti, 618 and fn. 732.

33. Lord, unpublished notes for *Giacometti*, as cited in Polizzotti, 618 and fn. 732.

34. André Breton, *Mad Love*, transl. Mary Ann Caws (University of Nebraska Press, 1987 [1937]), 28. Henceforth, *ML*.

35. Breton, *La clé des champs* (Paris: Fayard, 1977), 232; Dagmar Motycka Weston, "Surrealist Paris: The Non-Perspectival Space of the Lived City" in *Intervals in the Philosophy of Architecture*, ed. Alberto Pérez-Gómez and Stephen Parcell (Montréal: McGill University Press, 1996), 149–172, citations on 157 and 171, fn. 29 and 30.

36. *I*, 23.

37. See Carolyn Burke, endnotes for "Recollecting Dada: Juliette Roche" in *Women in Dada: Essays on Sex, Gender and Identity*, ed. Naomi Sawelson-Gorse (Cambridge, MA: MIT Press, 2011), 571–575.

38. Breton cites Craven in the Preface for a Reprint of the Manifesto (1929). See *Manifestoes of Surrealism*, 3.

39. Mina Loy, "Love Songs to Joannes" (1917) in *The Lost Lunar Baedeker*, ed. Roger Conover (New York: Farrar, Straus & Giroux, 1997), 53. Henceforth, *LLB*.

40. Peggy Guggenheim, *Out of this Century: Confessions of an Art Addict* (New York: Universe, 1979), 71.

41. Jessica Bernstein, *Cold Modernism: Literature, Fashion, Art* (University Park, PA: Penn State University Press, 2013), 152–153 and 159.

42. Kristin Gilger, "On Skid Row: Bowery Bums and the Politics of Waste." Paper presented at the annual meeting of the American Studies Association Annual Meeting, Hilton Baltimore. 17 August 2013.

43. In her introduction to the 2014 reprint of *Insel* (New York and London: Melville House, 2014), Sarah Hayden characterises Loy's engagement with the avant-garde as "ironic" and highly attuned to the movements' "performance politics" (Hayden, 3). In *Cultures of Modernism: Marianne Moore, Mina Loy & Else Lasker-Schüler* (Ann Arbor: University of Michigan, 2005), Cristanne Miller notes Loy's ambivalence towards the Paris art scene after she moved to New York in the 1930s, and her tendency to operate on the fringes of artistic circles (Miller, 72). See also Caroline Georgianna Miller, "Ephemeral Materiality: The Objects and Subjects of Mina Loy's Downtown New York," *Abstract Concrete: Experimental Poetry in Post-WWII New York* (University of Michigan: 2011), 16–53.

44. Sandeep Parmar, *Reading Mina Loy's Autobiographies: Myth of the Modern Woman* (London: Bloomsbury, 2011), 169.

45. Sara Crangle, "Mina Loy" in *A History of Modernist Poetry*, ed. Alex Davis and Lee M. Jenkins (Cambridge University Press, 2015), 275–302, citation on 293.

46. Mina Loy, *Insel*, 19.

47. My reading chimes with Tyrus Miller's assessment of Insel as "literally embod[ying] the predicaments of the [1930s] artist." Tyrus Miller, "More or Less Silent: Mina Loy's Novel *Insel*" in *Late Modernism: Politics, Fiction and Art Between the World Wars* (Berkeley: University of California Press, 1999), 207–221. Citation on 208.

CHAPTER 3

Samuel Beckett's *personnes perdues*: Human Waste in *The Trilogy*, *Texts for Nothing*, and *How It Is*

Towards the beginning of *Molloy* (1955), Samuel Beckett's titular protagonist abruptly interrupts an anecdote he is telling to correct his readers' expectations of a linear and exhaustive narrative.[1] It is impossible to tell a story in full, he argues, adding:

> if I failed to mention this detail in its proper place it is because you can-not mention everything in its proper place, you must choose, between the things not worth mentioning and those even less so. For if you set out to mention everything you would never be done, and that's what counts, to be done, to have done. Oh, I know, even if you mention only a few of the things there are, you do not get done either, I know, I know. But it's a change of muck. And if all muck is the same muck that doesn't matter, it's good to have a change of muck, to move from one heap to another a little further on, from time to time, fluttering you might say, like a butterfly, as if you were ephemeral. (*MO*, 41)

Molloy's is a meditation on what is worth keeping in a narrative and what can be disposed of (tempered by the comical recognition that rid-ding a story of surplus details will not necessarily accelerate its ending). "Muck" is used to equate the selection of one detail instead of another with a willingness to embrace variety—"it's good to have a change of muck"—as well as to call attention to how little that selection really mat-ters, all details being ultimately the same. However, having used muck

© The Editor(s) (if applicable) and The Author(s) 2016
R. Dini, *Consumerism, Waste, and Re-Use in Twentieth-Century Fiction*,
DOI 10.1057/978-1-137-58165-5_3

to carefully work through a kind of logic, Molloy shifts tack, adding an "ephemeral" butterfly "fluttering you might say" over heaps of shit to the mix—an apt metaphor for the alchemising task of the artist, but also a suggestion of how little weight he himself attributes to the task of narration. The passage's humour is heightened by the fact that Molloy himself spends much of the novel wading through *actual* "muck" of different kinds, and with far less grace than a "butterfly."

As in the passage just discussed, much of Beckett's late 1950s and early 1960s prose derives its humour from his characters' complex discussions of "muck" and value, from the characters' own apparent uselessness, and from the muck-ridden settings in which their endeavours take place. Waste is both the physical site in which their failures occur and a metaphor for their ineffectuality, inefficiency, and near-obsolescence. In what follows, I read the representation of waste and supernumerary humans in these works as salient counters to the culture of rationalised production and consumerism that spread throughout Western Europe after the Second World War, as exemplified by the ideas of Henry Ford and F.W. Taylor.[2] The principles of Fordism are particularly relevant to this discussion, as they sought to socialise workers to think of themselves as consumers (Harvey, 136). Thus the system's application in the post-war reconstruction effort profoundly altered not only European manufacturing and the consumer landscape but culture at large. In her study of post-war French culture, *Fast Cars, Clean Bodies*, for example, Kristin Ross shows how the growth of the automobile industry on the one hand, and of the personal care and domestic cleaning products industry on the other, helped shape a new rhetoric of efficiency.[3]

Against this backdrop, Beckett's novels imagine an existence in which the world of commodities is replaced by a world of unusable, perished goods, and in which time, divested of the need to work or consume, is devoted to idleness or various forms of infirmity. The waste-dwelling unemployed in Beckett's *Molloy* (1951 French; 1955 English), *Malone Dies* (1951/1956), and *The Unnameable* (1953/1958), and in his later prose novellas *Texts for Nothing* (1955/1967) and *How It Is* (1961/1964), exist on the cusp of the commodified social.[4] They resist the productivist paradigm by injuring their bodies and thus rendering them unusable; by embarking on useless narrative quests, commencing interminable inventory projects, or accruing useless objects; by leaving these self-imposed tasks unfinished; and by choosing to dwell in landfills and subsist on waste, thus abstaining from participation in the market economy. Finally, they draw attention to the extent to which their surplus status, habitation of dumps, and scavenging of discards render them, in the eyes of capital, remaindered entities undistinguishable from remaindered things. These readings chime with Laura Salisbury's analysis of the *Trilogy* as narratives about "minds and bodies that cannot be habituated to the temporality of early to mid-century capitalistic production nor to the linearity of its favoured mode—the nineteenth-century bourgeois novel or the classic Hollywood narrative film that races towards the production of a denouement" and her recognition that one would never give Beckett's characters a job.[5]

Beckett's condemnation of the nineteenth-century novel is well documented: the subversion of reification through stasis and waste-dwelling in his novels is thus bound up in a broader effort to destabilise the foundations of the form itself, to counter its totalising tendencies, and to shatter its logic.[6] In "The Reality Effect" (1968), as we saw in the previous two chapters, Roland Barthes argues that useless objects in the traditional novel are used to lend verisimilitude to the narrative, and to ultimately illuminate the character and intent of the players while stamping out the inexplicable (141–148). For Barthes, useless objects advance the plot, for the particularity of their features reveals the social and moral codes to which their owners are bound. Their presence substantiates the post-Enlightenment view that all things are readable. Beckett subverts that logic by using useless objects not to advance the plot, but to underscore its absence, and to allow the characters themselves to exist wholly outside the capitalist order. Beckett's character Molloy's assertion, at the very beginning of the Trilogy, that "to restore silence is the role of objects" and that "there could be no things but nameless things" suggests the material world's resistance to being made legible or productive (MO, 9; 31). This celebration of the irrational partly reflects Beckett's well-documented relationship to Surrealism and Dada, movements he however encountered only in their aftermath, when they were already succumbing to commercialisation.[7] And, indeed, his friendship with Marcel Duchamp and his translations of André Breton and Paul Eluard's poetry into English have led a number of scholars to read his depictions of waste in relation to descendants of Surrealism, or, relatedly, as celebrations of the irrational in the tradition of Georges Bataille's *Solar Anus* (1931).[8] The Beckett that emerges from these analyses is acutely concerned with excretion as a form of production, and with the subversive potential of scatological wordplay.[9] Without dismissing these approaches, I argue that where the historical avant-garde re-invests in waste only for its project to become, in essence, a recycling plant, Beckett in fact rejects the ethos of reuse through outright abstention. His depictions of waste propose a radicalism of idleness as opposed to recuperation and suggest the merits

Beckett's advances an boy's surprise + recuperation [handwritten annotation]

of dwelling in waste. Along will this radical abstention—if not inertness—of Beckett's supernumerary people, I focus on the extent to which the objects in the *Trilogy* resist our gaze, exemplifying what New Materialists including Maurizia Boscagli and Jane Bennett have termed matter's potential for "unruliness" (Boscagli, 3; Bennett, 4-6).

The radicalism described above bears certain affinities to that manifest in the work of Arman (Armand Fernandez), an artist closely associated with *Nouveau Réalisme*. Founded by Yves Klein and Pierre Restany in 1960, *Nouveau Réalisme* sought, in Restany's words, to reflect the "optimistic metaphor of European consumer society" through a "direct appropriation of the real" comparable to that of the French *nouveau roman*.[10] For Arman, this involved highlighting the centrality of waste to post-war consumption. But where his Surrealist and Dadaist predecessors sought to alter the everyday through the re-configuration of waste into new forms, Arman displayed his *déchets* untransformed and on their own terms, in what he called *Poubelles* ("Trash Cans").[11] These consisted of sealed polymer display cases filled with consumer waste and industrial by-products that he gathered from municipal dumps, the homes of friends, and the trash bins of upper-class neighbourhoods. The first of Arman's *Poubelles*, titled *Petits Déchets Bourgeois* (1959), reproduced on the cover of this monograph, features the residues of branded consumer products (Gitanes cigarettes, Le Petit Cleville Camembert), specifically chosen for their reflection of middle-class values.[12] The title of another, *Déchets Bourgeois (Et s'il n'en reste qu'un je serais celui-la)* ("Bourgeois Discards (and if there remains only one, it shall be me)"), makes the critique of consumption even more explicit through its ironic reference to the last line of Victor Hugo's "Ultima Verba" (1853). Playing on the poet's promise to stand against tyranny even if he is the last, Arman here suggests that the "last one standing" will not be the poet or artist intent on opposing tyranny: it will be mass of rubbish overflowing from their *poubelles*.[13] Each *Poubelle* presents waste not as a potential participant in collage or sculpture, but rather as an inevitable component of a society wedded to mass consumption, and, in that sense, a naturally occurring phenomenon—as reflected in Arman's assertion that "the objects themselves formed a self-composition. My composition was to allow them to compose themselves."[14] A "condensation of consumption," a "patinaed still-life or portrait of our civilization,"[15] the waste in these works *is* reality, unadulterated, and untransformed.

As in Arman's *Poubelles*, waste in Beckett's prose "just is," and his characters willingly make themselves at home in it rather than seeking to put it to use. Beckett's subversion of the taxonomic distinctions between objects and people, and his focus on figures of displacement, parodies the totalising effects of reification in the Lukácsian sense—that is, the "thingification" of human relations resulting from commodity exchange.[16] The depiction of characters as objects literalises the marketplace's obscuring of the human. Their very marginality is a reminder of the extent to which social inclusion is predicated on marketability. At the same time, their willingness to accrue worthless objects parodies consumerism. The emphasis on idleness—which is to say, wasting time—highlights the extent to which time itself is a commodity and reminds us of Marx's assertion that the "mutilat[ion]" of the worker "into a fragment of a man [or] an appendage of a machine" involves "transform[ing] his life-time into working time" (*C*, 604). And finally, the characters' own partial and digressive accounts of themselves provide a means to oppose the rationalising tendencies of the novel form itself.

The tendency of waste itself, in these novels, to absorb the characters or distract us from their stories serves to satirise reification (highlighting the extent to which exchange grants objects more importance than the humans trading them), and to posit the characters themselves as surplus entities. Beckett's unemployed qualify as Karl Marx's "reserve army of labour" (*C*, 781). Marx uses the phrase to denote a specific form of devaluation of labour under capitalism, whereby the perennial existence of others willing to do the job for less enables an employer to cut wages. While Beckett's characters are not jobseekers, they are very much surplus entities, and their surplus status is rooted in their abstention from taking part in the market economy. In the eyes of the market, they are human waste, or what Zygmunt Bauman terms "flawed consumers"—people without the means, and in this case, the desire, to participate in the cycle of production and consumption.[17] Like the defiant rubbish of Arman's *Poubelles* and accumulations of identical objects, which, in Jill Carrick's words, function as "barricades" against the "army" of industrial production, Beckett's characters resist post-war consumer culture's "pretension to regulate the planet through accumulation" (Carrick, 95). In what follows, I examine the many forms such abstention takes.

"[A]LL THESE QUESTIONS OF WORTH AND VALUE"[18]: PARTIAL INVENTORIES, FAILING BODIES

Beckett's *Trilogy* recounts a series of failed quests. The first volume, *Molloy* (1951/1955), features the first-person account of crippled vagabond Molloy's perambulations on his bicycle, followed by that of a private detective, Jacques Moran, and his son (also named Jacques). The elder Jacques has been commissioned by a man called Youdi to find Molloy, bring him home, and write a detailed account of the journey, as he has done on numerous occasions before with other vagabonds. His first-person narrative is precisely that account. But project and narrative ultimately fail, as the elder Jacques develops infirmities akin to those of his pursuant, loses his bearings in the wilderness, and is abandoned by his son. His account ends with him returning home empty-handed to record his journey and die alone in the courtyard of his ruined homestead. Left untended, his farm and henhouse have become gutted buildings strewn with the carcasses of the animals he once kept. Of Molloy we know only what we knew in the novel's opening: that he has been found by someone, isolated in a room, where he, too, is being forced to write his story. In both narratives, the characters' journeying results in a gradual decline into incoherence.

In combining these two enforced records, and emphasising the gradual erosion of his characters' productive capacity, physical strength, geophysical bearings, and mental stability, Beckett turns failure and unproductiveness into a joke, making pointlessness precisely the point:

> So many pages, so little money. Yes, I work now, a little like I used to, except that I don't know how to work any more. That doesn't matter apparently. What I'd like now is to speak of the things that are left, say my good-byes, finish dying. They don't want that [...] I don't work for money. For what then? I don't know. (*MO*, 8)

The subtext, that there is nothing to be gained, is an echo of Beckett's most quoted line—*Waiting for Godot's* "Nothing to be done."[19] But where *Godot's* surrender belies any kind of beginning, the absence of intent in *Molloy* is all the more fraught in that the characters continue, regardless of their diminishing ability to do their jobs. Molloy's explicit admission that he is working neither for money, nor for some other personal satisfaction, highlights how odd it is that we do things we would not otherwise do, in exchange for a quantity of something defined by someone else. Perhaps for this same reason, much of the novel, like the subsequent volumes, is really about the characters' efforts to rest—to not be of use. At the outset of *Molloy*, a policeman remonstrates Molloy for lying on the handlebars of his bicycle—a sleeping posture deemed indecent in public, and that slyly recalls the handlebars of Picasso's "Bull's Head" (1942), whose aesthetic re-deployment changed their original function. Where Picasso modified the original function of the handlebars (to navigate the bicycle) and turned them into components of an artwork, Molloy changes their function by using them as a headrest. Inactivity here is intimately linked with uselessness—the body at rest is a body abstaining from work.

Similarly, Molloy and Moran spend far more time nursing their bad legs or looking for places to perch than getting anything done. As the titular protagonist of *Malone Dies* (1956) pragmatically notes, his body is an obstruction:

> My body is what is called, unadvisedly perhaps, impotent. There is virtually nothing it can do. Sometimes I miss not being able to crawl around any more. But I am not much given to nostalgia. My arms, once they are in position, can exert a certain force. But I find it hard to guide them.[20]

The description of Malone's body as impotent is telling: literally, it is unable to perform sexually, but figuratively, it is unable to do or create or will itself to act. The body refuses to work for its owner, who becomes, in this figuration, an ineffectual line-manager, unable to guide his employees.

The body's use as an *excuse* for ineffectuality is evident from the degree to which its failures are recorded. Malone's characters are either intent on dragging themselves forward despite an aching limb or prolapsed sphincter, or they are entirely consumed by their corporeality, intent on recording each instance their bladder fails, or their bowel movement occurs on schedule. In *Molloy*, characters are described almost solely in terms of their secretions. Molloy's mother is incontinent "both of faeces and water" (*MO*, 18); Molloy himself smells of "ammonia" and "bowels" (*MO*, 18–19); the death of Teddy the old dog, whom Molloy runs over with his bicycle, is a blessing in disguise, ending the dog's incontinent old age and allowing him to "finish dying" as Molloy himself would like (*MO*, 19; 8). Similarly, Moran's son is nowhere depicted so vividly as when he is lying on the bathroom floor, ass up, waiting for his father to give him an enema to cure his upset stomach (*MO*, 113, 133). As Molloy puts it: "The most you can hope is to be a little less, in the end, the creature you were in the beginning, and the middle" (*MO*, 33). In this context, the body is just a maker of waste, on its way to becoming part of the waste through which it moves.

In "Beckett and Failure" Michael Kinnucan reads Beckett's preoccupation with the body and its limitations as endowing a unique function to the novel form itself: "In most novels the disposition of the body is merely a metaphor for the disposition of its soul; in Beckett the body shows up as a machine in its own right, breaking down constantly, in need of management."[21] Expanding this reading, we might consider how the perpetual breakdown of Beckett's body-machines subverts his characters' (however half-hearted) efforts to work, thus challenging the system of production.

For Marx, production under capitalism results in "the domination over, and exploitation of, the producers"—the means of development "mutilate the labourer into a fragment of a man [and] degrade him to the level of an appendage of a machine" (*C*, 604). In Beckett, the body-machine needs management its owner cannot give: its constituent parts (characters' limbs or bodily organs) are given rein to freely fail. The body as we see it in Beckett resists commodification (if we consider commodification in terms of Arjun Appadurai's delineation, as the putting-to-use of a thing). In relentlessly breaking down and obstructing the work of its owner, it remains in a constant state of waste—an object that, for the moment at least, cannot be put to use. Further, the body's failure in these texts underlines the inadequacies of the novel form itself. The novel, ultimately, will be unable to explain the events of this rambling narrative or give a definitive account of its ambiguous protagonists, whose very identities, like the onions in the glutinous stew the Morans eat before their journey (and which gives Jacques Junior indigestion), ultimately "go to nothing" (*MO*, 102). Where Jacques Moran rummages through the rubbish bin, seeking evidence that the charwoman has thrown the onions away, we have only the option of going back to the beginning, in hopes that perhaps we have missed something. Ontological meaning is as easily found by sniffing through a heap of dung as it is in "the mess of [a] poor old uniparous whore" (*MO*, 19).

One way of understanding failure in these texts is in terms of self-sabotage or unconscious subversion—what critics have termed Beckett's "aesthetics of failure."[22] The wasted attempt can be read as perversion, a wilful desire to remain unproductive. It is error in the tradition of Sterne—a return to narrative as feigned haplessness, the performance of an aborted project. Such time-wasting is exemplified by *Malone Dies*, whose narrator intersperses the real-time account of his dying days with a detailed list of his possessions, and a pastime he calls "playing"—that is, the making up of stories, which he tells in the third person. The novel itself amounts to fragments of Malone's narrative, interrupted by the speaker's second-guessing and diversions. The absence of structure is augmented by the absence of epistemological design, and both are figured in terms of waste. For instance, to distract himself from his incipient death, Malone tells himself a story about a married couple, Mr and Mrs Saposcat, whose life is "full of axioms, of which one at least established the criminal absurdity of a garden without roses and with its paths and lawns uncared for" (*MD*, 188). To counter this absurdity, they consider growing vegetables—but the high price of manure necessitates they move to a smaller house "in the country where, having no further need of manure, they could afford to buy it in the cartloads" (*MD*, 188). The rationale of domestic economy turns into a series of illogical decisions that result in stasis: old age in a cottage with overheads low enough to buy the functional objects that they no longer need. The manure's devaluation from inaccessible luxury to an affordable but ultimately useless item is akin to that which, according to Bill Brown, distinguishes an "object" from a "thing." For Brown, the "object" is that which we use for its intended purpose; the "thing" is the "object" after it breaks, stops working, or fails.[23] "We begin to confront the thingness of objects when they stop working for us [...] when their flow within the circuits of production and distribution, consumption and exhibition, [is] arrested" (Brown, 4). The story of the Saposcats' absurd efforts to acquire manure, and the changing status of the manure in relation to their house move, is the story of an object's lost use. The story plays on the degree to which our lives are shaped by supply and demand, the lengths we will go to make a living. Beckett shows that it little matters whether we are trading in gold or dung: the market determines where we put our faith. The manure in this instance is a commodity—and a valuable one at that—but in order to afford it, the Saposcats must make a series of decisions that ultimately negate its utility. In becoming affordable at the same time that it loses its use-value, the manure is rendered waste once more.

This parodying of capitalist logic relates to a broader concern that permeates the *Trilogy*—the absurd criteria by which we adjudicate value to people and objects, which manifests largely in the characters' efforts to determine what things are worth keeping, and what events are worth recounting. Early in his narrative, Molloy notes: "the things that are worthwhile you do not bother about, you let them be, for the same reason, or wisely, knowing that all these questions of worth and value have nothing to do with you, who don't know what you're doing, or why" (*MO*, 46). He thus focuses on gathering and inventorying things with no monetary value, while intentionally shirking the question of how these efforts might be monetised. Indeed, our doubt regarding their value grows as we notice how Molloy's meticulous recollections, like Jacques Moran's after him, stray into descriptions of things that are not even there. For instance, the departure from hospital concludes with an irrelevant comment about his boots, which "came up to where [his] calves would have been if [he] had had calves, and partly [...] buttoned, or would have buttoned, if they had had buttons" and which he thinks he "has still [...] somewhere" (*MO*, 46).

The meandering description highlights the many things Molloy lacks: functioning limbs, proper clothes, and knowledge of his possessions' whereabouts. It also draws attention to his narrative project's absurdity— a haphazard account comprising useless anecdotes, descriptions of things that might have been but are not, and approximations of events.

The concepts of collecting, hoarding, and ordering have been approached from a variety of different critical disciplines. Jean Baudrillard[24] and Jacques Derrida[25] both link collecting and archiving to the death drive: the collector is essentially staving off the inevitable end that is death. For Susan Stewart, after Bachelard, the process of collection is akin to self-articulation—a process, that is, which calls attention to the corporeality of the self and of the pieces from which the body is constituted.[26] For Scott Herring and Martin F. Manalansan, those who accrue objects of little or no worth—including trash—offer a rebuke to the normative ordering of the material world under capitalism.[27] For Michel Foucault, it is less the collection than its organisation that warrants attention. In *The Order of Things*, he reads taxonomic organisation as an attempt to affirm power.[28] Power asserts itself by the putting of things in their proper place: people and objects are designated roles to play and rules to follow according to social norms and practices. To question or exceed these categories is to challenge authority, and to invite increased measures of systematisation. In each of these analyses, objects in a collection fluctuate between the status of commodity and the status of waste: collecting frequently entails a valuation of objects that is entirely separate from, or at odds with, that of the market. Although economic value can often play a part (one thinks of the collection of stamps or antiques), the governing impulse for the collector is frequently personal and (in the eyes of the market), irrational. The collector's concern is the objects' place within the narrative of the collection (and their potential to help complete it), and their value is tied to their relationship to the other objects, as opposed to the price they might secure in the marketplace. André Breton's hoarding of junk in his house in late life, touched on in Chap. 2, exemplifies this idea (although ironically the objects he saved accrued value after he died, as objects that had belonged to him).[29] To put it in the terms of Michael Thompson's rubbish theory, collecting is not necessarily driven by a desire to transform the objects from "transients" or "rubbish" into "durables": one might as easily accrue pebbles, buttons, and food wrappers as out-dated but commercially valuable coins. Rather, it more often stems from a desire to imply a narrative and causation where none exist, or to stop—or shroud—time. Arman's *Poubelles*, alluded to at the opening of this chapter, can be seen as the counterpoint to the collection: the sealed polyester containers of waste make no effort to classify or distinguish between the objects accrued therein. They draw attention to the impossibility—and absurdity—of classifying rubbish. Relatedly, Arman's *Accumulations*—sculptures featuring mounds of identical, usually mass-produced, objects—sought to divest objects of *all* meaning: the use of repetition provided a way to reduce them to abstractions, while the works themselves embodied reified procedures of production (Carrick, 87). The act of accruing and archiving in these works results in the object's loss of social status which renders it akin to waste in its meaninglessness, while the sealing of the collection in polymer or plexiglass does the opposite, preventing the objects from disintegration—effectively suspending it in an a-temporal space. The *Accumulation* itself serves to counter what Arman described as the "automation, assembly-line production, and also serial-discarding" of post-war society.[30] Sealed in their display cases, the *Accumulations* provided "strata and geological layers full of all the *force of the real*" (Arman, 265, as cited in Carrick, 86).

In the case of Beckett's characters, too, the aims of accruing are in perpetual flux, while the objects they collect or inventory are of no value at all. The goal of their inventories is fundamentally unstable, subject both to whim and to changes in circumstance such as the emergence of a new object, the recollection of an object forgotten, or the loss of one prized. The only consistent factor in these collections and scatterings is the tension between the attempt to catalogue the useless objects and a profound awareness that such an attempt will likely fail. "Soon I shall be quite dead at last, and so on, without even going on to the next page, which was blank," Malone intones, drawing attention to the narrative's role in marking time and proving his existence before the inevitable end (*MD*, 210). The addition of each record serves to undermine the project itself, suggesting its futility—which is in turn heightened by Malone's inclusion in the list of his very pencil and exercise book. After all, what use is it to record the possession of an exercise book in that very exercise book, when in losing the book one would also lose the record? (*MD*, 210) Does the record's structuring ability only exist insofar as we keep it to hand? Does the order hold if we close the book or lose it? Malone suggests not:

> [It] must be in the natural order of things, [that] all that pertains to me must be written there [in his record], including my inability to grasp what order is meant. For I have never seen any sign of any, inside me or outside me [...] I gave rein to my pains, my impotence. (*MD*, 210)

*failure to make sense =
failure to order
failure to narrate
sense-making
= use value*

Molloy disproves his inventory's capacity to organise experience in the very same passage as he suggests it: thus, the inventory paradoxically confirms Malone's inability to produce. The description of impotence as something to which one *gives rein* is also telling, suggesting that such inability to do, or make, has an anarchic dimension. For all that Malone seeks to order his thoughts and produce a coherent whole, his instincts drive him to hinder the process.

The inventory-taker's unreliability is a recurring theme throughout the *Trilogy*. For instance, Jacques Moran, the private investigator commissioned to find Molloy, wonders whether he'll remember everything there is to remember when he returns home from his quest and writes his report. He acknowledges that any inventory of his possessions will inevitably be incomplete—even if he keeps them away from his son's grasping hands, he will either lose or forget he possesses them. Ironically, by the time he comes home, there is very little to record, his search having failed. We might read this turn of events as a broader acknowledgement of the futility of seeking ontological truth or design—but an investigator with a better work ethic and strategic approach (to put it in management terms) would have been more than capable of fulfilling the terms of the project. Is it an explicit choice on Beckett's part to play out a narrative in which the contracted worker is frankly uninterested in completing the job for which he was hired. The useless inventories and investigations described are not intended to suggest an outright absence of meaning or the limits of ascribing meaning—rather, they suggest an awareness of the extent to which interpretation is a form of use-value. By abstaining from extracting a narrative from their lists, Molloy, Malone, and Moran abstain from participating in (to use an anachronistic term) the "knowledge economy." The lists thus remain a record of items with next to no use-value (since they themselves admit not knowing what to do with it), rather than valuable data ripe for analysis. Put differently, they and the items within them remain in their waste-state, unable to re-enter the cycle of commodity-information.

We find a different kind of subversion in the *Trilogy*'s famous "stone-sucking" passage (*MO*, 74). As the name suggests, these are stones which Molloy sucks on in lieu of proper food and which he moves from pocket to pocket in order to feel that he is sucking on something new each time he fishes one out (*MO*, 63–60). The stones are waste objects, having no monetary value or established function other than which Molloy imposes on them, and serving as an alternative to the accrual of wealth. Where

Malone spends most of his narrative delaying his inventory-taking before finally acknowledging the futility of the entire enterprise, Molloy dismisses system and order within the very first pages of his story: "But of the other objects which had disappeared why speak, since I did not know exactly what they were" (*MO*, 45). It is beyond the scope of Molloy's project to impose a system on the objects he accrues—just as he himself is "willing to concede" it is "not natural enough to enter into [the] order of things, and appreciate its niceties" (*MO*, 44). The stone-sucking scene gains even greater meaning, however, when we consider how well Molloy is schooled in the rules of capital. He has already noted: "you cannot go on buying the same thing forever." And he has informed us that advertising itself is premised on repetition. Echoing Joyce's Leopold Bloom, who meditates that "for an advertisement to work you must have repetition. That's the whole secret" (and who then enacts this repetition by later stating "Good idea the repetition. Same thing with ads. Buy from us. And buy from us"), Molloy asserts that if you say something "often enough," you will "end up believing it. It's the principle of advertising" (*U*, 419; 492; *MO*, 53).

Similarly, the stone-sucking circuit can be seen to mimic capital's endless circularity. My analysis chimes with that of Félix Deleuze and Gilles Guattari, who cite the sequence in the opening of *Capitalism and Schizophrenia*, Volume I (1972), in order to illustrate what they view to be the affinities between capitalism and the workings of the schizophrenic mind.[31] The schizophrenic, Deleuze and Guattari argue, makes no distinction between people, nature, industry, and society (Deleuze-Guattari, 3). Further, the schizophrenic makes no distinction between the things s/he desires and those s/he has ceased to desire, between those s/he seeks to consume and those for which s/he no longer has a use. In the schizophrenic mindscape, there is thus little—if anything—to distinguish a commodity from waste, for there is nothing to identify where production ends and consumption begins (or ends). "[P]roduction is immediately consumption [...] without any sort of mediation" (Deleuze-Guattari, 4). For Deleuze and Guattari, these tendencies are a product of the capitalist ethos, which is solely intent on "continually producing production," but they represent the "*exterior* limit" of the system, which paradoxically necessitates containment (Deleuze-Guattari, 7). Capitalism "produces schizos the same way it produces Prell shampoo or Ford cars," but because "the schizos are not saleable," they must be contained (or shut away) in order to prevent the entire system from falling apart. Thus, the figure of the schizophrenic, while exemplifying the most extreme form of the capitalist ethos, is paradoxically both a positive and potentially subversive force, capable of disrupting the entire system.

Deleuze and Guattari only mention the stone-sucking passage in passing, and their readings of the *Trilogy* in later sections of the book take Molloy, Moran, and the anonymous protagonist of *The Unnameable* to be different fragments of a schizophrenic self, which I resist. However, the concept of the stone-sucking circuit as a productive machine—a mini recycling plant, in which the used is repeatedly transformed into the new—is indeed compelling, and corroborates my own understanding of the scene as effectively parodying the circulation of commodities, fulfilling their role through endless movement. Such a reading imbues the scene with a radical dynamism, rendering it a kind of protest or expression of dissent, and sheds new light on the transactions we have already examined in this chapter.

Examined more closely, the complex process of moving different sucking stones around and around so as to always have the impression of sucking a "fresh" one is a play on the logic of capitalist consumption, which relies on the lure of the new and seeks always to produce new desires. The designation of "new" the stones receive upon reaching a new pocket effectively amounts to a form of recycling. Although waste objects to us, the stones in this context are imbued with value, and the system itself does away with the category of waste, which in turn does away with any need to consume actual commodities. It is, in other words, a self-enclosed cycle. Moreover, taking into account the nature of the objects being circulated allows us to expand the reading further: for what renders the scene comic is the sheer oddity (not to mention unhygienic nature) of stone-sucking itself. The prizing of stones, and the effort taken to continuously reimbue them with meaning, amplifies the strangeness of the capitalist logic: Molloy's assignation of value to the stones parodies the arbitrary nature of capitalism's value system, reminding us that the system hinges on turning objects of dubious worth into commodities, often for all too spurious reasons. The collector of worthless things, like the schizophrenic, is radical, but s/he is, too, a child of capitalism—his/her creativity is merely a natural result of the system into which s/he was born. In depicting these very different engagements with objects of little or no worth—inventorying, collecting, and "playing" at consumption—each of which discloses a degree of irrationality, and none of which can be seen to have a true point, Beckett does away with both the narrative logic of the traditional novel and the logic that governs subject–object relations under capitalism.

"[I]N THE RUBBISH DUMP, WHEN SHE LAID HER HAND UPON MY FLY"[32]: FIGURATIONS OF HUMAN WASTE

Beyond suggesting the collection's capacity to enshrine items in a state of uselessness and exploring the list's capacity, in its potential interminability, to defer the production of a complete, and useful, end product, Beckett's texts explore the extent to which the valuation of a person as unfit for use— or unproductive—relegates them to the status of human waste. We see this most clearly in the treatment of people as if they were discarded objects— finds to be scavenged—and in the depiction of tramps whose appearance is indistinct from their surroundings. Inert (often through injury) and averse to working, going, or doing, these characters take on a thing-like quality. The figure of human-as-*objet-trouvé* is literalised in *Molloy*. The vagrant's first sexual encounter is with an old woman (who might be a man) called "Ruth or Edith," who "finds" him in a rubbish dump:

> We met in a rubbish dump, unlike any other, and yet they are all alike, rubbish dumps. I don't know what she was doing there. I was limply poking about in the garbage saying probably, for at that age I must still have been capable of general ideas. This is my life. She had no time to lose, I had nothing to lose. [...] Anyway it was she who started it, in the rubbish dump, when she laid her hand upon my fly. More precisely, I was bent double over a heap of muck, in the hope of finding something to disgust me for ever with eating, when she, undertaking me from behind, thrust her stick between my legs and began to titillate my privates. (*MO*, 57)

The first sentence of this passage reveals specific qualities about waste itself. As a whole, waste when grouped together looks like an undifferentiated mass; but considered closely, nothing could be more different from another thing than one dump from another. Moreover, the aim of Molloy's scavenging (not to find something to eat, but to "disgust himself" enough to lose his appetite) nullifies the very purpose of the act. He is not scavenging for food, but for food waste unattractive enough to dissuade him from putting it to use. The passage also frames Molloy as a find—human waste, it transpires, the old woman/man intends to put to use by paying him for engaging sexually. For a brief time, Molloy and Ruth-Edith inhabit the dump and she pays him regularly for penetrating her "arid and roomy" orifice. Once she dies, he feels the "pain of losing a source of revenue" and wonders whether she was, in fact, a man (*MO*, 60). The act of sex is thus turned into a monetary transaction, amplified by the fact that the woman/man's age, if not his/her gender, negates the possibility of procreation, while her "aridity" makes for rather uncomfortable "rubbing." The cycle of production–consumption would have continued ad infinitum, had s/he not died. Finally, the interchangeableness of the rubbish dumps ("they are all alike") explicitly comments on the homogeneity of waste, which is also an obstacle to its usefulness. If all waste is the same (dubious in itself, given the phrasing "unlike any other," which suggests that it is not), then what is the likelihood of finding something of interest within it? Where Dada's scavengers set out to unlock the poetry within things, Beckett's scavenger here is far more sceptical in his foraging. He recognises that in digging through a tip, one is less likely to find a treasure than get aggressively prodded in the perineum. No narrative belies the things amassed in the dump, and the scavenger himself will not find redemption.

The exchange of money between Molloy and "Ruth or Edith" is in turn characteristic of the transactional dimension of Beckett's characters' relationships. For Beckett's *personnes trouvées* are frequently cast aside or killed almost as soon as they are discovered: their finders engage with them only long enough to determine whether they are worth keeping. Analogously, the finds' recuperative potential is repeatedly negated. When Molloy depicts a cigar-smoking gentleman walking his dog (*MO*, 13), he changes his story mid-sentence, admitting that the cigar was just a fag, the gentleman a bum, and the dog a mutt he found on one of his many walks from here to nowhere:

[W]as not perhaps in reality the cigar a cutty [and] what prevented the dog from being one of those stray dogs that you pick up and take in your arms, from compassion or because you have long been straying with no other company than the endless roads, sands, shingle, bogs [and] the fellow-convict you long to stop, embrace, suck, suckle and whom you pass by, with hostile eyes, for fear of his familiarities? Until the day when, your endurance gone, in this world for you without arms, you catch up in yours the first mangy cur you meet, carry it the time needed for it to love you and you it, then throw it away. (*MO*, 12)

The stray dog in this configuration is merely a surrogate companion and, as the passage progresses, it takes on metaphorical significance as a symbol of the closest approximation to affection. What began as a fantasy of gentrification, in which walking is circumscribed within the order of everyday civilisation, quickly devolves into a bitter rumination over the transactional nature of companionship, in which one carries one's companion "the time needed for it to love you and you it" before "throw[ing] it away" (*MO*, 12). Gentleman and bum alike subscribe to this ethos, extracting a temporary use (companionship) from their fellow "mangy cur" before moving on.

Towards the end of *Malone Dies*, scavenging is framed ironically, as one of the (many) activities for which Malone seeks to find a methodology or governing logic. Here, Malone is looking to understand the parameters of his relations with an unnamed vagrant he has encountered on the road. The man is defined by the resemblance of his clothes to those of Molloy and Moran, and to the greatcoat to which Malone had referred in passing at the beginning of the narrative (*MD*, 273). The meticulous description, with its paradoxical intimations of the interchangeable and fundamentally malleable nature of identity, provides the catalyst for a two-page-long proposed list of questions and commands:

> I shall tear a page out of my exercise-book and reproduce upon it, from memory, what follows, and show it to him to-morrow, or to-day, or some other day, if he ever comes back. 1. Who are you? 2. What do you do, for a living? 3. Are you looking for something in particular? What else? 4. Why are you so cross? 5. Have I offended you? 6. Do you know anything about me? 7. It was wrong of you to strike me. 8. Give me my stick. 9. Are you your own employer? 10. If not who sends you? 11. Put back my things where you found them. 12. Why has my soup been stopped? 13. For what reason are my pots no longer emptied? 14. Do you think I shall last much longer? 15. May I ask you a favour? 16. Your conditions are mine. 17. Why brown boots and whence the mud? 18. You couldn't by any chance let me have the butt of a pencil? 19. Number your answers. 20. Don't go, I haven't finished. Will one page suffice? There cannot be many left. I might as well ask for a rubber while I am about it. 21. Could you lend me an India rubber? (*MD*, 274)

That Malone is only *proposing* to compose the list endows this passage with a meta-fictional element. More to the point, what we have is a parody of the traditional novel form's efforts to order events into a narrative divested of ambiguity. The list's interruption, the interlocution of an absent other, the depiction of the vagrant as a surplus entity to be assimilated and made coherent, and the entire scene's imagined setting parody the novel form's efforts to organise lived experience. By speaking in the second person, Malone reaches out to an Other who straddles the boundary between narrative and world, and makes one final bid for logic to render the unknown knowable. Indeed, his combination of these seemingly unrelated things—actual events, speculations, side-notes, and questions to the reader—recalls Michel Foucault's reading, in the preface of *The Order of Things*, of the Chinese encyclopaedia entry Jorge Luis Borges describes in "The Analytical Language of John Wilkins" (Foucault, xvi–xx).[33] According to Borges, this list of animals (imaginary and real, embalmed and alive) draws attention to the sheer arbitrariness of all ordering practices. For Foucault, the "monstrosity" of the encyclopaedia entry comes from "the fact that the common ground on which such meetings [of unrelated things] are possible has itself been destroyed. [...] Absurdity destroys the *and* of the enumeration, making impossible the *in* where the things enumerated would be divided up" (Foucault, xviii). Borges in other words highlights the significance of the "site" of order by removing it. In a similar way, the absence of order in Malone's list draws attention to its importance elsewhere. The fact that his story culminates in a series of different, competing, and ultimately unresolved narratives spectacularly undermines his effort to impose order on his experiences. Material possessions, human relationships, ontological, epistemological, and theological systems collide in a haphazard heap of non-sequiturs (*MD*, 274). And it is precisely this haphazardness—in which the list-maker must interrupt the account of his meeting with the vagrant to ask his reader to loan him a rubber in order to enable him to erase what they have just read—that renders the passage comedic. Is Malone intending to erase the whole record and start again? Does that record include the novel we are reading? And, if so, what was the *point* of everything we have just assimilated? The novel itself, at this moment, is caught in a limbo between use-value and waste—if it continues, which of course it will, we can assume this record will have some kind of use (if only that of furthering the novel's efforts to sabotage its own narrative design); but if it hadn't continued, the pages of erased writing would have become waste. The mere suggestion of erasure draws our attention to the tenuousness of the writing process, and to the waste potential of literature itself, while distracting us from the narrative's original concern—what to do with the vagrant and how to put him to use within the story. In casting doubt on his capacity to complete his story, Malone turns our attention away from the question of human surplussage, allowing his vagrant to remain human waste—unattended, left to his own devices, and free to be of no commercially productive use.

Beckett extends this preoccupation with the thingness of human beings and their capacity to be deemed human waste in his last novel, *How It Is* (1964).[34] The very notion of social relations is inverted here, as the narrator blindly wades through an endless expanse of mud and encounters an anonymous man. Where a traditional novel might see the two converse, Beckett's protagonist subjects the unknown Other to a process of tactile identification and allocates him the name of "Pim," before meditating on how—and if—to put him to use. Crucially, Pim's thing-like quality is implied from the outset. His identity amounts to the cumulative sum of his body parts—the corporeal equivalent of the "bits and scraps" via which the narrator's own narrative is murmured (*H*, 43). His skin-like texture, the human-like blabber he emits, and the possession of hair and limbs and nails merely underline the absence of something else: utility, and personality. As such, he is not quite human, but rather an uncanny imitation of the human.

My use of the word "uncanny" relates specifically to Freud's delineation of it in his seminal essay, "The 'Uncanny'" (1919).[35] Freud identifies the unease evinced by inanimate objects that appear animated and that of people who appear inanimate: these phenomena elicit our fear due to their primordial associations. This, to an extent, is how Pim is framed: as a not-quite-human entity whose surplus status and pliability inspires barbaric tendencies in the narrator, including the solicitation of speech via clubbing. The depiction extends one of the central tropes of the historical avant-garde: the potential for our mechanising processes, and our compulsion to put things and people to use, to take on a life of their own, in a vein akin to Charlie Chaplin's *Modern Times* (1936).[36] The key difference is that the thing threatening to revive, in this case, *is human*. Beckett's narrative centres on the disquieting effect of reification: to look upon an inert human who acts like a faulty automaton, and to be angered by their uselessness, is to glimpse the effects of our ordering systems.

The slippage between human and automaton is augmented by Beckett's emphasis on Pim's different anatomical parts and on their identification via means other than sight. The narrator ascertains Pim's gender via a process of blind groping and attentive listening to the anonymous voice murmuring the action to him as he performs it. The framing has a distancing effect, severing actor(s) from action, as well as from each other, suggesting a system of actors and acted *upon*:

> having rummaged in the mud between his legs I bring up finally what seems to me a testicle or two [...] to feel the skull it's bald no delete the face it's preferable mass of hairs all white to the feel that clinches it he's a little old man we're two little old men. (*H*, 46)

Rummaging brings to light evidence as to the nature of the proverbial beast. This reconstruction, however, highlights the ease with which Pim can be disassembled: the narrator is able to "bring up" the "testicle or two," as if his anatomical parts were detachable. Such an impression is later heightened: having pulled up Pim's arm to check the time on his wrist watch—an act that further amplifies his function as a device or utilitarian object—the narrator throws it back down again. The arm flops down, lifeless, recalling the inertness of an automaton, which depends upon its manipulator to imbue it with a semblance of liveliness. Without such intervention, it amounts to little more than a useless cast-off:

> A few more movements put the arm back where I found it then towards me again the other way [...] until it jams one can see the movement grasp the wrist with my left hand and pull while bearing from behind with the right on the elbow or thereabouts. [...] Released at last the arm recoils sharp a little way then comes to rest it's I again must put it back where I found it way off on the right in the mud Pim is like that he will be like that he stays whatever way he's put but it doesn't amount to much on the whole a rock. (*H*, 50)

Pim is thus figured as human waste insofar as he cannot be made to do anything and insofar as his very limbs lack functionality. He is a thing not only without agency but unable to respond to simple orders to fulfil simple tasks, and thus the very embodiment (from the perspective of production) of superfluity. The narrator further emphasises this in the slippage between Pim and the narrator's malfunctioning wristwatch: "It keeps me company that's all its ticking now and then but break it throw it away let it run down and stop no something stops me it stops I shake my arm it starts no more about this watch" (*H*, 51). As he has just been talking about Pim, the "it" here could be either Pim or the watch. The dismissive "no more about this watch"—which echoes the format the narrator deploys elsewhere to clarify potentially ambiguous pronouns (e.g. "what about it my memory we're talking about my memory" (*H*, 10); or "it comes the words we're talking of words" (*H*, 21))—makes clear that the ambiguity is intentional. "It" isn't the man—it's the watch. But that temporary moment of uncertainty has been enough to destabilise the narrative, to make us imagine a malfunctioning man-watch in the process of being used, breaking, and being cast aside. Indeed, the narrator has already implied as much at the outset of Part II, in his suggestion that it is he who enables Pim to be more than human waste: "but for me he would never Pim we're talking of Pim never be but for me anything but a dumb limp lump flat for ever in the mud but I'll quicken him" (*H*, 10). Pim's existence is contingent upon the narrator's locution—it is in giving utterance to him that he endows Pim with the momentary semblance of a human being with a purpose, and amenable to being rendered more efficient ("quicken[ed]").

One way that the narrator seeks to put Pim to use is by training him to respond to violent thumps of a can opener on the skull or spine. One thump, and Pim speaks. A longer thump, and he sings. The narrator's use of a tin opener to evince these responses renders Pim analogous to the tins in the narrator's bag—a thing from which to extract a function via a mechanical act (screwing the opener into the tin, or wacking Pim on the head with it). Indeed, the narrator himself draws attention to the mechanical nature of the act:

> I take the opener in my right hand move it down along the spine and drive it into the arse not the hole not such a fool the cheek a cheek he cries I withdraw it thump on skull the cries cease it's mechanical end of first lesson series rest and here parenthesis. (*H*, 57)

Just as a tin is useless without an opener or sharp object to extract its contents—and thus, to all intents and purposes, waste—Pim is only useful when he is made to work. Once the process ceases, he goes back to being an inert object without use-value. This cycle uncannily reflects the ease with which the commodity slips from essential to obsolete.

Paradoxically, the greatest obstacle to putting Pim to use is his humanity. Habituated to clawing Pim in the armpit to evince particular responses, the narrator deliberates over "try[ing] a new place," one more sensitive, for instance his eye or "glans," before deciding that this would "only confuse him fatal thing avoid at all costs" (*H*, 54). The process is governed by the need to ensure that the man-machine operates according to the machinist's will—but what is also evident is the need to adapt the commands to the man-machine's capabilities.[37] Thus, it is precisely the objective limitations imposed by Pim's body, and faculties of comprehension, that obstruct the efficiency of the process. Where a machine can be programmed to tease out blips and loopholes, the body remains impassive: where a broken part can be replaced, the body's capacity to heal is limited. Pim's humanity is ultimately what renders him unfit for the purposes for which the narrator wants to use him and renders him human waste once more.

Beckett explores human waste and scavenging from a different standpoint in *Malone Dies*, through Malone's account of the failures of a man called Macmann (known, earlier in the novel, as Sapo) to work as a street sweeper. Due to a near-pathological distractedness, Malone tells us, Macmann cannot help but further sully the spaces he is meant to be cleaning: despite his "hop[e] of [...] being a born scavenger," Macmann is incapable of either scavenging or properly disposing of that which he accrues (*MD*, 237). Just as he himself is prone to tripping and stumbling, as if his body were somehow incapable of situating itself in the proper order of things, so, too, his efforts to clean and tidy successively fall short. In this parallel divagation of the body, and sullying of the streets through which it moves, Macmann enacts the very essence of vagrancy, erring from his course and succumbing to one physical failure after another while failing to fulfil the one task with which he was originally entrusted. The depiction reflects both Macmann's lack of biomechanical control and his lack of agency in the face of external circumstances:

> For he was incapable of picking, his steps and choosing where to put down his feet (which would have permitted him to go barefoot). And even had he been so he would have been so to no great purpose, so little was he master of his movements. And what is the good of aiming at the smooth and mossy places when the foot, missing its mark, comes down on the flints and shards or sinks up to the knee in the cow-pads? (*MD*, 238)

The intricacy of the narrative here is telling—Malone spares no detail, delving into the events as they unfold, and how these differ from how one might have expected them to. "In theory," for instance:

> his hat should have followed him, seeing it was tied to his coat, and the string twisted itself about his neck, but not at all, for theory is one thing and reality another, and the hat remained where it was, I mean in its place, like a thing forsaken. (*MD*, 239)

In this meticulous account, Malone contradicts our aesthetic assumptions, and highlights the degree to which objects defy narrative design via their very inertness. We expect art to give an aesthetic patina to experience, to locate beauty in the malfunctioning or mundane. Malone demonstrates the fallacy of such assumptions. Sometimes the mundane is just that: mundane. Where Surrealism was predicated on finding an epiphanic dimension to waste, and in fact explicitly espoused searching the city for inspiration, Beckett tells us not to bother. You won't achieve ontological clarity by sifting through mud or excrement. You'll just get dirty.

"[S]OMEWHERE SOMEONE IS UTTERING"[38]: DWELLING AND SPEAKING IN WASTE

Beckett's characters not only resist work by accruing waste objects and by pursuing tasks destined to fail. They also find ways to resist being assimilated into the society of producers and consumers by dwelling in landfills, ditches, and mud piles, and making waste a space in which to live outside the remit of capitalist production and consumption. Waste sites in Beckett thus have another socio-political dimension beyond the resistance to human reification, functioning as spaces in which his human waste characters can move freely. Beckett's insistence on setting his narratives against a backdrop of rubbish piles and muddied wastelands is a gesture towards the polysemy of objects and spaces, and to their significance beyond the values attributed to them within the system of capitalist consumption and urban planning. Beckett opens mud up as a field of enquiry in its own right, a space worthy of attention despite its evident obstruction to processes such as manufacturing, circulation, and distribution. Outside the field of capitalist production there is a use for mud—one that has nothing to do with its commodity potential, but rather with surviving outside the capitalist sphere of production and consumption. In this sense, his characters do indeed put waste to use—but their methods of doing so are very different from those of the historical avant-garde, insofar as the use-putting never finds its way back into the cycle of commodity exchange.

What we might call the politics of Beckett's wastelands becomes self-evident when we consider his characters' geospatial movements and their object relations as manifestations of de Certeauvian tactics. de Certeau essentially extended Foucault's power relations to address how everyday activities such as shopping and walking can function as manipulations of space.[39] He deployed military lexicon in his analysis of these cultural practices and uses of space, using the concept of "strategies" to denote actions and movements practiced by entities in power (state, private sector), and "tactics" to refer to the actions of the weak (citizens and consumers).[40] Strategies rely on an established place from which to plan, envision, and stockpile, and they rely on visual cues to do so, while tactics are defined by dislocation, relying on mobility and creative initiative, often without the privilege of sight (de Certeau, 36). The absence of a legitimate headquarters or home prevents them from growing their wealth: they have to use up what they accrue, or else leave it behind (de Certeau, 37). Their strength thus lies in pure action. This dynamic of randomness and ingenuity lends itself to our reading of waste in Beckett: like de Cereau's tactics, Beckett's characters use their displacement and mobility to their own advantage. As *Waiting for Godot*'s Estragon says to his fellow bum, Vladimir, "We don't manage too badly. [...] We always find something [...] to give us the impression we exist" (*G*, 69). The flippant sarcasm of Vladimir's retort, "Yes yes we're magicians" (*G*, 69), is deceptive. It is precisely on such apparently menial recuperative efforts, or what de Certeau, after Lévi-Strauss, terms "making do" (the direct translation of *bricolage*), that tactics gain their strength.[41] Vladimir's own assertion, earlier, that he "get[s] used to the muck as [he] go[es] along" reflects an ethos of survival contingent upon persuasion and (self)-deception. Similarly, where Estragon is all too keen to bum five or ten francs off the first passer-by, Vladimir's indignant objection, "We are not beggars!" reflects the tactic's peculiar self-reliance—the preference for stealing scraps or digging through a landfill as opposed to accepting alms (*G*, 39). Emphatically creative, and unapologetically disingenuous, tactical use is contingent upon the capacity to "throw one over" power, be it a police officer, parent, or personage to whom they are in debt. Indeed, it verges on the criminal. To use cannily is also, often, to *mis*-use or transgress. To assign an alternative use to something is to challenge its place in the official narrative or order of things, and thus to (however obliquely or subtly) undermine authority.

In *The Unnameable,* knowledge of the world itself is depicted as requiring re-purposing, if it is to be of any use to the novel's protagonist. The protagonist dismisses what others have taught him as essentially inapplicable to his own marginalised state, but he "[declines] to say it was all to no purpose. I'll make use of it, if I'm driven to it" (*U*, 299). The alienated self makes use of the scraps society throws it—it re-appropriates facts and so-called truths and assembles them in new and unexpected ways. Like Levi-Strauss' *bricoleur*, he deconstructs civilised society's hierarchical values, recognising that "the thing to avoid [...] is the spirit of system" (*U*, 294).

Beckett's characters move through and deploy mud tactically partly because they recognise its "useful" qualities. In its very obscuring and stalling capacities, mud offers both the possibility of concealment and respite—a surrogate home. Darkness allows concealment from others; an enforced pause is also a chance to rest. In *Malone Dies*, it is in a muddied ditch that the protagonist of Malone's framed narrative, Macmann, finally lies down to sleep and is retrieved by the caretakers of a rest home. While his fall reprises those of Molloy and Moran in the *Trilogy's* previous volumes and Pozzo's towards the end of *Godot* (*G*, 81), it differs in its explicit intentionality. Sapo/Macmann *chooses* to fall. He seizes upon the mud as a space for rest, identifying its *useful* properties. "Caught by the rain far from shelter Macmann stopped and lay down" Malone tells us (*MD*, 239), before meticulously detailing his logic: that in lying down, he might be less exposed to the pelting rain. "So he lay down, prostrate, after a moment's hesitation" (*MD*, 239). This deployment is important on two counts: where Malone's trajectory remains unexplained, and Molloy and Moran are subject to chance and their own failings, Macmann displays an ability to thoughtfully manipulate circumstance—to use the bog to his own ends, and thus to wrest a kind of agency out of chance, however fraught. Rather than an obstruction, mud becomes a shelter. What society views as requiring expulsion or avoidance (embodying negative associations of alterity, filth, danger, ambiguity, and opacity) becomes, for the vagrant, a medium in which to lay low—to literally wait out the storm. Mud and muck are thus recast as useful, and as *protective*—offering a sense of wrested parentage or homeliness constructed out of necessity. A fundamentally malleable entity, mud acts as a temporary, makeshift shelter. This use-putting is a form of tactical manipulation, where the thing deployed is eventually left behind, a vestige of its transient user's ingenuity and skill.

Beckett's vagrants' manipulation of wasted spaces involves accepting the spaces' unaccommodating, and in many ways *estranging*, nature. Mud sticks, stops, and gets in the way: it is revolting to the touch and repellent to our aesthetic sensibilities, and our systems of order and cleanliness. To rest in the spaces that mainstream society avoids is to perform an act of resistance as well as to gesture towards an alternative metrics. Where mainstream society seeks self-improvement, promotion, and peer validation, the marginalised *I* cultivates inertia and distances itself via an open acknowledgement of its own impotence. For instance, Malone refers to his body as an external casing that he would throw out the window, were he able to: "If I had the use of my body I would throw it out of the window. But perhaps it is the knowledge of my impotence that emboldens me to that thought" (*MD*, 219). In their willingness to dwell in the spaces eschewed by the rest of society, Beckett's characters show how we might desist from productivity.

My concern throughout this analysis of waste in Beckett has been his characters' resistance to being put to use and the many creative ways they find to sabotage both their work and the production of a coherent narrative whole. Before concluding, however, I want to expand this discussion to consider how, while resisting being put to productive use, his characters implicitly affirm, in their accounts, the narrative potential of waste. The entire meandering yet static narrative of *The Unnameable* ultimately builds towards two admissions: that the narrator has "never stirred from here," and that it is from a position of stasis that he has spawned "all these stories about travellers and paralytics" (*U*, 416), including, as his allusions to "Malone," "Murphy," and "Watt" suggest, all the protagonists that have preceded him in his author's previous novels. An "absentee" (*U*, 417) with no discernible identity, he has nevertheless been able to create a multitude of (albeit conflicting and rarely logical stories) out of a void (*U*, 414). From his "parlour, where [he] wait[s] for nothing," and aided only by simple tricks of rhetoric (*U*, 414), he creates a linguistic "something" (*U*, 414).

In scavenging sticks and hats and mouldy food, in rummaging through heaps of dung, in contemplating their own bodily emissions, Beckett's characters enact a process of survival on the margins resistant to commercial paradigms or social mores. They show how one can make one's self at home in one's homelessness and make do without profit or gain, basing our actions on chance and circumstance rather than logic or bureaucratic order:

> we leave our sacks to those who do not need them we take their sacks from those who soon will need them we leave without a sack we find one on our way we can continue on our way [...] more sacks here then than souls infinitely if we journey infinitely and what infinite loss without profit there is that difficulty overcome. (*H*, 97)

In these narratives, it is not waste itself that causes fear: it is the process of iteration, the process of making *sense* of waste, of putting it to use through thought and logic, that horrifies. To bed down in waste is to abstain from meaning-making. The waste Beckett's characters inhabit is where words and scraps of phrases can pile up or decompose at will, where the absence of adverbs or pronouns is irrelevant, where inexplicability, lack of progress, or disorientation is of little or no issue. Thus:

> brief black long black no knowing and there I am again on my way again something missing here only two or three yards more and then the precipice only two or three last scraps and then the end end of part one leaving only two leaving only part three and last something missing here things one knows already or will never know it's one or the other. (*H*, 38)

There is no coherent order, narrative structure, or epistemological framework here, as attested by the absence of "something" that may or may not fall within the bounds of what the self knows or understands.

Rather, the concern of the narrator (and of the other voices he implies are vying to be heard) is to continue saying.

It is through narrative that the characters discover what we might term, after Breton, *l'espoir trouvé*. The concluding section of *Texts for Nothing* opens with a declamation of authorial defeat, only to seize upon that gesture, detecting a kernel of hope and narrative continuity in the very statements of negation. Having asserted that "it's nothing new, I'm nothing new," the narrator realises that "Ah so there was something once, I had something once" (*TN*, 50). The present is defined by absence, which belies a *previous presence*. The narrator inhabits a wasteland, but waste, by very definition, is the remainder of what once was: a wasteland is the remainder of a once-functioning world. This, in turn, affirms the existence of *a* world, however fractured. Hence, the narrator's change of heart:

> This is most reassuring, after such a fright, and emboldens me to go on, once again. But there is not silence. No, there is utterance, somewhere someone is uttering. Inanities, agreed, but is that enough, is that enough, to make sense? (*TN*, 50)

Not only is there a world: it is a world populated by voices. The reference to sense is both rhetorical and ironic, underlining the absurdity of expecting "sense" from a narrative defined by obscurity. However, the mention of "enough" implies that despite the paucity of signification, cardinal direction, discernible identities, or clear geographic landmarks, the presence of "utterance" and the absence of "silence" belie potential. The very muddle of self-contradictory, anachronistic "buts" in which the narrator has caught himself suggests that if nothing else, he is not at a loss for excess words. Beckett's narrating wastrel confirms the power of language and his own capacity to use it to whatever unintelligible intent he chooses.

In abstaining from turning waste into art, Beckett's characters show us the inherent limitations of the aesthetic of re-use: by its very nature, re-use becomes part of the system that generated waste in the first place. The *objet trouvé*, once recognised as such, becomes a commodity in the art market, codified within a new system of values. Via abstention—a constipated sitting-still—Beckett's characters obstruct the system and its capacity to subsume them. To be sure, the characters themselves prove useful to the creation of the novels we hold in our hands. But beyond this they suggest the radical potential of resisting use-putting and the radical potential of dwelling *in* waste—what we might term a poetics not of re-use, but of immersion. Beckett's figuration of failed inventorying, worthless collections, and pronated, ailing bodies offers different ways into thinking about how one might resist participating in the market economy, while parodying our tendencies to evaluate humans in terms of their capacity to produce and consume.

NOTES

1. Samuel Beckett. *Molloy* (1955) in *Trilogy* (London: John Calder, 1959), Henceforth, *MO*.
2. Braverman, *Labor and Monopoly Capitalism*, 66–82; David Harvey, "Fordism" in *The Condition of Postmodernity* (Oxford: Blackwell, 1991), 125–140.
3. Kristin Ross, *Fast Cars, Clean Bodies*, 19; 25; 26.
4. For insight into Beckett's engagement with the historical avant-garde, see Peter Fifield, "Samuel Beckett and the Interwar Avant-Garde" in *The Edinburgh Companion to Samuel Beckett and the Arts*, ed. Stan E. Gontarski (Edinburgh University Press, 2014), and Enoch Brater, *Ten Ways of Thinking About Samuel Beckett* (London: Bloomsbury, 2011).
5. Laura Salisbury, *Samuel Beckett: Laughing Matters, Comic Timing* (Edinburgh University Press, 2012), 100; 98. Susan Signe Morrison like-wise draws attention to the "corrosive" slippage between material waste and metaphorical in *Endgame*—where she notes the ash bin-dwelling char-acters experience waste psychologically and spiritually, perceiving their interior selves as "wasted and meaningless" (Morrison, 93).
6. Sardin and Germoni, for example, note Beckett's mockery of what he termed "the 'chloroformed world' of Balzac" (Sardin and Germoni, 741).
7. See Pascale Sardin and Karine Germoni, "Scarcely Disfigured: Beckett's Surrealist Translations," *Modernism/Modernity* 18. 4 (November 2011): 739–753. Peter Fifield notes Beckett's frustration with the involvement of art editor and curator Herbert Read in his translation of Paul Eluard's poems: Read's involvement with the commercial world of sales suggested a "troubling commercial repackaging of Surrealism," representing a "mar-ketable avant-garde" (Fifield, 173; 176).
8. See, for instance, Anna Katharina Schaffner and Shane Weller, *Modernist Eroticism: European Literature after Sexology* (London: Palgrave Macmillan, 2012).
9. Ivan Fónagy associates pronunciation itself, in the *Trilogy*, with defecation, relating Molloy's reference to his mother as "Countess Caca" to the anal impulse in speech. Ivan Fónagy, *La vive voix: Essais de psycho-phonétique* (Paris: Payot, 1983). Keir Elam reads the reference, in *How it is*, to "word-shit," which most readers assume to be a description of his logorrhea, as a literal description of him losing control of his bowels. Keir Elam, "*Not I:*

Beckett's Mouth and the Ars(e) Rhetorica" in *Beckett at Eighty/ Beckett in Context*, ed. Enoch Brater (Oxford University Press, 1986), 124–148. Citation on 146. Beci Carver extends this investigation of scatology in "Waste Management in Beckett's *Watt*" in *Granular Modernism* (Oxford: Oxford University Press, 2014), 142–170. See esp. 162.

10. Pierre Restany, "*Nouveau Réalism*: The Richness of the World of Objects," in *Nouveau Réalistes*, transl. Editha Carpenter (New York: Zabriskie, 1988), 8, as cited in Jill Carrick, *Nouveau Réalisme, 1960s France, and the Neo-Avant-garde: Topographies of Chance and Return* (Farnham: Ashgate, 2010), 4. Carrick notes that although Restany's articulation of the movement's aims led many to view it as a "naïve pastiche of capitalist spectacle," critics have more recently identified, in the work of its individual artists, an underlying criticism of post-war consumerism and hitherto unacknowledged oppositional intent (Carrick, 4; 7).

11. Susanne Hauser makes a similar point in "Waste into Heritage: Remarks on Materials in the Arts, on Memories and the Museum," arguing that Arman "showed garbage as garbage, merely transferring it from the dustbin to the gallery and obstinately putting it on display." See *Waste-Site Stories: The Recycling of Memory*, Brian Neville and Johanne Villeneuve (Albany: State University of New York Press, 2002), 39–54, citation on 44. For an in-depth analysis of Arman's work with waste and a discussion of its political underpinnings, see Carrick, 77 and 95, and Gillian Whitely, *Junk: Art and the Politics of Trash* (London: I.B. Tauris, 2010), 47 and 109–114.

12. See Arman, *Le Nouveau Réalisme* (Paris: Editions du feu de Paume, 1999).

13. For further discussion of this aspect of the work, see Gérard Bartolini, *Montre-moi tes déchets: L'art de faire parler les restes* (Paris: L'Harmattan, 2011), 9–13.

14. Arman, as cited in Daniel Abadie, *Arman: L'âge de fer et ses monuments* (Paris: Galerie Beaubourg, 1977), 80.

15. "Nouveau Réalisme: The Sociology of the Object," in *Art of the 20th Century*, ed. Karl Ruhrberg et al. (Köln: Taschen, 2000), 519.

16. Georg Lukács, *History and Class Consciousness* (London: Merlin, 1967 [1968]), 83.

17. Zygmunt Bauman, *Wasted Lives*, 39.

18. *Molloy* (1951/1955) in *Trilogy* (London: John Calder, 1959), 46. Henceforth, *M*.

19. Samuel Beckett. *Waiting for Godot* (London: Faber, 1956 [1954]), 1; 14; 60; 66. Henceforth, *G*.

20. *Malone Dies* (1956), *Trilogy* (London: John Calder, 1959), 186. Originally published in French as *Malone meurt* (Paris: Minuit, 1951). Henceforth, *MD*.

21. Michael Kinnucan. "Beckett and Failure" in *The Hypocrite Reader* 5 (June 2011), accessed 10 May 2015. http://www.hypocritereader.com/5/ beckett-and-failure.

22. See James Knowlson and John Pilling, *Frescoes of the Skull* (London: Calder, 1979); Susan Brienza, *Samuel Beckett's New Worlds: Style in Metafiction* (University of Oklahoma Press, 1987) and Marcin Tereszewski, *The Aesthetics of Failure: Inexpressibility in Samuel Beckett's Fiction* (Newcastle upon Tyne: Cambridge Scholars, 2013).

23. Bill Brown, "Thing Theory," *Critical Inquiry* 28. 1 (Autumn, 2001), 1–22, citation on 3–4.

24. Jean Baudrillard, "The System of Collecting" in *The Cultures of Collecting*, ed. John Elsner and Roger Cardinal (London: Reaktion Books), 7–24.

25. See *Archive Fever: A Freudian Impression*, transl. Eric Prenowitz (Chicago: University of Chicago Press, 1996), 10.

26. Susan Stewart, *On Longing: Narratives of the Miniature, the Gigantic, the Souvenir, the Collection* (Duke University Press: Durham and London, 1993), 132–169.

27. Scott Herring, *The Hoarders: Material Deviance in Modern American Culture* (Chicago: University of Chicago Press, 2014); Martin F Manalansan IV, "The 'Stuff' of Archives: Mess, Migration and Queer Lives," *Radical History Review* 120 (Fall 2014): 94–107.

28. Michel Foucault, *The Order of Things* (London and New York: Routledge, 1989 [1966]).

29. Polizzotti, *Revolution of the Mind: The Life of André Breton*, 618 and fn. 732.

30. Arman, "Réalisme des accumulations," in *1960: Les Nouveaux Réalistes* (Paris: MAM, 1986), 265, as translated by and cited in Carrick, 86.

31. Félix Deleuze and Gilles Guattari, *Anti-Oedipus: Capitalism and Schizophrenia*, transl. Robert Hurley, Mark Seem and Helen R. Lane (Minneapolis: University of Minnesota Press, 1983 [1972]). 3.

32. *Molloy*, 57.

33. Jorge Luis Borges, "The analytical Language of John Wilkins," transl. Lilia Graciela Vásquez (Alamut: Bastion of Peace and Information). Accessed 10 February 2016: https://ccrma.stanford.edu/courses/155/assignment/ex1/Borges.pdf.

34. *How It Is* (New York: Grove, 1964). Originally published in French as *Comment c'est* (Paris: Minuit, 1961). Henceforth, *H.*

35. Sigmund Freud. "The 'Uncanny,'" 228–256.

36. *Modern Times* (1936), directed by Charlie Chaplin [Film]. USA: United Artists Corporation.

37. For further insight into the machine-like nature of Beckett's bodies, see Hugh Kenner, "The Cartesian Centaur" in *Samuel Beckett: A Critical Study* (New York: Grove Press, 1961); Phil Baker, *Beckett and the Mythology of Psychoanalysis* (London: Macmillan, 1998), 143; Ulrika Maude, *Beckett, Technology, and the Body* (Cambridge University Press, 2011); and Yoshiki Tajiri, *Samuel Beckett and the Prosthetic Body: The Organs and Senses in Modernism* (New York and London: Palgrave Macmillan, 2007).

38. Samuel Beckett, *Stories and Texts for Nothing* (New York: Grove, 1967), 50. Henceforth, *STN*.

39. Michel de Certeau, *The Practice of Everyday Life*, transl. Steve Rendall (Berkeley: University of California Press, 1986), 35.

40. de Certeau, 35.

41. Claude Lévi-Strauss, *The Savage Mind* (Chicago, IL: University of Chicago Press, 1966 [1962]), 17, 21), as cited in de Certeau, 29–30.

CHAPTER 4

Waste in Donald Barthelme, J.G. Ballard, and William Gaddis

J.G. Ballard's early short story "The Subliminal Man" (1963) imagines a UK entirely colonised by freeways, supermarkets, and offices.[1] While men work 12-hour days, women scrutinise TV advertisements and scour the shop aisles for incentives to trade recent purchases for new ones. The roads feature rubber studs designed to damage vehicles driving over them, ensuring they never last more than six months. And every day, commuters drive by billboards that block from view a series of towering landfills and junkyards teeming with the things they have thrown out:

> The areas on either side of the expressway were wasteland, continuous junk-yards filled with cars and trucks, washing machines and refrigerators, all perfectly workable but jettisoned by the economic pressure of the succeeding waves of discount models. Their intact chrome hardly tarnished, the metal shells and cabinets glittered in the sunlight. Nearer the city the billboards were sufficiently close together to hide them but now and then, as he slowed to approach one of the flyovers, Franklin caught a glimpse of the huge pyramids of metal, gleaming silently like the refuse grounds of some forgotten El Dorado. (SM, 569)

In this society enslaved to built-in obsolescence, advertising tantalises commuters while physically obscuring their cast-offs. The billboards' placement in front of the landfill literalizes advertising's role in confusing

© The Editor(s) (if applicable) and The Author(s) 2016
R. Dini, *Consumerism, Waste, and Re-Use in Twentieth-Century Fiction*,
DOI 10.1057/978-1-137-58165-5_4

needs with wants, and actual use-value with perceived use-value. The subliminal incitements to which the title refers—flashing messages concealed under seemingly innocuous traffic signs, and that command commuters to "BUY NOW BUY NOW BUY NOW"—are shown to be integral to this system. While the hoardings distract consumers from the landfills, the subliminal messages persuade them to participate at ever-greater speed in the cycle of consumption and disposal. Consumers' need for money to fund this frantic consumption of discretionary goods in turn guarantees that they will acquiesce to a seven-day working week (SM, 576).

Ballard's story anticipates themes explored by a number of Anglo-American and European novelists writing between the late 1960s and late 1970s, while building on the ideas we have discussed thus far: the landfill-pyramids lining the motorway recall de Chirico's estranging waste objects, while the story's emphasis on lives spent perpetually repeating the same, ultimately meaningless, tasks—driving, working, buying—recalls the senseless actions of Beckett's bums. Ballard's text differs however in its economistic framing: it is not merely waste objects that estrange, but the characters' detailed discussions about the financial merits of their transactions and their role in supporting the nation's economy. *Everything* in this story is reduced to a use-value.

This chapter examines a selection of texts that examine waste in similarly economistic terms: Donald Barthelme's *Snow White* (1967)[2]; J.G. Ballard's "urban disaster" trilogy, *Crash* (1973),[3] *Concrete Island* (1974),[4] and *High-Rise* (1975)[5]; and William Gaddis' *JR* (1975).[6] The tendency of these novels to view waste in catastrophic—even dystopian—terms aptly reflects the intense socio-economic upheavals of the period in which they were written, which included the first major post-war recession, the Arab Oil Crisis, the breakdown of the Bretton-Woods agreement, and the dissolution of Fordism-Keynesianism.[7] But as well as questioning the cultural toll of consumerism, each text deploys waste to extend the novel form. While they have been termed postmodern by many, I contend that these texts, and their recuperative practices, are in fact indebted to the Surrealist tradition.[8] To be sure, each of these novels grapples with what Frederic Jameson, in his study of postmodernism, terms the "logic of late capitalism"—a cultural paradigm shaped by "the frantic economic urgency of producing fresh waves of ever more novel-seeming foods (from clothing to airplanes), at ever greater rates of turnover."[9] My concern however is to explore the avant-gardist strategies they deploy to counter that paradigm, which is also to say, the ways in which waste becomes a tool for, and the site in which to, negotiate this new socio-economic terrain.

Barthelme, Ballard and Gaddis were not the only novelists of the 60s and 70s to consider the relationship between shortened product cycles and the growth of landfills. Much of Thomas Pynchon's *V.* (1963) takes place in the sewers of Manhattan, where protagonist Benny Profane has been hired to hunt a swarm of alligators.[10] The alligators are the result of a passing fad for baby alligators among children of the Manhattan elite, having been flushed down the toilet when the fad ended. Profane is in turn aware that once he has killed all the alligators, he will be out of a job. Pynchon thus parodies progressive obsolescence and the cycles of employment and redundancy. Commodity culture's excretions, out of sight, are not out of mind: their traces are there to remind us of the fickleness of our market-driven desires (*V*, 146; 148).[11] In Italo Calvino's *Invisible Cities* (1972), the city of Leonia is defined less by the things its inhabitants produce than by those they excrete to "make room for the new," and by the sense of purification resulting from such disposal.[12] Calvino posits consumer waste as a threat to our assumptions about sovereignty: the ultimate irony of capitalist imperialism is that its posterity is measured in rubbish. By contrast, the homosexual landfill worker in Michel Tournier's *Gemini* (1975), already alluded to in the Introduction, presents rubbish as the highest status to which an object can aspire, and (recalling Beckett's Molloy), the landfill itself as a cruising ground. In a humorous passage titled "Aesthetic of the Dandy Garbage Man," he explains that "[f]ar from trying to arrest the process of production-consumption-disposal, I pin all my hopes on it since it ends at my feet. The refuse dump is not an abyss in which the object is swallowed up but the repository where it finds a home after successfully passing through a thousand ordeals" (75). Consumption is merely a means to arrive at an object's true essence: "the empty bottle, the squeezed tube [...] the hard, durable parts of the product, the elements of the inheritance which our civilization will bequeath to the archaeologists of the future" (76). Consumer waste is ironically recast as a precious entity, and its right to burial rather than incineration protected by valiant garbage-men-qua-custodians who endure tapeworms and dysentery for their cause (80; 87).

The texts we are about to discuss amplify and complicate these depictions of overconsumption: extending the avant-gardist practices of de Chirico, Breton, Loy, and Beckett, they reclaim waste to create radically innovative narrative forms.

THE WRITING OF "DRECK": DONALD BARTHELME'S *SNOW WHITE* (1967)

Donald Barthelme's fairy-tale pastiche, *Snow White* (1967), situates the 1937 Disney version of Snow White in modern-day New York, re-casting Snow White's seven dwarfs as labourers Bill, Clem, Hubert, Henry, Kevin, Edward, and Dan. The dwarfs earn their living by manufacturing Chinese baby food and washing buildings (except for Dan, who works at a plastic hump-making plant), and they share a passion for "dreck" (Yiddish for excrement, nonsense, or junk, and whose first known use in English was James Joyce's *Ulysses*[13]). While the dwarfs work or ponder the hidden value of waste, Snow White tends to the housekeeping (*SW*, 111). In their leisure time, they all enjoy sex together in the shower. The novel's villains are Jane, "the evil stepmother figure," and Hogo, a millionaire who has fitted a General Motors advertisement into the ceiling of his mansion and who disposes of his garbage by throwing it out of the window (*SW*, 82; 134). Like Barthelme's short fiction, *Snow White* is disjointed and at times even nonsensical, featuring partial dialogues, lists of seemingly unrelated objects, and frequent references to waste and its disposal. And it is *very* funny. Considered by many to be the archetypal postmodernist text, it has more recently been recognised as a descendant of the historical avant-garde.[14] Barthelme himself acknowledged this debt in an interview with *The Paris Review* published in the summer of 1981, in which he recalled receiving a copy of Marcel Raymond's *From Baudelaire to Surrealism* from his father (a renowned modernist architect), and noted its enduring influence on his imagination.[15] In the same interview, Barthelme described his fondness for "all the filth on the streets" of New York, elaborating:

> it reminds me of Kurt Schwitters. Schwitters used to hang around printing plants and fish things out of waste barrels, stuff that had been overprinted or used during makeready, and he'd employ this rich accidental material in his collages. I saw a very large Schwitters show some years ago and almost everything in it reminded me of New York. Garbage in, art out.

The testimonial is fascinating not only because of its suggestion that we bring Schwitters' aesthetic to bear on Barthelme's work, but because it suggests that *all* city writing, if not the urban experience itself, has been indelibly shaped by the historical avant-garde and its appreciation for waste: to view collage is to be reminded of urban waste, and to view urban waste is to be reminded of collage. The two are intertwined. This identification of the inherent interrelation of the historical avant-garde, the city, and waste is key to Barthelme's aesthetic, as is the notion that the fiction writer, like the collage artist, might put waste to aesthetic use. The latter is comically voiced by a character in Barthelme's story, "See the Moon" (1966), who envies painters, since:

> They can pick up a Baby Ruth wrapper on the street, glue it to the canvas (in the right place, of course, there's that), and lo! People crowd about and cry 'A real Baby Ruth wrapper, by God, what could be realer than that!' Fantastic metaphysical advantage. [...] Fragments are the only forms I trust.[16]

The waste we find on the street is in fact more authentic than any representation, and fragments convey truth more than a whole. In turn, the parenthetical aside, "(in the right place of course, there's that)," amusingly suggests that there is a logic underlying the placement of collage fragments. Barthelme's own predilection for collage is well documented— he explained it at length in a series of correspondences with Jerome Klinkowitz between 1971 and 1972, and confessed, in the introduction to *Guilty Pleasures* (1974), his "secret vice" of "cutting up and pasting together pictures."[17] It would likewise be difficult to name a text of his that does not make reference to waste and its potential hidden meanings. The fragment-loving character in "See the Moon" mounts old objects from his past onto his wall in the hope that they "will someday merge, blur—cohere is the word, maybe—into something meaningful. A grand word meaningful" (*SS*, 91). "Brain Damage" (1970) opens with the narrator recounting his discovery of a book "in the first garbage dump," implying that each of the following disjointed passages takes place in other, different, dumps.[18] "Sakrete" (1983) recounts a male artist's efforts, at his wife's instigation, to find out who has been stealing the neighbourhood garbage cans.[19] Perhaps most famously, "The Indian Uprising" (1965), which imagines the defeat of the US empire by a tribe of Native Americans and their ghetto-dwelling allies, features multiple references to pollution, mobile garbage dumps, and barricades made out of household items (*SS*, 102–109), which the story's first reviewers assumed to be references to the New York City garbage crisis and critiques of "the sense of unreality created by television when newsreels of carnage run smoothly into advertisements for the good life."[20] In each of these instances, Barthelme deploys waste to disrupt the narrative and hint at a broader malaise underlying popular culture.

Studies of the relationship between waste and the governing aesthetic of *Snow White* tend to focus on Barthelme's deployment of "verbal waste"—advertising slogans, slang—while reading the physical waste in his work allegorically. William Gass' oft-quoted summary of Barthelme's project as "constructing a single plane of truth, of relevance, of style, of value—a flatland junkyard—since anything dropped in the dreck *is* dreck, at once, as an uneaten pork chop mislaid in the garbage" is emblematic of critics' focus on the semantic slippage between trash as "low-brow" culture and trash as physical waste.[21] In what follows, I aim to demonstrate the fruitfulness of a more literal reading. I read Barthelme's waste objects as the physical evidence, or counterparts, to the lexicons of marketing and advertising that so preoccupied him. These objects are semiotic to be sure, but they call attention, as well, to their materiality.

Towards the end of *Snow White*, the dwarfs are faced with the quandary of disposing of a "well-known aesthetician" tasked with judging the merits of their shower curtain. They contemplate shredding him in their electric wastebasket:

> The electric wastebasket is a security item. Papers dropped into it are destroyed instantly. How the electric wastebasket accomplishes this is not known. An intimidation followed by a demoralization eventuating in a disintegration, one assumes. It is not emptied. There are not even ashes. It functions with a quiet hum digesting whatever we do not wish to fall into the hands of the enemi [*sic*]. The record of Bill's trial when he is tried will go into the electric wastebasket. When we considered the destruction of the esthetician [*sic*] we had in mind the electric wastebasket. First dismemberment, then the electric wastebasket. That there are in the world electric wastebaskets is encouraging. (*SW*, 135)

This is but one of many passages in which we are alerted to the bureaucratic nature of Barthelme's dwarfs, with their staunch work ethic (Bill, the only one to leave a vat of baby food unattended, is dutifully tried and hanged) and their adhesion to rigorous research methods. Indeed, the above-mentioned aesthetician is only deemed unsuitable, and hence disposable, because he lacks a reputable methodology with which to adjudicate value. This leaves the "truth" of his judgement that theirs is the "best" curtain open to doubt. Likewise, the reference to "First dismemberment, then the electric wastebasket" brings to mind the efficiency of the electric chair. What Larry McCaffery describes as Barthelme's tendency to confront his characters with "worn-out systems [that] fail to operate successfully"

(McCaffery, 104) is embodied in a technological device that removes all trace of past mistakes, or those who make them, including the out-dated criteria by which aesthetic value itself is judged. The passage's comedy lies in the idea of disposing with those in charge of deciding what is worth keeping—a fine solution for dealing with one's critics!

Barthelme's conceptualisation of waste and value however is embodied in the novel's oft-quoted landfill scene. Here, Dan asserts the value of the ""'blanketing' effect of ordinary language"'—those words that "'fill in"' sentences rather than straightforwardly signifying. "'That part, the "fill-ing" you might say, of which the expression "you might say" is a good example"' is "'the most interesting part,'" as it comprises the largest part of our exchanges (SW, 111). The seemingly value-less has value. One is reminded of Moretti's conceptualisation, after Barthes, of narrative "fill-ers"—those non-events that furnish the nineteenth-century novel without our really noticing them, but that in the early twentieth century, I argued in Chap. 2, become quasi-protagonists. In this instance, however, it is the narrative value of individual words that is in question.[22] What other value can words have, beyond advancing plot or meaning? Perhaps it depends on what Dan means by the "'blanketing' effect of ordinary language.'" In the context of a novel whose characters constantly parrot the language of corporate board meetings, advertisements, and market forecasts, we can assume the expression refers to what Paul Maltby terms the proliferation of "easily consumable" language forms and the "diminished use-value of language" resulting from late capitalism's emphasis on maintaining and improving the conditions of commodity production and consumption (Maltby, 36; 57; 54). It is what Barthelme himself describes in one of his last essays as the "pressure on language from contemporary culture in the broadest sense—I mean our devouring commercial culture—which results in a double impoverishment: theft of complexity from the reader, theft of the reader from the writer."[23]

Dan suggests as much when he draws a parallel between the "stuffing" of this ordinary language and the plastic buffalo humps produced by his manufacturing plant:

> [T]he per-capita production of trash in this country is up from 2.75 pounds per day in 1920 to 4.5 pounds per day in 1965, the last year for which we have figures, and is increasing at the rate of about 4 % a year. [...] I hazard that we may very well soon reach a point where it's 100 %. Now at such a point, you will agree, the question turns from a question of disposing of this "trash" to a question of appreciating its qualities [...] because it's all there is,

and we will simply have to learn how to "dig" it—that's slang, but peculiarly appropriate here. So that's why we're in humps, right now, more really from a philosophical point of view than because we find them a great money-maker. They are "trash," and what in fact could be more useless or trash-like? It's that we want to be on the leading edge of this trash phenomenon [...] and that's why we pay particular attention, too, to those aspects of language that may be seen as a model of the trash phenomenon. (*SW*, 112)

The logic governing the mass production of the "useless" plastic buffalo humps is the same, essentially misguided, logic governing mass consumption and mass disposal, which are, in turn, driven by the language of mass marketing and mass media. The interrelation of meaningless lexicons, mass production of useless products, and material waste in this passage goes some way towards explaining scholars' interpretation of Barthelme's *oeuvre* as piecing together and imbuing new meaning into popular culture's vacuous jargon(s). Such readings however tend to obscure the causal relationship between the mountains of waste described by Dan and the language—in the form of advertising campaigns and market research reports—that has contributed to their growth. The invitation to appreciate the hidden qualities of trash is an exhortation to recognise not only the verbal trash of commercial culture *but the physical relics that testify to its power*. The trash phenomenon which so fascinates the dwarfs comprises not only commercially-inflected idioms, but useless product categories (such as the plastic humps they themselves produce despite their dubious utility) rendered marketable by the persuasive deployment of such idioms, and the landfills where those products ultimately end up. Barthelme thus draws attention to the symbiotic relationship between marketing-speak and the remainders of products purchased and disposed of at its behest. In turn, there is an underlying radical potential in Dan's contention that the objects circulating from factory to shop floor to home to landfill have a narrative, perhaps even anthropological, value.

This becomes clearer when we consider the extent to which Barthelme recognises, and in fact gestures towards, the status of his own texts as physical entities and commodities. A page-long description of Snow White's scouring of the dwarfs' books to rid them of "book lice" underscores the volumes' physicality, positing them as objects that must be cleaned and looked after if they are to escape the Thompsonian category of "rubbish" (Thompson, 7). But Barthelme then undermines this by specifying that Snow White is cleaning the books with a "5 % solution of DDT" (*SW*, 43).

This detail is acutely significant. DDT is a toxic pesticide that was made infamous, and subsequently banned, following Rachel Carson's revelation, in *Silent Spring* (1962), of its carcinogenic effects. First published in three instalments of *The New Yorker*, the magazine for which Barthelme regularly wrote, *Silent Spring* is generally credited with spawning the environmental movement in the USA, augmenting existing anxieties about the effects of super-industrialization and influencing much of the American subculture of the 1960s and 1970s.[24] Barthelme would have been familiar with the book, and DDT's dangers. His figuration of his fairy-tale housewife spraying "book lice" with the twentieth century's most powerful and maligned chemical pesticide is almost Beckettian in its absurdity, re-enacting the irony of the original DDT scandal: that the thing meant to prevent crops being consumed by pests (and become waste) was in fact a mass killer. It can likewise be seen as a comment on the erosion of culture, embodied, here, in a library being given cancer by one of modernity's failed attempts at efficiency.

Maurizia Boscagli's identification, after Zygmunt Bauman, of the ontological threat to hygiene, security, and stable categories that waste in modernity is perceived to pose provides a further way of reading the passage. Boscagli notes how:

> Trash, refusing to give up its foreignness and otherness, becomes a threat, for it suspends any opposition between a classificatory order and the chaos of hybridity. The spaces and time scales of waste are disturbing because they seem to collapse in the *métissage* of a new category. Disused or decaying matter, in its liminality, plasticity, and abjection, occupies space in new, unexpected ways. (Boscagli, 231)

From this perspective, the eradication of book lice and the effort to preserve the books in their current state reads as an attempt to stamp out ambiguity. It is an attempt to prevent the books from "breeding" new and unfamiliar forms or devolving into something "other." Snow White's cleaning of the books is not only ecologically unsound and absurdly toxic in a literal sense. It is also a fascistic attempt at maintaining order and the status quo: in this case, the categories of good literature and bad, and of classical fairy-tales and "contaminated" ones such as the adulterated version of *Snow White* the reader holds in their hands. The irony of course is that that adulteration has already occurred: there is nothing this fairy-tale heroine can do to undo the corruption of the story in which she is housed. From a New Materialist perspective, then, the passage reads as a parody of the role of consumerism and the lexicons of hygiene and efficiency in the environmental crisis, but also as a comment on capitalism's peculiar affection for fixed categories of value/worthlessness, cleanliness/uncleanliness, which exists alongside a paradoxical devaluation of language and literature.

A similarly absurd meditation on the physicality, value, and (limited) durability of books emerges in the following passage:

> I read Dampfboot's novel although he had nothing to say. It wasn't rave, that volume; we regretted that. And it was hard to read, dry, breadlike pages that turned, and then fell, like a car burned by rioters and resting, wrong side up, at the edge of the picture plane with its tyres smoking. Fragments kept flying off the screen into the audience, fragments of rain and ethics. Hubert wanted to go back to the dog races. But we made him read his part, the outer part where the author is praised and the price quoted. We like books with a lot of dreck in them, matter that presents itself as not wholly relevant (or indeed, at all relevant) but which, carefully attended to, can supply a kind of "sense" of what is going on. This "sense" is not to be obtained by reading between the lines (for there is nothing there, in those white spaces) but by reading the lines themselves—looking at them and so arriving at a feeling of […] having read them, of having "completed" them. (SW, 112)

The startling image of "a car burned by rioters and resting, wrong side up, at the edge of the picture plane" brings to mind Compte de Lautréamont's description, celebrated by the Surrealists, of a youth's beauty as "the chance meeting on a dissecting-table of a sewing-machine and an umbrella."[25] But the image is soon replaced by that of a movie screen from which fragments of "rain" and "ethics" fly, and then a physical book once more, identifiable by the promotional material and price on the back cover. Each sentence undermines the meaning of the last as well as the physical shape, genre, and form of the text discussed. Together with the ensuing explanation of the dwarfs' preferred reading material, the passage self-consciously gestures towards the ambiguous form and content of the novel we are holding in our hands, which is similarly composed of "matter that presents itself as not wholly relevant." The dwarfs' preference for literature that does not require one to "rea[d] between the lines (for there is nothing there, only white spaces)" is both a playful recommendation and a reminder of the novel's own status as a physical object, of which some aspects (e.g. the lines of text) are worth more than others (the space between them).

These different meditations on value and waste coalesce in a consumer survey with which the reader is faced mid-way through the novel:

1. Do you like the story so far? Yes () No ()
2. Does Snow White resemble the Snow White you remember? Yes () No ()
3. Have you understood, in reading to this point, that Paul is the prince-figure? Yes () No ()
4. That Jane is the wicked stepmother? Yes () No ()
5. In the further development of the story, would you like more emotion () or less emotion? ()
[...]
8. Would you like a war? Yes () No ()
[...]
13. Holding in mind all works of fiction since the War, in all languages, how would you rate the present work, on a scale of one to ten, so far? (Please circle your answer) 1 2 3 4 5 6 7 8 9 10
14. Do you stand up when you read? Lie down? () Sit? ()
15. In your opinion, should human beings have more shoulders? () Two sets of shoulders? () Three? (). (*SW*, 82–83)

The passage parodies the concepts of the consumer survey and consumer research, which emerged as a discipline in the late 1950s out of "motivation research," an earlier field that combined anthropology, sociology, and clinical psychology to understand consumer behaviour.[26] Among the earliest instances of such research were Franklin B. Evans' 1959 study of the personality differences of Chevrolet and Ford owners, which challenged established ideas regarding automobile brand imagery and, more importantly, raised public awareness of the discipline, and Arthur Koponen's 1960 study of 9000 cigarette smokers, which found that male cigarette smokers scored higher than average for aggression and need for sex and dominance.[27] The passage's comedic element stems from its treatment of literature as a product to be improved upon by finding out what the reader-qua-customer wants, and from the suggestion that the writer apply the basic principles of consumer research to ensure their book's success. Question 8, "Would you like a war?" is particularly telling in this regard. Potentially referring to the reader's predilection for violent conflict in literature, it can also be interpreted as gauging the reader's views on America's involvement in Vietnam—a reference to the treatment of war as entertainment as well as to the tendency of market researchers to advise companies to adapt their messaging to the political views of their target audience. Barthelme's survey both demonstrates the economic imperative underlying cultural production under late capitalism and makes fun of it, asking the reader to assist in the development of the ideal product-qua-book—a paradoxical and self-defeating exercise, given that by its very definition a new aesthetic must shock and surprise.

A true descendent of the historical avant-garde, Barthelme grapples with the repercussions of treating works of art as commodities to be valued or disposed of. One is reminded of his bemused acknowledgement, in interview, of the fact that his short stories published in *The New Yorker* were inevitably flanked by—if not interspersed with—advertisements for luxury products. In a context in which a vitriolic piece of fiction titled "The Rise of Capitalism" is interrupted by ads for luxury watches and yachts, it is perhaps not so unrealistic to imagine a novel being interrupted by an invitation to the reader to rate their customer experience. The 12 December 1970 edition of *The New Yorker*, in which "The Rise of Capitalism" was first published, also features full-page print advertisements for brands including Boda Crystal and DeBeers Diamonds (see Figs. 4.1 and 4.2). The tagline of the former, "Art you use," suggests the objects' value lies in their utility—where most art has no purpose, here is art with which to impress one's guests. It also uncannily confirms Barthelme's own assertion, in "On Not Knowing" (1983), that "it takes [...] about forty-five minutes for any given novelty in art to travel from the Mary Boone Gallery on West Broadway to the display windows of [the luxury women's clothing retailer] Henri Bendel on Fifty-seventh Street" (*NK*, 18–19). The tagline of the De Beers ad, "Diamonds are for now," is a tongue-in-cheek reference to "Diamonds are forever," the slogan De Beers coined in 1947 to promote diamonds as the only suitable gem for an engagement ring.[28] Where the original tagline promoted diamonds as a symbol of enduring love, the emphasis on the "now," the numerous rings, and fist in the 1970 ad play on the themes of instant gratification, conspicuous consumption, and power in an effort to reflect shifting ideals brought about by the women's rights movement. Female empowerment, here, amounts to the freedom to buy things "now" (while diamonds are posited as the ideal accessory for the "now" of second-wave feminism). As with the Boda Crystal ad, the statement is ludicrously at odds with the radical ethos of Barthelme's story.

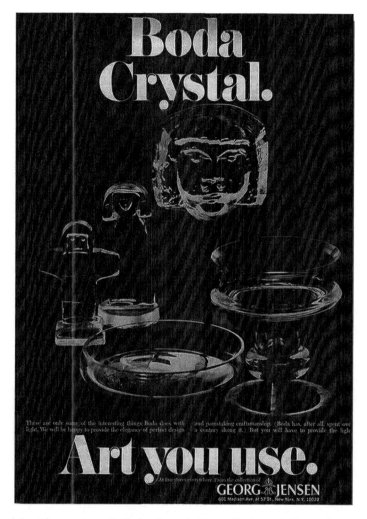

Fig. 4.1 "Art you use." Boda Crystal, Kosta Boda and Georg Jensen, *The New Yorker*, 12 December 1970, p. 59. Reproduced with the permission of Kosta Boda and Georg Jensen

Fig. 4.2 "Diamonds are for now." De Beers, *The New Yorker*, 12 December 1970, p. 62. Reproduced with the permission of De Beers

The world Barthelme seeks to represent is a world in which works of art are products to be consumed or, more frequently, disregarded entirely—as attested by the depiction of Paul (the "prince-figure" who paints) upon completing a painting:

> "It is a new thing I just finished today, still a little wet I'm afraid." [...] Paul leaned the new thing up against our wall for a moment. The new thing, a dirty great banality in white, poor-white and off-white, leaned up against the wall. "Interesting," we said. "It's poor," Snow White said [...] "Yes," Paul said, "one of my poorer things I think." "Not so poor of course as yesterday's, poorer on the other hand than some," she said. "Yes," Paul said, "it has some of the qualities of poorness." "Especially poor in the lower left-hand corner," she said. "Yes," Paul said, "I would go so far as to hurl it into the marketplace." (*SW*, 54)

Never referred to as a painting or a work of art, Paul's "thing" is dismissed in the same breath as it is acknowledged—and once its poor quality has been determined it is relegated, not to the dustbin, but to the marketplace, where any old trash will sell. As well as anticipating Barthelme's quip in "On Not Knowing" regarding the speed with which art is appropriated by commercial culture, the passage anticipates what he describes, in the same essay, as the writer's doubt, upon completing his or her work: "Am I masterpiece or simply a pile of junk?" (*NK*, 18; 19). As in the passages discussed thus far, Barthelme inverts our understanding of value and suggests that it is through commodification (or technological efficiency, as in the case of the DDT) that things become waste. The marketplace in late capitalism is an immense dustbin, the objects circulating in it financially valuable but frequently void of aesthetic or semantic worth.

"THINGS PLAYING A MORE IMPORTANT PART THAN PEOPLE"[29]: BALLARD'S URBAN DISASTER TRILOGY

Set in junkyards, abandoned waysides and disaster zones, and addressing the different forms of social devolution that occur in these settings, J. G. Ballard's fiction assumes waste to be integral to the post-war landscape and to reveal discomfiting truths about both industrialisation and consumerism. Nowhere is this more evident than in his 1970s trilogy, where waste is the catalyst for each narrative. This analysis is corroborated by Ballard's own description of the three texts, in a 1975 interview, as "a kind of trilogy," and his specification that the term "disaster" was inaccurate, since his concern was "to show a new kind of logic emerging, and this is to be embraced, or at least held in regard."[30] The statement suggests a self-conscious attempt to recuperate meaning from the waste-laden contexts being critiqued and an acknowledgement that it is from waste that his narratives emerged.

The prominence of waste in Ballard has not gone unnoticed: for example, for Will Viney the endless fluctuation of Ballard's objects between Thompsonian "rubbish" and "durable"[31] reflects a faith in fiction's capacity to "negotiate and re-negotiate value," while Jeanette Baxter reads the recurring concern with cleanliness and expulsion in his later work as a critique of fascism's legacy.[32] However, little attention has been paid to its importance in Ballard's rejection of realism. Waste, particularly in the trilogy, serves a dual function: to expose the fallacies of mass consumerism and hyper-industrialisation, and the incapacity of the realist novel to contend with those fallacies. The obscuring of humans by remnants of objects amplifies this. Ballard suggests that the story of the 1970s is best told through the residues of things purchased and the anxieties these elicit.

Ballard's scepticism towards realism's utility in the post-war era, which he famously expressed in his introduction to the 1995 edition of *Crash*, and the well-documented influence of Surrealism and de Chirico's Scuola Metafisica on his work, offer insights into his aesthetic approach.[33] In the introduction to *Crash*, Ballard notes that the "balance between fiction and reality has changed":

> We live in a world ruled by fictions of every kind—mass-merchandising, advertising, politics conducted as a branch of advertising, the pre-empting of any original response to experience by the television screen. We live inside an enormous novel. It is now less and less necessary for the writer to invent the fictional content of his novel. The fiction is already there. The writer's task is to invent the reality.[34]

Throughout his career, Ballard explicitly linked this task with Surrealism: in a 1966 book review titled, "The Coming of the Unconscious" he identified Surrealism as the approach best suited to addressing the collapsing distinctions between "real" and "false" in the artifice-laden era of advertising and celebrity culture.[35] In a much later interview he commented that he had "needed something more charged [than realism]. I embraced surrealism—like a lover."[36] The crashed cars, dismembered mannequins, and shattered domestic objects in Ballard's novels are central to this aesthetic credo. These objects captivate us with a "liveliness" that dulls the sheen of the commodities with which we ourselves are surrounded.

"[T]he Deformed Metal and Plastic That Forever Embraced Him": Crash (1973)

Waste in the first novel of the Trilogy manifests itself in the form of wrecked automobiles as well as remaindered mannequins, semen, vaginal fluid, and excrement. The novel follows the lives of two men—TV advertising executive James Ballard and scholar-qua-crash obsessive Vaughan—who derive sexual pleasure from watching and participating in car crashes. Much of the novel's plot takes place in and around wrecked cars, while the few indoor scenes occur in spaces that give onto crash sites, or in which crash re-enactments are staged. Through these depictions, the novel attends to what we might call the acceleration of obsolescence, which Ballard first examined in the two works that first inspired the novel: an exhibition of wrecked automobiles he held in London in 1969 and 1970, and *The Atrocity Exhibition* (1969), which first inspired the exhibition.[37] *Crashed Cars* featured three iconic car models—the Pontiac, the Austin Cambridge A60, and the Mini—which became indistinguishable once demolished, exemplifying Vaughan's assertion, in *Crash*, that "every car crash looks the same" (*C*, 104). The brand and make of an object are irrelevant once it has become waste. The discrepancy between the car's original status as a luxury item, and its new status as waste, was amplified by the placement of a price tag for £3000 on one of the cars—a spoof thought up by the photographer for the *Daily Mirror* who had come to document the exhibition.[38]

Like this real-life exhibition, *The Atrocity Exhibition* also provides the reader of *Crash* with vital clues. Consisting of a series of disconnected and individually titled vignettes, the novel envisages crashed cars, peeling advertisements, and litter on the street as emblems of a fractured modernity. One of the protagonists asserts:

apart from its manifest function, redefining the elements of time and space in terms of our most potent consumer durable, the car crash may be perceived unconsciously as a fertilizing rather than a destructive event—a liberation of sexual energy. [...] In the Eucharist of the simulated auto-disaster we see the transliterated pudenda of Ralph Nader, our nearest image of the blood and body of Christ. (*AE*, 27)

This emphasis on the automobile rather than on the individuals involved in the crash anticipates the obscuring of people by things in *Crash* (of which I will have more to say later), while the figuration of the automobile as the "most potent consumer durable" highlights its status as a commodity and indicates why the novelist might be interested in its appearance once destroyed. Ballard made this view even more explicit in "The Car, The Future" (1971), where he described the automobile as embodying the ethos of twentieth-century capitalism—the "speed, drama and aggression, the worlds of advertising and consumer goods, engineering and mass manufacture, and the shared experience of moving together through an elaborately signalled landscape."[39] Where the essay suggests that the car is the quintessence of the twentieth century, *The Atrocity Exhibition* posits journalist Ralph Nader, best known for his seminal study of car crashes, *Unsafe at Any Speed* (1965), as the twentieth century's closest approximation to Christ. The reference implicitly equates the car crash with the crucifixion, suggesting it is a sacrificial rite that transcends the laws of consumption and disposal, reconfiguring body, car, and landscape into something entirely alien and new. By describing the crash as a "Eucharist," Ballard relates it to Christ's last supper and Holy Communion—suggesting that the transformation that occurs as vehicle(s) and driver collide with the asphalt is nothing short of transubstantiation (the Catholic term for the literal transformation of Christ's body and blood into bread and wine). These readings are confirmed by the revised version of the passage, which was re-printed in the *Crashed Cars* exhibition leaflet, and where Ballard explicitly states: "In twentieth-century terms the crucifixion would be enacted as a conceptual car crash."[40] Note the absence of both human and God in this revised version: Ralph Nader and the blood and body of Christ have been removed, leaving only car and crash.

Ballard's understanding of the crash as a moment both destructive and fertile—a transubstantiation of the car-as-consumer-good into another entity freed of its original use-value—allows us to see the wrecked cars in *Crash* as rendering the grotesqueness of consumerism explicit. The fetish for novelty is recast as a fetish for *disposal*, recalling what Ballard once described, in interview, as the intention behind his work:

> When I began to write, Britain was beginning to change. The supermarkets were arriving, motorways were being built, we had television for the first time, the first jet planes. We had the beginnings of a consumer culture. I became aware of these huge undercurrents flowing through our lives and wanted to reflect them.[41]

Ballard's novel challenges the assumption that pleasure arises from replacing an old product with a new one, suggesting it comes instead from its disposal. Crashing a car is not only arousing because it goes against our impulses for self-preservation but because it involves profligacy—the destruction of something of substantial monetary value. A car crash both accelerates the process of obsolescence and goes against the dictum that one look after one's investment. In that sense, the car crash re-enactments in the novel are equivalent to the stone-sucking routine in Beckett's *Molloy*, which we discussed in Chap. 3, mimicking the process of becoming-waste and exemplifying the schizophrenic impulse described by Deleuze and Guattari as simultaneously literalising the consumerist ethos, and providing a radical alternative to it.[42] Ballard himself, in the notes to the 1993 expanded edition of *The Atrocity Exhibition*, acknowledges that it was this paradox that fascinated him when he first started writing about crashes:

> The car crash differs from other disasters in that it involves the most powerfully advertised commercial product of this century, an iconic entity that combines the elements of speed, power, dream and freedom within a highly stylised format that defuses any fears we may have of the inherent dangers of these violent and unstable machines. (*AE*, 157)

In the Ballardian imagination a crashed car is essentially a more reproachful kind of waste. The sight of a crashed car alerts us to the destructive potential of all cars, which flies in the face of the significance that the car has come to assume in contemporary culture (indeed, Joe Moran notes that the publication of Ballard's novel almost exactly coincided with the waning of public anxieties over car safety, as the worst year for road deaths in Britain, before and since, was 1966[43]). The car-as-waste exposes what advertising conceals. It debunks the myth of the car-as-paragon-of-freedom, literalizing the destructive potential of consumerism itself in a way that other waste objects seen individually do not.

Most notably, Vaughan himself embodies waste's anarchic potential. Introduced to us in the novel's opening lines lying inert in a mess of wrecked metal and splattered blood, Vaughan comes to us first and foremost as waste. We witness the aftermath of the novel's climax (the crash we are told killed him) before we witness the climax itself, and our sense of Vaughan as the novel unfolds is entirely bound up with our awareness of his inevitable death. In turn, we learn to see him in relation to waste, sex, and death—and to see these as intimately conjoined. This sense is borne out by James' descriptions of Vaughan: "I see him in the stolen cars he

drove and damaged, the surfaces of deformed metal and plastic that forever embraced him" (*C*, 2). Vaughn is depicted throughout the novel as
the entropic force hurtling the novel to its close. The relationship between
waste and sex is likewise made clear from the outset. James recalls Vaughan
copulating "in the crushed rear compartments of abandoned cars in break-
ers' yards" and later describes how he and Vaughan showed their scars to
each other after having had sex in a breaker's yard, in order to "celebrat[e]
the re-birth of the traffic-slain dead, the deaths and injuries of those we
had seen dying by the roadside and the imaginary wounds and postures
of the millions yet to die" (*C*, 3; 203). In each instance, the eroticism of
the car crash relates to the fact it results in wreckage. The waste object
functions to highlight the flouting of social norms, amplify the novel's
preoccupation with destruction, and convey the characters' understanding
of the re-birth that destruction precedes. In the last instance, the reader
cannot but recall the end of Marinetti's *Futurist Manifesto*:

> When I came up—torn, filthy, and stinking—from under the capsized car,
> I felt the white-hot iron of joy deliciously pass through my heart! [...] And
> so, faces smeared with good factory muck—plastered with metallic waste,
> with senseless sweat, with celestial soot—we, bruised, our arms in slings, but
> unafraid, declared our high intentions to all the *living* of the earth.[44]

James' figuration of the crash as a site of renewal, and the intimation
that from such wreckage might emerge insight into the twentieth century
itself, is an explicit reference to Marinetti's account of Futurism's origins,
which he claimed emerged from his experience of a violent car crash. Like
their Futurist forebears, James claims he and Vaughan are reborn after
each crash. In Marinetti's text, the junked car metaphorically gives birth
to the Futurist artist, who emerges from the wreckage livened with the
aesthetic possibilities of speed, industrial technology, and destruction. In
Ballard's, the junked car facilitates orgasm: sex in a wrecked car, or the
sight of a car in the midst of crashing into something, culminates in violent
ejaculation, which James meticulously and graphically describes. Where
waste in Marinetti's text produces the artist, waste in Ballard's produces
ejaculate that is then shaken off or smeared on the waste object, and, insofar as it does not serve to impregnate anyone, becomes more waste. But
in both cases, waste produces the text we hold in our hands—Marinetti's
account hinges on the accident, and Ballard's novel claims to be a record
of the protagonist's awakening to the sexual possibilities of accidents. In
this sense, they both perform an act of recycling.

Crash is also, however, indebted to de Chirico's project: the enigmatic relics strewn throughout the text recall de Chirico's metaphysical waste in their liveliness. The attention Ballard pays to the waste resulting from both real and staged crashes leaves us wondering which of these is more "real"; how one determines the difference between "real" and "unreal" waste; and whether this ambiguity might be intended to undermine the novel's potential to either convey reality or to authentically reflect the experience of the artifice-laden post-war era. For example, when Vaughan stares, not at the victims of a car crash, but at the shattered car, "almost about to embrace it," or when the spectators' eyes in witnessing a later crash "[a] re fixed, not on [the] human victims, but on the deformed vehicles at the centre of the stage," the relics of irrational destruction take the place of the human beings involved in it (*C,* 10; 182). In this way, Ballard's crashes draw our attention not only to the end of the purchase cycle but to the extent to which the collapsing distinction between "real" and "false" is entwined with reification: the fact that "the events in the world at large have the conviction and reality of those depicted on giant advertisement hoardings" is a result of the liveliness granted to the objects depicted on those hoardings. The shattered remnants of cars and de Chirico-esque mannequins (in this case, crash test dummies) alert us to this boundary slippage while resisting our efforts to situate them logically. Their use, if they can be said to have one, is to alert us to the irrationality underlying consumer culture. Where the resemblance of de Chirico's partial mannequins to figure drawing aids serves to underscore his paintings' artifice—that they are representations of modern alienation—the crash test dummies in the novel's car crash enactments invite us to consider both the enactments themselves and the crashes they emulate as works of art.

"Like a Dying Pavement Artist in A Rich Man's Cast-Off":
Concrete Island (1974)

Like *Crash, Concrete Island* is concerned not only with what waste says about us but also what imagining ourselves in different scenarios involving waste might teach us about the neuroses and desires that post-war consumerism masks. Ballard makes this explicit in the introduction to the 1994 edition of the novel:

> As we drive across a motorway intersection, through the elaborately signalled landscape that seems to anticipate every possible hazard, we glimpse triangles of waste ground screened off by steep embankments. What would

happen if, by some freak mischance, we suffered a blow-out and plunged over the guard-rail onto a forgotten island of rubble and weeds, out of sight of the surveillance cameras?[45]

Concrete Island imagines one such scenario. In the novel's opening, protagonist Robert Maitland crashes his Jaguar while driving down the exit lane of the Westway interchange in Central London and is catapulted onto a small traffic island "that l[ies] in the waste ground between three converging motorway routes" (*CI*, 12). Despite its location "at the centre of this alienating city" (*CI*, 129), the island is invisible to the cars speeding along the highway. Ballard is keen to emphasise that this is a setting at the centre of civilization but paradoxically lost to it. Referred to repeatedly as a wasteland (*CI*, 11; 69; 84; 92; 132), the island exists in a now-defunct past, as evidenced by the presence of a former World War II air-raid shelter now buried in gravel (*CI*, 38), a few crumbling headstones signalling the former presence of a churchyard (*CI*, 41), a derelict pay-box indicating a former cinema (*CI*, 69), and a broad valley marking out "the line of a former neighbourhood high street" (*CI*, 40). Grass has grown over these relics, while one part of the island has become an illicit garbage dump for local restaurants to dispose of food scraps (*CI*, 128). The space is both a monument to obsolescence and to tenacious survival:

> Comparing it with the motorway system, he saw that it was far older than the surrounding terrain, as if this triangular patch of waste ground had survived by the exercise of a unique guile and persistence, and would continue to survive, unknown and disregarded, long after the motorways had collapsed into dust. Parts of the island dated from well before World War II. The eastern end, below the overpass, was its oldest section, with the churchyard and the ground-courses of Edwardian terraced houses. The breaker's yard and its wrecked cars had been superimposed on the still identifiable streets and alleyways. In the centre of the island were the air-raid shelters among which he was sitting. Attached to these was a later addition, the remains of a Civil Defence post little more than fifteen years old. (*CI*, 69)

While the rest of the world goes about its business, here lie the things its citizens no longer need—not because they have thrown them away, necessarily, but because civilization has outgrown them. In fact, Maitland begins to perceive even himself in the past tense. Sifting through his overnight case, he is struck by the anachronistic quality of his once-familiar possessions, which have no use on the island: "The overnight case [is] almost literally a time capsule—he could easily reconstitute a past world from these scents and surface textures" (*CI*, 44). Likewise, wearing his dinner jacket makes him feel "like a dying pavement artist in a rich man's cast-off"—a shocking description that hinges on our association of "dying pavement artist" with avant-gardism and "rich man's cast-off" with home-lessness and social inequality (*CI*, 62). In both descriptions, our attention is drawn to the displaced nature of the objects in question—toiletries and a dinner jacket belong to a previous life, and Maitland's condition as a tramp makes using or wearing these items appear absurd. Being of no use here, they are waste akin to the detritus littered throughout the island—as worthless as the "cigarette packs, stubs of burnt-out cigars, confection-ery wrappers, spent condoms and empty match-books" through which Maitland digs to find food (*CI*, 41).

Ballard thus introduces us to a world similar to Ellis Sharp's *The Dump* and the wastelands of Beckett's novels, where the characters roaming through waste are often indistinguishable from it. Indeed, Maitland him-self frequently refers to himself as an extension of the wasteland:

> Identifying the island with himself, he gazed at the cars in the breaker's yard, at the wire-mesh fence, and the concrete caisson behind him. These places of pain and ordeal were now confused with pieces of his body. He gestured towards them, trying to make a circuit of the island so that he could leave these sections of himself where they belonged. He would leave his right leg at the point of his crash, his bruised hands impaled upon the steel fence. He would place his chest where he had sat against the concrete wall. At each point a small ritual would signify the transfer of obligation from himself to the island. (*CI*, 70)

Where the body in *Crash* exists in relation to the process of turning a car into waste, and where the self is reaffirmed each time one witnesses or survives a crash, in *Concrete Island* both the body and the self are described as already defunct, and beyond saving. Notice how Maitland imagines his limbs to be disposable, the various "pieces of his body" encumbrances to be relinquished to the island as part of a broader disavowal of responsibility. Likewise, his claim elsewhere that "'[he is] the Island'" is an act of self-era-sure (*CI*, 70). The person he was prior to the crash has been supplanted by the persona of a tramp who identifies with the wasteland he inhabits and who is increasingly unconvinced by the utility of his own body: hence the descrip-tion of "his right leg, as useless as the scabbard of a broken lance" trailing behind his body rather than enabling it to move more efficiently (*CI*, 144).

It is also noteworthy that the only driver to see Maitland assumes he is a tramp—and that as the narrative proceeds, there is little to distinguish him from one. He sleeps in his wrecked car; he drinks water out of the car's windshield wipers; and he survives his first 36 hours on the island by scavenging a half-eaten sandwich the aforementioned driver has thrown out of his window, and some greasy chips out of a pile of "cigarette packs, tattered newspapers and refuse lying around him at the foot of the embankment" (*CI*, 63). By the time he encounters the two permanent residents of the island—a prostitute and a mentally retarded former circus performer, who live, respectively, in the abandoned cinema and former air-raid shelter—Maitland has in fact become what Zygmunt Bauman would term "human waste."[46] Able to view the (literal and metaphorical) traffic of modern life but unable to join it and conscious that his unfelt absence by the world indicates his lack of value, he is physically at the centre of things, but socially cast out of them. My reading chimes with David Punter's view, echoed by Sebastian Groes, that *Concrete Island* in fact replaces the utopian impulse of post-war urban planning with "a wish for abdication" which involves the self reasserting a "useless sovereignty, apparently free from technological compulsion."[47] Maitland's recess on the island functions as a paradigm of uselessness. Unable to work, shop, drive, or socialise—unable, that is, to participate in the market economy— he has no recognised "use." Thus, not unlike the story of Vaughan and James Ballard's fetish for technological destruction, Maitland's recess on the traffic island is a meditation on value, the alienating effects of modernity, and the interrelation of the two. We are told that Maitland's absence is likely to have gone unnoticed by his wife, lover, and colleagues (each of whom, he reckons, will assume he is with the other) and that on the day of the crash, his wife was on her way to buy herself a new car (*CI*, 38). Since Ballard does not explicitly say whether Maitland ever leaves the island or not (on the last page we see him sitting and watching the cars on the freeway while contemplating escape), we might deduce that the new car ends up taking his place, effectively replacing the obsolete husband—reaffirming the Ballardian credo of "things playing a more important part than people" (*AE*, 127).

That this modern-day *Robinson Crusoe* is a meditation on value becomes apparent when we consider Maitland's interactions with Proctor (the ex-circus performer), and Jane (the prostitute). Maitland repeatedly bribes Proctor with enough money to "*buy* this island!" in exchange for help in escaping, and Jane demands payment in exchange for sex (*CI*,

158; 142). But these transactions are essentially meaningless, since money serves no actual purpose in this context: Jane notes, "'as far as I know, there's nowhere here to spend it'" (*CI*, 113). Thus, money is ultimately divested of value: far from marvelling at the handfuls of notes Maitland throws him, Proctor is made uneasy by them and begs "'Mr Maitland ... please ... no more flying money'" (*CI*, 158). Likewise, when Maitland and Jane have finished having sex, she takes the notes and puts them back in his wallet—she only requested payment to divest the sexual encounter of any affect and ensure its transactional nature (*CI*, 142). In the context of this wasteland, money has no meaning—just as the wrecked Jaguar being slowly buried by grass is no longer a status symbol (*CI*, 146). Ballard's novel thus explores what it means to watch modernity from the margins and to perceive one's self as obsolete and one's possessions as worthless.

Waste "Recombined in Unexpected But More Meaningful Ways": High-Rise (1975)

Where *Crash* uses car wrecks to explore the dehumanising effects of modernity, and *Concrete Island*'s story of an abandoned traffic island imagines how it feels to be marginalised by modernity, *High-Rise* depicts a disintegrating apartment block to explore the primordial impulses that modernity conceals. The novel takes place in one of five newly built luxury apartment blocks two miles east of the City of London, in the middle of a square mile of abandoned dockland and warehousing on the north bank of the Thames. The square mile of new-builds is surrounded on all sides by "decaying nineteenth-century terraced houses and empty factories already zoned for reclamation," but the novel's protagonist, Dr Robert Laing, perceives it to be entirely separate from both these relics and the City of London (*HR*, 3). This dislocated, futuristic space proves to be an ideal breeding ground for primordial behaviour, which the novel traces from the perspective of Laing and two other residents: the building's architect, Anthony Royal, and documentary film-maker, Richard Wilder. The novel itself is written in a style that self-consciously emulates what Ballard called the "invisible literature of market research reports, company in-house magazines, promotional copy, press releases, science abstracts, internal memoranda, sex manuals and government reports," which lends a clinical, distancing tone to the scenes depicted.[48]

Although it is a series of minor malfunctions in the building's infra-structure that expose the tensions between the building's inhabitants,

Ballard makes it clear that these tensions were already present. The faults in the building's air-conditioning conduits and garbage disposal chutes merely lay bare the residents' own deep-seated psychopathologies and reveal civilization to be an illusion. Indeed, the building is seen to *facilitate* psychopathological behaviour:

> The more arid and affectless life became in the high-rise, the greater the possibilities it offered. By its very efficiency, the high-rise took over the task of maintaining the social structure that supported them all. For the first time it removed the need to repress every kind of anti-social behaviour, and left them free to explore any deviant or wayward impulses. (*HR*, 37)

These deviant impulses lead to rape, murder, and the ransacking of apartments, but also—and more frequently—to the smearing of faeces on walls and the construction of barricades out of rubbish. Thus, the LeCorbusieresque "machine designed to serve" its residents becomes a "high-priced tenement, [a] hanging palace self-seeding its intrigues and destruction" (*HR*, 5; 45).

To an extent, *High-Rise* transposes the conflicts of nineteenth-century naturalism, where tensions arise between people living in close proximity to one another, to the post-war landscape. Dust emanating from faulty air-conditioning units, the smell of faeces, urine, and waste crammed into stairwells—we are not so far from the tenements described in the urban narratives of Dickens, Zola, or Norris. But Ballard's novel differs from these, for the conflicts here are not triggered by deep-seated poverty or poor sanitation, but by petty disputes over blocked garbage disposal chutes and littering between wealthy, supposedly "well-bred" tenants— thus putting paid to the equating of "class" and "propriety." This plot was partly inspired by the petty conflicts Ballard himself witnessed between tenants in an apartment building in Spain where he holidayed with his family in 1973. In a 1978 interview, Ballard recalled seeing someone taking photographs of residents on the upper floors throwing cigarette butts onto the balconies below; a notice appeared a few days later asking them to refrain from littering or risk photographs of the act being circulated.[49] That someone would spend an expensive holiday documenting such a small act of impropriety struck him as absurd. A similarly absurd concern with cleanliness shapes the first half of the novel: residents with no children persecute those who allow their children to urinate in the swimming pool (*HR*, 15); others are angered by the residents who leave their

WASTE IN DONALD BARTHELME, J.G. BALLARD, AND WILLIAM GADDIS 125

garbage in the corridor, or by the female resident "endlessly re-decorating her apartment on the 33rd floor" who regularly blocks the garbage disposal chute with the remnants of the décor she has replaced (*HR*, 40). Once the violence starts, however, waste becomes a tool of aggression: the tenants fling human faeces on walls and block the ventilation shafts with dog excrement. Ballard thus presents the dismantling of civilisation as a gradual habituation to living amid waste:

> Along corridors strewn with uncollected garbage, past blocked disposal chutes and vandalised elevators, moved men in well-tailored dinner jackets. Elegant women lifted long skirts to step over the debris of broken bottles. [...] The scents of expensive aftershave lotions mingled with the aroma of kitchen wastes [...] marking the extent to which these civilised and self-possessed professional men and women were moving away from any notion of rational behaviour. (*HR*, 103–104)

By the novel's end, the building's social hierarchy has spectacularly fallen apart, together with the technologies that kept the building itself functional: once discreetly disposed of, the tenants' unseemly secrets are evident for all to see. The piling up of foetid waste is material evidence that humanity has given into its atavistic impulses.

Of the trilogy's three novels, *High-Rise* is perhaps the closest to the realist tradition, providing a clear narrative arc in which waste objects render palpable the devolution into civil unrest. But waste also serves to dismantle the tidy linearity of realism. Where the casual flinging of garbage from the apartment balconies is explicitly likened to the customs of nineteenth-century tenements, the obsolescence of domestic appliances (no longer needed), of television (which the residents no longer watch), and even of the garbage disposal chutes themselves (supplanted by the now malfunctioning elevators) is interpreted by Laing as dislocating the high-rise from linear time. It is no longer clear whether these objects are relics of the past or emblems of the future. They are merely evidence of change, as attested by Laing's inability to remember the original function of his "derelict washing-machine and refrigerator, now only used as garbage bins" (*HR*, 167). Divested of their original use, they have "taken on a new significance, a role that he ha[s] yet to understand"—a transformation that recalls the historical avant-garde's re-purposing efforts. In the new world order of the high-rise, "everything [is] either derelict or, more ambiguously, recombined in unexpected but more meaningful ways" (*HR*, 167).

Ballard complicates the dystopian impressions we might derive from these passages, however, by also imbuing waste with positive associations. The characters in fact perceive waste as affirming reality itself, as exemplified by Wilder's impression of the debris surrounding the high-rise upon his return from work every evening:

> For Wilder, this brief period away from the apartment building was almost dreamlike in its unreality. [...] Even the debris scattered at the foot of the building, the empty bottles and garbage-stained cars with their broken windscreens, in a strange way merely reinforced his conviction that the only real events in his life were those taking place within the high-rise. (*HR*, 64)

It is no coincidence that it is a documentary film-maker—one who at the beginning of the novel was intent on documenting the experiences of the building's residents—who thinks these thoughts. Recalling Ballard's own comments, in "The Coming of the Unconscious" and in the introduction to *Crash*, regarding the peculiar blurring of reality and fiction in the age of television and celebrity, the passage suggests that the appeal of the high-rise and the waste accruing therein, like the appeal of car wrecks for Vaughan and James, is rooted in their authenticity, which contrasts with the hyper-real quality of the nearby office blocks and television studios. The high-rise accrues authenticity as it falls into disarray and exposes the artifice of the world surrounding it. The disintegration of social codes in the building, symbolically rendered in the gradual accrual of waste, is interpreted as evidence of a reassuring and all-too-rare reality.

This is rendered explicit in a later passage, as Laing considers his resentment of daylight:

> The true light of the high-rise was the metallic flash of the Polaroid camera, that intermittent radiation which recorded a moment of hoped-for violence for some later voyeuristic pleasure. What depraved species of electric flora would spring to life from the garbage-strewn carpets of the corridors in response to this new source of light? The floors were littered with the blackened negative strips, flakes falling from this internal sun. (*HR*, 123)

In this synthetic version of photosynthesis, the flashbulb of the camera coaxes new life out of the "soil" of the high-rise: a "metallic flash" of the Polaroid camera has replaced the sun, while corridors carpeted in waste have taken the place of seeds and dirt. The re-imagining of the high-rise in biological terms invites the reader to imagine the garbage inside to be sentient and productive. This becomes more evident a few paragraphs later: "In the bedroom a broken mirror lay on the bed, the pieces flickering like the fragments of another world trying unsuccessfully to reconstitute itself" (*HR*, 124). Moreover, through these mirror fragments, Ballard calls attention to the disintegration of the world of the high-rise—reflected in the mirror's shards—as well as to the constructed nature of this space. Where Shakespeare's Hamlet asserted that the purpose of theatre is to "represent reality, holding a mirror up to virtue, to vice, and to the spirit of the times" and Bertolt Brecht is said to have claimed "Art is not a mirror held up to reality but a hammer with which to shape it," Ballard suggests that art's role is to *shatter the illusion* of postwar reality and to draw attention to artifice through the act of shattering.[50] Waste is rendered narratively useful in both passages, serving to both underscore the fictitiousness of the text and draw attention to the artifice that the text seeks to expose.

Ballard's Trilogy posits waste as simultaneously estranging and reassuring—that which resists coherent understanding but lays bare the artifice of post-war consumerism, revealing the truth beneath the multifarious mirages constructed by advertising and television. The waste objects in these novels prove very useful indeed, providing a means to approach the surreal quality of lived experience in advanced capitalist societies.

"What America's All About, Waste Disposal and All"[51]: William Gaddis' *JR* (1975)

In one of the final scenes of William Gaddis' *JR* (1975), a character named Rhoda gawps at a steak broiler that has just been delivered to the apartment where she is squatting, and at the language in the accompanying promotional leaflet:

> Like it says right on it man Steakwatcher, I mean like it really says solid state computer programmed for broiling steaks and chops to perfection I mean somebody really paid money for these, man [...] I mean like a lot of fucking money man, like they're scared if they gave you something somebody might like really need you'll think it's this fucking insult ... [...] like I mean things are really screwed up. (*JR*, 555)

Rhoda then proceeds to challenge the categorisation of a stockholder report as "literature":

Literature? You call this literature man? [...] This reduced fully diluted shares outstanding by sixteen percent which had the effect after imputed interest on like you call that literature man I mean I call it bullshit. (*JR*, 556)

These two characteristically comical passages are emblematic of Gaddis' use of waste, throughout *JR*, to question the ambiguous categorisation of worth under capitalism. "[L]ike I mean things are really screwed up" and "I call it bullshit" are the novel's rallying cries, pointing to an economic system in disarray. *JR* recounts the story of an 11-year-old boy (the titular JR) who applies the lessons in trading he has learned on a school field trip to build a paper empire and in the process ruins the lives of everyone with whom he comes in contact. Among these are two failed writers, Dan Eigen and Jack Gibbs (whose abandoned manuscript, *Agape Agape*, bears the same title as Gaddis' last novel), and the composer Edward Bast, all three of whom spend the novel seeking and failing to produce great works of art and avoiding penury. *JR*'s central lesson (voiced, aptly, by a stockbroker) is that "anything is worth whatever some damn fool will pay for it" (*JR*, 201), but the undoing of its characters demonstrates the consequences of subscribing to this credo. The novel stages the dizzying speed with which the value of commodities under capitalism—be the commodity a stock option, real estate, a patented invention, or a work of art—grows and declines.

While much has been written about the representation of money, capitalist exchange, and art in *JR*, less has been written about the novel's striking engagements with the worth*less* and about what the text's depictions of actual and metaphorical waste say about capitalism, the speculative nature of finance, and, indeed, about the novel form itself.[52] The few analyses that do engage with Gaddis' waste follow a similar pattern to those of Barthelme, examining it from a linguistic perspective rather than attending to the waste objects themselves.[53] In what follows, I show how Gaddis makes use of waste objects to critique the financialisation of capital and the extent to which he conceives waste and value—most often figured as shit and money—to be inextricably linked. By interlacing his story of free-market enterprise with references to faeces and items of dubious value (fluctuating stock, unfinished art), and having his characters repeatedly deploy waste-based invectives and aphorisms to describe commercial failures, Gaddis suggests that capitalism essentially deals in waste. The implied ending to the unfinished phrase "what America is all about"—repeated, throughout the novel, by the entrepreneur and atomic shelter designer Major Hyde—is not money but commodification. "America is all about" turning anything, however worthless, into a sellable item or an investment opportunity (*JR*, 201).

Gaddis' novel opens with a discussion about the nature of money:

—Money ...? in a voice that rustled.—Paper, yes.—And we'd never seen it. Paper money.—We never saw paper money till we came east.—It looked so strange the first time we saw it. Lifeless.—You couldn't believe it was worth a thing.
—Not after Father jingling his change. (*JR*, 3)

The passage is an explicit meditation on the discrepancy between the actual worth of paper money and the apparent triviality of its physical appearance. "You couldn't believe it was worth a thing" provides a first intimation of the irreverent stance of the novel, its continuous disbelief (echoed in Rhoda's wonder at the steak broiler) at the arbitrary ways in which value is attributed and just as easily lost, and the extent to which these surges and declines shape culture. Such disbelief underpins Edward Bast's outburst to JR: "Can't you see it's trash it's just trash it's always been trash all of it! The net assets the nickel deductions the man of vision all of it, can't you see that now?" (*JR*, 656). His point—that JR's company is built on speculation, or glorified gambling, and that the marketing rhetoric it adopts merely obscures the fact that it deals in the purchase and sale of things of negligible worth—is lost on JR:

where I'm trying to find out what I'm suppose to do so you say it's trash? where this here paper says I'm this man of vision so you say it's trash? where I'm leading this parade where there's this groundswill of I'm like fit for this big career in public life. (*JR*, 661)

JR's obtuse belief in the PR stories that have been constructed around him, and in the value of his enterprise, is a direct counter to Rhoda's "I call it bullshit"—it is the voice of capital, seeking to assert itself as something more than, better than, waste.

Gaddis explores these ideas on both a formal and thematic level, and in different ways. At the level of form, waste objects are frequently deployed for what Barthes, as we saw in the prior chapters of this study, terms their "reality effect"—a means to connect the characters and scenes together and "furnish" the narrative with suitable props.[54] The number of references to garbage cans (*JR*, 290; 362; 548; 599; 609; 632; 633) and the disposal of things (*JR*, 55; 67; 109; 165; 187; 292; 374; 485; 549; 660; 712) is staggering, even for a novel of this length, and the attentive reader will notice that such references serve both a descriptive and metaphorical function. Indeed, for matter that by definition is of no worth, waste is paradoxically very valuable in the economies of meaning that the novel itself generates and in the specific stories it tells.

The crushed beer can that moves through three of the novel's initial scenes provides a case in point (*JR*, 66). The can, which Bast picked up in his aunts' backyard in order to throw away, is first mentioned as he enters their living room. The two women are appalled to see him holding it and ask him to dispose of it somewhere outside the house, for they "don't care to have it seen in [their] trash, thank you" (*JR*, 67). And so we follow Edward and the can into his writing shed, where he gesticulates with it while arguing with his cousin Stella, before flinging it at her as she steps into a cab. Stella in turn tries to leave the can in the back seat of the cab, but the driver demands she remove it. She takes it with her into the train station, where she runs into Jack Gibbs. As they exchange angry words, she throws the beer can into an empty trash bin on the train platform (*JR*, 73).

In each of these scenes, the can serves a realist function, insofar as it helps develop our sense of the individual characters—thoughtful Edward Bast, who first takes it upon himself to clean up the yard; the fussy aunts, who baulk at the prospect of this type of rubbish being found in their garbage, let alone in their living room; distracted Stella, who remains impervious to Edward's anger and will just as unthinkingly leave trash at the back of a cab. The crushed can also links the scenes together, and connects the characters, helping the reader follow the plot as it switches, often abruptly, between different interactions. And, of course, the focus on the can extends the novel's thematic concern with the distinction between worth and worthless (including narrative worth—what is worth recounting and remembering).

However, the empty beer can also has another function. It is a shadow or underside to the preoccupation with money that pervades the scenes discussed, the physical embodiment of Bast's claim that "it's just trash it's always been trash all of it!" (*JR*, 656). The sight of the can interrupts Edward's aunts' discussion about the family business and their recently deceased brother's legacy, before punctuating (and bringing to an end) Edward's conversation with Stella, who is looking to obtain his shares of the company, and Stella's conversation with Jack Gibbs, from whom she is also seeking to obtain shares. Its disruption of these different scenes foreshadows the general disarray that characterises the last third of the novel, during which stock markets collapse, Bast's writing project falls apart, and the headquarters of JR's company is filled with worthless merchandise.

The scene discussed above is but one of many instances in which Gaddis deploys waste objects to counterbalance or disrupt the discussion of money and value throughout the novel. For instance, a discussion about the expensive teaching equipment in which JR's school has invested, and which has not yet been unpacked, leads to the acknowledgement by one of the administrators that "no one understands how to use [it]" (*JR*, 23). The equipment is expensive, but worthless unless someone figures out how to put it to use. When businessman Mr Angel notices his secretary has left out the "s" in "metal scraps" in a memo aimed at persuading his client to invest, the humour hinges on the typo's disruption of the assumed difference between valued commodity (metal scraps) and worthless (crap) (*JR*, 153). As well as potentially undermining a business deal, the typo discloses the true nature of the things being traded and the absurdity of the exchange process itself.

This concern with the relationship between value and waste—and with how capitalism recycles waste—is highlighted in one of the novel's first scenes, where a group of teachers and administrators is gathered to discuss expenses for the year ahead, while a live stream of the individual classes currently taking place plays on a series of television screens in the background. Gaddis interrupts the fragments of the teachers' dialogue with slices of the filmed lessons playing on the screens; and in each lesson—on the workings of a combustion engine, the principles of investment, the process by which a silkworm makes thread, and the life of Mozart—waste emerges as a central metaphor or literal concern:

—We call the fuel that this machine uses, food. We measure its value...
—the value of the fuel for this engine the same way
—that the engine has an alimentary system just like the human machine...
[...]
Money that isn't out working and earning something is just like a lazy partner who...
—in the bowel, where this raw material is converted for use as ... all kinds of raw silk...
—when the silkworm starts to spin it discharges a colorless ... that happens in the large bowel before ... billions of dollars, and the market value of shares in public corporations today has grown to...
—treatment of waste silk, called discharging...
—beautiful colors, but the smell of this waste silk fermenting is so offensive that...
—improving production knowhow and eliminating waste in the cause of human better...
—elimination of waste and is fitted with a muscular mechanism, or sphincter. (*JR*, 29; 45–46)

Note, here, the contrast between the dialogue fragments that define inert money, needless expenditure, and the by-products of production as waste, and those in which waste is defined as matter to be alchemised— that which the silkworm turns into silk, or that an engine discharges as it "digests" fuel in order to run. The juxtaposition of fragments results in a dual impression of waste: idle money versus raw material, a profit loss versus silk-in-the-making, foul smelling but capable of creating beauty. Waste is that which efficient industrial production seeks to minimise, but it is also a vital component in the biological production of silk and in the working of an engine. It is an obstruction to economic growth and human progress, but it is also a simple biological or mechanical outcome. In the case of the silkworm, it is valuable: waste is a necessary component to the production of silk. Meanwhile, the absurd mixing of partial dialogues, without some effort on the reader's part, amounts to little more than gibberish, revealing the ease with which the narrative itself can be reduced to meaningless words, particularly in the context of the discussion of commercial transactions.

Gaddis extends this exploration of value and waste in his depiction of Edward Bast's televised lecture on Mozart (for which Bast is fired, in turn catalysing his involvement with JR's company). In his lecture, Bast lingers on Mozart's life-long poverty and his predilection for scatological humour, before reading from some of Mozart's letters to a female cousin:

> —money, he wrote three of his greatest symphonies in barely two months while he was running around begging for loans wherever he ... [...] he apologizes to her for not writing and he says Do you think I'm dead? Don't believe it, I implore you. For believing and shitting are two very different things ... um, his um playful sense of humor yes he tells her you wouldn't be able to resist me much longer and our arses will, will um, will be the symbols of our peacemaking and then he, then he tells her down here about an imaginary village called Tribsterill where the, where the muck runs down to the sea ... village called Burmesquik where the crooked arseholes are manufactured and um, in the um, his um playful sense of humor. (*JR*, 40–42)

Bast's fellow teachers and the school administrators are scandalised both by Bast's use of waste-related profanities in the lecture and his depiction of Mozart as a foul-mouthed pauper, governed by material needs, base humour, and an implied fetish for faeces and anal sex. Bast's figuration breaks with traditional narratives of artistic genius (although Mozart's scatological humour is actually well documented[55]), conjoining biological waste, aesthetic worth, material wealth, and faith ("believing and shitting are two very different things"). Shit, music, money, and ideology are brought together in an apparently incoherent diatribe that in fact encapsulates Gaddis' concern with the blind belief that governs his characters' actions: belief in the stock market and the principles of trading and off-shore investment; belief in the capacity of art to uplift, instruct, or elevate; and belief in the systems in which we ourselves participate, be these economic, ideological, or semantic, even in the face of material inequality, madness, or failure. Waste is connected to the moral value of art and the economic imperatives of work, while the passage ultimately undermines art's capacity to rise above material concerns. Indeed, Bast argues, Mozart's humour:

> help[s] make him something you can understand too...—to humanize him because even if we can't um, if we can't rise to his level no at least we can, we can drag him down to ours...—what the um, what democracy in the arts is all about. (*JR*, 42–43)

It is not art that elevates us, but rather we who debase it—an irreverent view that foreshadows Bast's own failure to financially support himself while completing the opera he set out to write. The aphorism "believing and shitting are two very different things" articulates the distance between the abstractions of faith and its reality. In this instance, the faith in question is that of the artist, but elsewhere in the novel, it extends to faith in the market to accurately determine the worth of human beings and things, and in the capacity for a commercially-driven culture to foster the production of good art, let alone recognise it.

This concern with how one actually determines value—what distinguishes worth from waste—is rendered explicit in the novel's oft-quoted field trip scene, in which stockbroker Crawley attempts to explain the principles of financial speculation to JR and his classmates. The passage highlights the inability of financiers themselves to articulate its logic:

> Now first off, what's the whole point of this stock market, anyhow. It's to bring together people who want to buy with people who want to sell. Now if you're selling something, something definite … He shaped the space before him with empty hands into—A basket, baskets let's say. You may have a tough time finding somebody that wants to buy exactly your kind of baskets. But if you own stock in a company that makes baskets, you can sell it in a minute. There's always a buyer waiting somewhere. […] Are you with me? (*JR*, 84)

JR implicitly detects the leap from tangible thing (the basket) to intangible (stock in a company that makes baskets) when he interjects:

> Yeah but what about all these baskets? Like suppose this here company makes all these baskets which they can't sell them either? [...] They're stuck with all these here lousy baskets they made which nobody wants to buy them, so who wants their stock? [...]—So this old law of supply and decline with all these baskets happens with their stock too so what's the difference? Like everybody's buying it and selling it which they all want to get rid of it at once so like how does anybody know how much it's worth? Like we saw all these guys tearing up all this paper all over the floor which nobody knew what they were doing, so like now we buy this stock of Diamond Cable with our money so what if there's all this here cable nobody wants like nobody that didn't buy all those baskets so it just ends up with all these guys are running around tearing up paper all over the floor like where does that leave us? (*JR*, 84)

JR is challenging how a stockbroker can know that something is a sound investment, but he is also challenging the feasibility of the trading process itself: how can an economic system run on the hope that things will retain—and accrue—value, on the belief that we won't all end up "running around tearing up" our worthless stock options in despair? (*JR*, 84). Crawley's reassurance that no one is "going to get stung with Diamond Cable" and that those involved in the stock market are "specialists" rings hollow in this context, while the plot itself ultimately disproves him, as the markets repeatedly collapse (*JR*, 85). The scene is eerily prescient, essentially anticipating the debates that took place, throughout the 1980s (and onwards) between proponents of free-market capitalism and its detractors, while reminding us of Gaddis' own concern with what he described, in interview, as "a free enterprise system running out of control."[56]

This concern, and the tension between what Beckett's Molloy would term "all these questions of worth and value,"[57] is most evident in Bast's increasingly desperate efforts to write good music while managing JR's company. Each of these scenes takes place in waste-ridden settings. The first of these is the shed where Bast, and his father before him, composes music. The shed however has been broken into, and as he contemplates the space's importance to his father James (also a composer), Bast reflects:

> it's one place it's the one place an idea can be left here you can walk out and close the door and leave it here unfinished the most, the wildest secret fantasy and it stays on here by itself in that balance between, the balance

between destruction and realization until [...] he could come back the next day a week a month later he could open the door and find it here this same unfinished vision here just like he'd left it, this same awful balance waiting undisturbed just like he'd left it here to, to tip it and. (*JR*, 69–70)

Prior to the break-in, the shed offered sanctuary, appearing immune to time's passage and to the workings of the outside world. Significantly for a text in which all things appear on their way to collapse, the room is also framed as having been—until the break-in—immune to entropy. According to the third law of thermodynamics, entropy refers to the measure of the disorder or disorganisation of a closed system: the more entropy, the more disorder.[58] The law states that while there are finite ways to order a closed system, there are *infinite* ways of throwing that order into disarray. The concept is often illustrated with the example of a room, in which there are more ways for the furniture or objects to be disordered than ordered. Bast's description of his shed implies a suspension of entropy— that in this space, things remain in balance. The break-in shatters that illusion, and constrained by the practicalities of running JR's company, Bast decides to rent an apartment in the city from Gibbs and Eigen, which reveals itself to be the antithesis of the shed-sanctuary. Phone calls, visits, and mail from lawyers, brokers, and salespeople arrive at all hours. A constant stream of water runs from the broken faucets of the bath and kitchen sink, while mountains of paper—mail for JR, Bast, and other employees of the JR empire; rolls of music scores; Gibbs' and Eigen's unfinished book manuscripts—accumulate on every surface. A radio sits at the bottom of one of these mounds and is buried so far down that no one can turn it off. The place where the different characters' aspirations converge, it is also where they are encroached upon by the commercial world. As Gibbs aptly describes it, the apartment is entropy in action:

Problem Bast there's too God damned much leakage around here, can't compose anything with all this energy spilling you've got entropy going everywhere. Radio leaking under there hot water pouring out so God damned much entropy going on think you can hold all these notes together know what it sounds like? Bast? (*JR*, 285)

The radio and telephone receiver emitting disembodied sales pitches and the toppling stacks of unread promotions and worthless inventory are conducive to little artistic creation. They are capital coming unspooled—

evidence of what Gaddis himself described, in the aforementioned interview, as the entropic tendencies of "the charade of the so-called free market, so-called free enterprise system" (ZoltÃ¡n AbÃ¡di-Nagy).

The stylistic approach Gaddis uses to describe the objects that furnish this dilapidated setting further contributes to our sense that this is *capitalist* entropy and *capitalist* waste. For rather than referring to a crate, a newspaper, and a can of oil, Gaddis chooses to name them by the brand or title emblazoned on these objects. Thus, Gaddis describes things being placed on, or falling off of, "Wise Potato Chips Hoppin' With Flavor!" rather than a simple carton (*JR*, 276; 282; 726). A disembodied voice emanates from behind "36 Boxes 200 2-Ply" (*JR*, 277). On the novel's last page Eigen drops the telephone on "24-One Pint Mazola New Improved" while JR's ramblings down the receiver about "success and like free enterprise and all" and "[Ameri]ca's all about like" are only heard by an audience of "500 Novelty Rolls 1-Ply White" (*JR*, 726). Likewise, we see Gibbs reach a bottle by climbing

> past the fleet of cartons and over the film cans, up 24-One Pint Mazola New Improved across bales of the Morning Telegraph toppling a peak of lampshades to mount Appletons' Cyclopaedia of American Biography at the sill of the window to the rear where light squared the window across the airshaft. (*JR*, 279)

The consequences of this approach are several. On a formal level, the substitution of names of objects with names of manufacturers and advertising slogans is not only jarring but a form of intrusion. Whether s/he is conscious of it or not, the reader is obliged to translate the slogan or title into non-commercial language in order to interpret what is being said. This in turn leads us to two potential interpretations. Either a series of marketing slogans has replaced the realist waste object (the reader is not looking at an old can of oil, but at an old Pint Mazola New Improved), or a series of marketing slogans has *enhanced* the realism of the waste object. That is—it is "New Improved" and "Mazola" that make this waste (and the scene itself) appear more real. The latter interpretation, however, also fetters the waste object to the signifying system in which it participated as a consumer product: the brand name has a "reality effect" that in turn impedes the waste object from being interpreted as anything other than a relic of its former self. Pint Mazola New Improved *remains* Pint Mazola New Improved even as it forms rust, accumulates dust, and becomes a resting place for teacups and junk mail rather than a receptacle for oil. These waste objects, in other words, do not have the freedom of those we might find in a Surrealist text or metaphysical painting or in Beckett, Barthelme, or Ballard, where they explicitly resist our gaze or take on new meanings. Referring to them by the brand name renders them wholly legible as consumer relics, residues of a business deal most likely gone bad.

Moreover, the waste objects that interrupt the apartment scenes and that render them comical—the drinks spilled on Bast's music scores, the mail-order business training manuals that no one ever reads, the plastic carnations in which JR has invested, but no one will buy—serve to dismantle JR's own vision of his company. They serve, that is, a similar function to the beer can in the novel's opening: where the beer can interrupts the reader's absorption of the discussions about company shares and inheritance law, the trash accumulating in and around the apartment dispels JR's idealised notion of himself as a capitalist magnate. This is rendered explicit in the disappointing outcome to a school trip to the apartment, which JR orchestrated in order to see the business he founded with his own eyes. Far from the majestic office buildings he had been expecting, the headquarters is little more than a "dump" and certainly unsuitable for a PR stunt such as the school trip and photo shoot he had been planning:

> —So there's suppose to be this photographer and these here box lunches and you're suppose to excort [*sic*] us and take us around like, so now you come down this street with these wrecked up cars and garbage cans all over in this here funny looking suit with these ripped pants and your eye and all I mean didn't Mister Davidoff even say to … […]
> —You wanted a low-cost operation didn't you!
> —Sure but holy, I mean, I mean holy…
> —Sixty-one forty a month what did you expect for sixty-one forty! What do you think I've been…
> —No but, no but I mean holy, I mean that was it this here whole world headquarters? that, that dump…?
> (*JR*, 633–637)

The reality—what we might call the "shit"—of the headquarters' location undermines JR's "belief" in the myths that have been spun about him as a "man of vision" (*JR*, 661) and his company as a global empire. The "wrecked up cars and garbage cans" are the other side—the shadow, but more importantly, the counter-truth—of JR's dreams of limousine rides and plush offices. As well as satirising and undermining the very principles of public relations (an industry in which Gaddis himself worked to support himself while writing), the scene extends the novel's thematic concern with entropy. Relatedly, it undermines, once more, our sense of where value lies. JR's headquarters is revealed to be a dump—and yet the apartment is still the site of an immensely successful operation. JR's discovery thus reveals the "shit" obscured by "belief" in the market, but it is also comparable to the climax of the silkworm story: the foul-looking apartment is where the "silk" of JR's empire is produced, just as JR's pile of papers featuring stock tips, which the adults in the novel repeatedly refer to as "trash," is in fact worth thousands of dollars (*JR*, 227–228).

Donald Barthelme's *Snow White*, J. G. Ballard's urban disaster trilogy, and William Gaddis' *JR* extend the historical avant-garde and Samuel Beckett's experimentations with language and form to critique the rhetoric of market research, advertising, and finance, and to debunk the myths of post-war consumerism. Like Beckett, they carry on the avant-garde's legacy by placing waste at the centre of this critique. By tracing the many paths objects travel on their way to and from the landfill and the frequency with which things under capitalism gain and lose value, Barthelme, Ballard, and Gaddis show waste to be a tenuous category that underscores the tenuousness of capitalism's ascriptions of worth. In turn, the unique ways in which their characters put waste to comedic use evidence the enduring potential for countercultural literature to give voice to other discourses and throw into relief the humour at the heart of our systemic failures.

NOTES

1. J.G. Ballard, "The Subliminal Man" (1963) in *The Complete Short Stories Volume 1* (London: Fourth Estate, 2014 [2001]), 559–577. Henceforth, SM.
2. Donald Barthelme, *Snow White* (New York: Simon and Schuster, 1965). Henceforth, *SW*.
3. J.G. Ballard, *Crash* (London: Fourth Estate, 2011 [1969]). Henceforth, *C*.
4. J.G. Ballard, *Concrete Island* (New York: Noonday Press, 1994 [1974]). Henceforth, *CI*.
5. J.G. Ballard, *High-Rise* (London: Flamingo, 1993 [1975]). Henceforth, *HR*.
6. William Gaddis, *JR* (London: Dalkey Archive, 2012 [1975]). Henceforth, *JR*.
7. For an in-depth account of these changes, see David Harvey, *The Condition of Postmodernity*, 141–188 and *A Brief History of Neoliberalism* (Oxford: Oxford University Press, 2005), 1–38.
8. Brian Nicol summarises the different ways Ballard's work has been likened to Noel King's concept of postmodern "ficto-criticism" in Chapter Eight of *The Cambridge Introduction to Postmodern Fiction* (Cambridge: Cambridge University Press, 2009), 184–204. In *Dissident Postmodernists: Barthelme, Coover, Pynchon* (Philadelphia: University of Pennsylvania Press, 1991), 43–81, Paul Maltby reads Barthelme's *Snow White* as emblematic of a politicised

postmodernism reacting against the corruption of language in late capitalism. For a sense of the debate around the categorisation of Gaddis' work as postmodernist, see Joseph Tabbi and Rone Shavers' edited essay collection, *Paper Empire: William Gaddis and the World System* (Tuscaloosa: University of Alabama Press, 2007). Most recently, Brian McHale has cited *JR* as a quintessential "postmodern megafiction." See McHale, *The Cambridge Introduction to Postmodernism* (Cambridge: Cambridge University Press, 2015), 77).

9. Fredric Jameson. *Postmodernism, or, The Cultural Logic of Late Capitalism* (London and New York: Verso, 1991), 4. It is also worth highlighting Ernest Mandel's *Late Capitalism* (1972) and David Harvey's *The Condition of Postmodernity* (1989), whose traces can be found in much of the scholarship on which I draw in this chapter and the next.

10. Thomas Pynchon, *V.* (London: Jonathan Cape and Vintage, 1995 [1963]), 43.

11. Although it is less concerned with waste than *V*, Pynchon's second novel, *The Crying of Lot 49* (1965), can be seen to build on these ideas: its entire plot is driven by a quest for a grail-like mailbox, which is eventually revealed to be nothing more than a trash can with the painted initials "W.A.S.T.E." Every object in the novel, including the mailbox-trash can, is entirely self-referential, as attested by the acronym of W.A.S.T.E, which is ultimately shown to stand for nothing but itself.

12. Italo Calvino, *Invisible Cities*, transl. William Weaver (New York: Harcourt Brace Jovanovich, 1974 [1972]), 114. Henceforth, *IC*.

13. David L. Gold. *Studies in Etymology and Etiology: With Emphasis on Germanic, Jewish, Romance and Slavic Languages* (Alicante: Publicaciones de la Universidad de Alicante, 2009), 218.

14. See, for instance, Philip Nel, *The Avant-Garde and American Postmodernity: Small Incisive Shocks* (Jackson, MS: University Press of Mississippi, 2002), 73–95 and Nicole Sierra, "Surrealist histories of language, image, media: Donald Barthelme's 'collage stories,'" *European Journal of American Culture* 32. 2 (1 June 2013): 153–171.

15. J.D. O'Hara, "Donald Barthelme, The Art of Fiction No. 66," *The Paris Review* 80 (Summer 1981).

16. *Sixty Stories* (New York: Penguin, 1981), 91. Henceforth *SS*.

17. Barbara L. Roe, *Donald Barthelme: A Study of His Short Fiction* (New York: Twayne, 1992), 98; Donald Barthelme, *Guilty Pleasures* (New York: Farrar, Straus and Giroux, 1974).

18. Barthelme, "Brain Damage" (1970) in *City Life* (New York: Farrar, Straus, and Giroux, 1970), 149.

19. Barthelme, "Sakrete" (1983) in *Forty Stories* (New York: Penguin, 2005), 183.

20. Jack Kroll. "The Comanches Are Here," *Newsweek* (6 May 1968): 112; "Social Science Fiction," *Time* (24 May 1968): 106, as cited in Philip Nel, *The Avant-Garde and American Postmodernity* (Jackson, MS: University Press of Mississippi, 2002), 81.

21. William Gass, "The Leading Edge of the Trash Phenomenon," *Fiction and the Figures of Life* (New York: David R. Godine, 1970), 97–103, citation on 101. For a sense of readings following this vein, see Larry McCaffery, "Donald Barthelme: the Aesthetics of Trash" (1975) in *The Metafictional Muse: The Works of Robert Coover, Donald Barthelme, and William H. Gass* (Pittsburgh: University of Pittsburgh Press, 1982), 99–150; Michael du Plessis, "The Postmodern object: commodities, fetishes and signifiers in Donald Barthelme's writing," *Journal of Literary Studies*, 4:4 (1988), 443–458; Jaye Berman Montresor, "Sanitization and its discontents: refuse and refusal in Donald Barthelme's *Snow White*," *Studies in American Humor* (1989), 74–84; and Nicholas Sloboda, "Heteroglossia and Collage: Donald Barthelme's *Snow White*," *Mosaic* 30.4 (1997): 109–23.
22. Franco Moretti, "Serious Century" in *The Novel, Volume I: History, Geography and Culture*, 364–399.
23. "Not Knowing" (1987), in *Not Knowing: The Essays and Interviews of Donald Barthelme*, ed. Kim Herzinger (New York: Random House, 1997), 15.
24. See Scott MacFarlane's summary of Carson's impact in *The Hippie Narrative: A Literary Perspective on the Counterculture* (Jefferson, NC: McFarland, 1997), 86.
25. Comte Lautréamont, *Maldoror*, transl. Guy Wernham (New York: New Directions, 1965 [1869]), 263.
26. See Donald A. Fullerton, "The Birth of Consumer Behavior: Motivation Research in the 1940s and 1950s," *Journal of Historical Research in Marketing* 5.2 (2013): 212–222. Adam Ardvisson provides an excellent account of the history of market research from the immediate aftermath of the World War I to the present in "On the 'Pre-History of the Panoptic Sort': Mobility in Market Research," *Surveillance and Society* 1. 4 (2003): 1–19, noting that the sector's exponential growth throughout the 1950s coincided with its establishment as a scientific discipline. Accessed 5 January 2016. www.surveillance-and-society.org/articles1(4)/prehistory.pdf.
27. Franklin B. Evans, "Psychological and Objective Factors in the Prediction of Brand Choice: Ford versus Chevrolet," *Journal of Business* 32 (October 1959): 340–69; Arthur Koponen, "Personality Characteristics of Purchasers," *Journal of Advertising Research* 1 (1960): 6–12.
28. For an in-depth discussion of the history of these marketing tactics, see Vicki Howard. *Brides, Inc: American Weddings and the Business of Tradition* (Philadelphia: University of Pennsylvania Press), 2006, esp. 33–70. Howard notes that promoting diamonds as the quintessential symbol of enduring love helped the company claw back its share of the American market in the aftermath of the Second World War.
29. *The Atrocity Exhibition* (London: Fourth Estate, 2006 [1969]), 127.
30. Interview by David Pringle and Jim Goddard, *Science Fiction Monthly* (4 January 1975): 30–31. See also Peter Brigg, *JG Ballard* (Mercer Island, Washington: Starmont House, 1985), 67.

31. Will Viney, "A Fierce and Wayward Beauty." *Ballardian.* 11 December 2007. Accessed 30 October 2015 11 December 2007. Accessed 30 October 2015. http://www.ballardian.com/a-fierce-and-wayward-beauty-parts-1-2 and http://www.ballardian.com/a-fierce-and-wayward-beauty-part-3.

32. Jeanette Baxter, "Visions of Europe in *Cocaine Nights* and *Super-Cannes*" in *J.G. Ballard: Contemporary Critical Perspectives,* ed. Jeanette Baxter (London: Continuum, 2009), 94–106.

33. Jeanette Baxter, *J.G. Ballard's Surrealist Imagination: Spectacular Authorship* (Farnham: Ashgate, 2009).

34. "Introduction" (1995) in *Crash* (London: Fourth Estate, 2011), i.

35. "The Coming of the Unconscious," *New Worlds* (July 1966), 141–142.

36. James Campbell, "Strange Fiction: Interview with J.G. Ballard," *The Guardian* (14 June 2008).

37. J.G. Ballard, *The Atrocity Exhibition* (London: Fourth Estate, 2006 [1969]). Henceforth, *AE.*

38. I am indebted to David Pringle for making me aware—over the course of an informal conversation about Ballard—of the role the newspaper photographer played in the price tag's placement.

39. "The Car, The Future" (1971), in *Users' Guide to the Millennium* (London: Flamingo, 1996), 262, as cited in Simon Ford, "A Psychopathic Hymn: J.G. Ballard's 'Crashed Cars' Exhibition of 1970," *Slash Seconds 1* (November 2005). Accessed 30 October 2015.

40. Jo Stanley, "Ballard Crashes," *Friends 7* (29 May 1970): 4–5, as cited in Simon Ford, "A Psychopathic Hymn: J.G. Ballard's 'Crashed Cars' Exhibition of 1970."

41. Jason Cowley, "Interview with J.G. Ballard," *Prospect 33* (August 1998). Accessed 24 November 2015.

42. Félix Deleuze and Gilles Guattari, *Anti-Oedipus,* 3.

43. See Joe Moran, *On Roads: A Hidden History* (London: Profile Books, 2009), 189–192.

44. Filippo Tommaso Marinetti, "The Founding and Manifesto of Futurism" (1909) in *Futurist Manifestos,* ed. Umbro Apollonio (*Tate Publishing:* London, 2009), 21, emphasis in the original.

45. "Author's Note," in *Concrete Island* (London: Fourth Estate, 2014 [1994]), vii.

46. Bauman, *Wasted Lives,* 5; 15; 39.

47. David Punter, "Alone Among the Murder Machines" in *The Hidden Script: Writing and the Unconscious* (London: Routledge, 1985), 17, as cited by Sebastian Groes, "The Texture of Modernity in J.G. Ballard's *Crash, Concrete Island* and *High-Rise*" in *J.G. Ballard: Visions and Revisions,* eds. Jeanette Baxter and Rowland Wymer (London: Palgrave Macmillan, 2011), 133. Simon Sellars likewise reads Maitland's habitation of the island as a form of "reclamation, recovering and recycling of territory" that echoes real-life efforts, in the late 1960s and early 1970s, to create micro-nations free from government production quotas. Like the real-life cases of Sealand and

Akhzivland—two micro-nations formed, respectively, in Western Australia and Israel—Maitland's island exists as an "adjunct to civilised society, forgotten and discarded." Sellars, "'Zones of Transition': Micronationalism in the Work of J.G. Ballard" in *J.G. Ballard: Visions and Revisions*, 234.

48. "J.G. Ballard," *Books and Bookmen* 15.10 (9 July 1970): 6, as cited in Vivian Vale and Andrea Juno, *Re/Search: J.G. Ballard, 8/9* (San Francisco, CA: Re/Search, 1984), 156.

49. *Extreme Metaphors: Interviews with J.G. Ballard, 1967–2008*, edited by Simon Sellars and Dan O'Hara (London: Fourth Estate/HarperCollins, 2012), 108.

50. William Shakespeare, *Hamlet* Act III Scene 2 (London: Wordsworth, 1992), 17–24. Whether Brecht in fact said this is disputed: the quote was attributed to him by Peter McLaren and Tomaz Tadeu da Silva in *Paulo Freire: A Critical Encounter*, ed. Peter McLaren and Peter Leonard (New York: Routledge, 1993), 80.

51. *JR*, 27.

52. For insights into this discussion, see John Johnston, "JR and the Flux of Capital," *Revue Française d'Études Américaine* 45 (1990): 161–71; Tabbi and Shavers, eds. *Paper Empire*; and Michael W. Clune, *American Literature and the Free Market, 1945–2000* (Cambridge: Cambridge University Press, 2010).

53. For a sense of such readings, see Tom LeClair's chapter on Gaddis in *The Art of Excess*, which examines *JR*'s mixing of lexicons and dialects as a form of literary bricolage that reflects the "quantitative values and uncontrolled bigness" of capitalist America. Tom LeClair, *The Art of Excess: Mastery in Contemporary American Fiction* (Urbana and Chicago: University of Illinois Press, 1989), 87–105, and Dieter Paul Polloczek's analysis of linguistic waste in "Recycling Semiotic Junk in William Gaddis' J R," *Compar(a)ison* 1 (1996): 203–29.

54. Barthes, "The Reality Effect" (1967), *The Rustle of Language*, 141–148.

55. See David O. Schroeder, *Mozart in Revolt: Strategies of Resistance, Mischief, and Deception* (New Haven: Yale University Press, 1999); Robert Spaethling, *Mozart's Letters, Mozart's Life: Selected Letters* (New York: WW Norton, 2000).

56. Zoltán Abádi-Nagy, "William Gaddis, The Art of Fiction No. 101," *The Paris Review* 105 (Winter 1987). For insights into the growth of free market capitalism—also known as neoliberalism—see Harvey's *A Brief History of Neoliberalism*, which identifies the significance of the policies implemented between 1978–1980 to curb the power of labour, increase the remit of global financial markets, and deregulate industry, agriculture, and resource extraction. I will have more to say about these in Chaps. 5 and 6.

57. Beckett, *Molloy*, 46.

58. J.S. Dugdale, *Entropy and its Physical Meaning* (London and New York: Taylor and Francis, 1996), 62. I am also indebted to Paolo Dini for explaining entropy to me in layman's terms.

CHAPTER 5

"Most of Our Longings Go Unfulfilled": DeLillo's Historiographical Readings of Landfill Waste and Nuclear Fallout

It is World War III. A nameless astronaut and his colleague, Vollmer, orbit the earth, waiting for a war base called "Colorado Command" to tell them what to blow up, while performing safety drills and participating in voice-recognition exercises to reassure Colorado Command—and themselves—that they are still there. For entertainment, they listen to a defective radio that endlessly replays soap operas and news broadcasts from the Second World War. So begins "Human Moments in World War Three" (1983), a little-known short story by Don DeLillo.[1] In the story, the narrator marvels at the fragments of sound emanating from the radio, wondering:

> What odd happenstance, what flourish or grace of the laws of physics enables us to pick up these signals? Travelled voices, chambered and dense. At times they have the detached and surreal quality of aural hallucination, voices in attic rooms, the complaints of dead relatives. Cars turn dangerous corners, crisp gunfire fills the night. It was, it is, wartime. Wartime for Duz and Grape-Nuts Flakes. Comedians make fun of the way the enemy talks. We hear hysterical mock German, moonshine Japanese. (*HM*, 38–39)

This uncanny montage of radio plays, advertising jingles, slogans, and news stories from a defunct era, with their archaic humour and nationalistic piety, re-affirm the narrator's sense that "all wars refer back" (*HM*, 30). It is only fitting that the war to end all wars is experienced to the soundtrack of the last one's mediated responses. To keep their sanity, the astronauts make lists of the things that remain and contemplate the mementos in their

R. Dini, *Consumerism, Waste, and Re-Use in Twentieth-Century Fiction*,
DOI 10.1057/978-1-137-58165-5_5

"personal preference kits"—boxes containing worthless objects collected specifically to remind them of life on earth. The narrator refers to these objects as "human moments," but as the story progresses, he extends the definition to include other items, too—memories, the astronauts' hammocks, even Vollmer's native Minnesota (*HM*, 27). A human moment is another term for waste that has been rendered subjectively meaningful and for any fragment of lived experience that can aid recollection (*HM*, 34–35). At the same time, these souvenirs are a reminder of the other, far less benign, souvenir of nuclear holocaust—fallout. They thus paradoxically gesture to that which cannot be recuperated. The term "human moment" is connotative of our capacity to attach meaning to matter as well as our capacity to destroy it and misread the remains.

Meditations on waste, recuperation, and value can be found in much of DeLillo's writing. The author himself has described his work as opposing a culture "filled with consumption and waste," noting that "even if one doesn't write about it in specific terms as I did [...] in *Underworld*, [...] a writer may feel that he is standing in opposition to this, and perhaps in a very general way to the idea of power itself."[2] DeLillo's fascination with waste reflects a broader shift in late twentieth-century western culture's relationship with consumption and disposal in the wake of environmental movement. This aesthetic project is fundamentally entwined with the culture of late capitalism, already mentioned in Chap. 4, and best understood in relation to the seismic economic events that in the 1970s and 1980s changed its nature.[3] The Volcker Shock of 1979—when the US Federal Reserve Bank deliberately plunged the US economy and much of the rest of the world into recession in an effort to shock the global economies out of stagflation—is generally recognised as marking the beginning of a new phase of capitalism. The decades following saw the privatisation of social services, deregulation of markets, normalisation of debt (otherwise known as the financialisation of markets), and globalisation of finance—all in the name of fostering competition and entrepreneurialism and rendering citizens "self-sufficient." Although the terms used to describe it have varied (the most well-known being "post-industrial society," "post-Fordism," "flexible accumulation," "media capitalism," and "global" or "transnational" capitalism, each of which served to emphasise different aspects), this economic model, since the 1990s, has been referred to as neoliberalism.[4] The rhetoric of neoliberalism emphasises individualism rather than collectivism, as exemplified in Margaret Thatcher's famed assertion that "there is no society, only individual[s]."[5] On the consumer end, manufacturers came to rely on ever-shortening product cycles and on what Frederic Jameson, in his seminal analysis of postmodernism, terms consumerism's reliance on commodity fetishism.[6] Meanwhile, disinvestment in the state sector led to phenomena such as the garbage barges endlessly circling New York in the 1980s—as Benjamin Miller and Heather Rogers both note in their respective historical studies of the New York and US garbage industries (Miller, 284–292; Rogers, 200).

I am not concerned, here, to explore DeLillo's relationship to postmodernism—itself a highly contested term. However, Jameson's study does offer useful parameters for thinking about subject–object relations in a globalised economy, and, specifically, about the "freedom" from guilt that results from the "effacement of the traces of production" from our purchases (Jameson, 315). The privilege of being a consumer is the ability to forget about the exploited labourers involved in producing your things or the many who cannot afford them: the product "somehow shuts us out even from a sympathetic participation, by imagination, in its production. It comes before us, no questions asked, as something we could not begin to imagine doing ourselves" (Jameson, 315; 371). Reification in late capitalism goes beyond rendering social relations transactional, to effectively annihilating our sense of responsibility towards others. In turn, the ecological view of waste somehow stands in for or occludes the socio-economic view of the object itself: we worry about discarded plastic in lieu of worrying about the cheap labour that went into making the plastic in the first place. DeLillo's waste representations redress that erasure: the commodity-turned-waste asks us to participate in its backstory. The dissimilarity between the waste object's appearance and what it looked like on the shop shelf requires an imaginative leap, inviting us to attend to the origins of the product and its potentially ethical dubiousness. DeLillo's novels allow us to explore the complex inter-play of meanings we attribute to the different forms of waste produced in the late twentieth century. Where for the 1950s plastics industry, "America's future [was] in the garbage wagon," DeLillo's novels suggest that its past, and its historical identity, is in the landfill (Rogers, 3).

"Garbage for 20 Years"

At the time of *Underworld*'s publication, DeLillo noted that he "had been thinking about garbage for 20 years."[7] This is evident in the frequent references to waste in his previous novels. The first of these, *Americana* (1971), tells the story of Dave Bell, a bored television executive who drives across

the USA to film the "essence of the nation's soul"—which amounts to buying, selling, and throwing things away.[8] The novel itself opposes the logic
of late capitalism and pays tribute to the historical avant-garde in its non-
linear juxtaposition of everyday ephemera with flashbacks to Bell's suburban
youth. What emerges is not a plot-driven narrative, but a series of insights
into the stuff "behind the smoke and billboards" of consumer culture (*A*,
111). For Bell, American culture is better told through its discards: "in
the last analysis, it is the unseen janitor who maintains power over us all"
(*A*, 60)—a view that uncannily recalls Marguerite Duras' description, in
"Madame Dodin" (1954), of the all-seeing nature of the streetsweeper:
"Nothing gets done, indeed, nothing happens, without his witnessing it."[9]
A Manhattan apartment building custodian reiterates this later, telling Bell
that collecting garbage "gives you clues to human nature" (*A*, 190).

The above-mentioned discussions effectively anticipate the central
tenets of 1970s "garbology." An academic discipline initiated in 1973
by the University of Arizona, garbology approached consumer waste as a
matter of archaeological inquiry, even suggesting that consumer researchers examine domestic waste to glean insight into consumers' purchasing
practices.[10] But garbology came to encompass a broader critical re-assess-
ment of waste over the course of the decade: while the environmental
movement gained traction with the public, the FBI looked for incriminat-
ing evidence in the garbage of suspected mobsters (substituting what they
stole with "fake" trash[11]), and the New Journalists sifted through the waste
of politicians. The custodian's sarcastic reply to Bell's remark that it must
be "satisfying to help keep the city clean" ("It overjoys me") tells us however that DeLillo's is an ironic garbologist (*A*, 190). The "unseen janitor
who maintains power over us all" is a source of unease, *hinting* at hidden
truths to be gleaned from the nation's refuse and yet abstaining from telling us what they are (*A*, 60). He is the antithesis of Walter Benjamin's
allegorical conceptualisation, after Baudelaire, of poetry as rag-picking—
the nineteenth-century industry based on collecting and re-selling scraps
for re-use.[12] For Baudelaire, the rag picker exemplifies the spirit of industrial modernity, which looks to turn all things into use-values.[13] Benjamin
extended this notion to the rehabilitation of culture in urban modernity,
seeing the rag picker's putting-to-use of effluvia as analogous to the poetic
method, which likewise seizes upon the imaginative potential of the overlooked. The poet-as-rag picker is willing to embrace capitalism's paradoxes
and contradictions in order to "produce" a new work that will in turn take
part in the commodity cycle.[14] DeLillo's custodian is the antithesis of the

rag picker since he extracts no insight—poetic or otherwise—from the
garbage he collects. The unseen janitor merely divests domestic spaces
of their narratives: the secrets he discovers remain unexpressed. What we
have is not a full disclosure—or aesthetic re-working—but the suggestion
of something significant. It is a first embryonic effort by DeLillo to think
otherwise about waste.

DeLillo's second novel, *End Zone* (1972), conflates the lexicon of nuclear
holocaust with that of American football, anticipating *Underworld*'s twinning of the military industrial complex and baseball.[15] The novel, whose
title and thematic concern with excrement has invited parallels with
Beckett's *Endgame,* charts the efforts of a team of football players to find
meaning in language while contemplating the prospect of nuclear annihilation.[16] Their explorations take them through the lexicons of thermonu-
clear warfare, advertising, and product innovation. DeLillo draws parallels
between American post-war technology and "the lampshades, the soap"
Nazi scientists made out of human skin, and suggests that advertising
rhetoric could easily be put to use in masking the "crop failures, genetic
chaos [and] scorched bodies" of nuclear war (*EZ*, 198). These meditations
culminate in protagonist Gary Harkness' startling realisation, upon seeing
a mound of excrement, that all matter is waste in the making and that the
lexicons that interest him are merely ways of dressing up shit. Thus, he
meditates upon the:

> nullity in the very word, shit, as of dogs squatting near partly eaten bod-
> ies; faeces, as of specimen, sample, analysis, diagnosis, bleak assessment of
> disease in the bowels; dung, as of dry straw erupting with microscopic eggs;
> excrement, as of final matter voided, the chemical stink of self disconti-
> ued; offal, as of butchered animals' intestines slick with shit and blood; shit
> everywhere, shit in life cycle, shit as earth as food as shit, wise men sitting
> impassively in shit, armies retreating in that stench, shit as history, holy men
> praying to shit, scientists tasting it, volumes to be compiled on colour and
> texture and scent, shit's infinite treachery, everywhere this whisper of inex-
> istence. (*EZ*, 88–89)

Harkness' fragmented thoughts draw attention to waste's resistance to
narration as well as the degree to which it lends itself to *multiple* narratives. "Shit" connotes nullity, but it connotes many different forms of nullity. The conflation of animal entrails, chemical spillage, saints' relics, and
academic studies on shit is likewise characteristic of DeLillo's approach
to waste throughout his work. "I had been thinking about garbage for

twenty years" prior to *Underworld*'s publication should not be read as a
reference to one specific form of waste but to the interrelation between
different forms: the narrative that connects the "chemical stink of self dis-
continued" and "shit as history" to "holy men praying to shit" and "shit's
infinite treachery."

Great Jones Street (1973) expands DeLillo's critique of capitalist excretion. Titled after Manhattan's Great Jones Street (known, in the 1970s, as
a hangout for junkies), the novel follows the relocation of rock star Bucky
Wunderlick to a squalid tenement building inhabited by marginalised characters including a struggling writer and a brain-damaged babbling teenager
whose father has spent the last 15 years trying to put him to use as a carnival
act and a medical subject (*GJS*, 269). While journalists hound Bucky to
extract a marketable story from his exodus, an illicit drug-manufacturing
branch of his record company works on a wonder drug that renders its
consumers speechless.

Great Jones Street thus interlaces meditations on language, marketability, and the dynamics of obsolescence. Bucky's neighbour Hanes notes
that in the eyes of the market—be it the music industry, bookselling, or
the drugs trade—our value is measured in terms of what we produce, and
how much people want it: "The market is a strange thing, almost a living
organism. It changes, it palpitates, it grows, it excretes. It sucks things in
and spews them up" (*GJS*, 28). In an effort to distance himself from this
"living organism," Bucky ends up taking the music company's silencing
drug and wandering through the Bowery, mutely observing the homeless
who, like nineteenth-century rag pickers, scavenge and sell the city's waste.
Among these is a woman "loudly cataloguing" the trash littering the pavement: "NEWSPAPER GLASS SHIT GARBAGE BOTTLE CARTON
BOTTLE PAPER STOCKING SHIT GARBAGE SHIT GARBAGE"
(*GJS*, 246). DeLillo gives voice to the city's human waste—its supernu-
mary people—in a manner akin to Mina Loy (see Chap. 2). In contrast
to Loy, however, the novel posits this inchoate babble as sound(s) waiting
to be put to use—with the right agent, the logic goes, these bums, too,
might become valuable commodities in their own right.

Running Dog (1978) expands on these ideas to explore the taxonomic
distinction between objects of value and objects of waste.[17] Narrating the
frenzied search for a pornographic home movie rumoured to have been
filmed during Hitler's last days, DeLillo shows that what saves objects
from the scrap heap is myth. In a 1988 interview, DeLillo identified the
novel's central concern as the "the terrible acquisitiveness in which we live,

coupled with a final indifference to the object. After all the mad attempts to acquire the thing, everyone suddenly decides that, well, maybe we really don't care about this so much anyway."[18] DeLillo ironises this by revealing that far from pornography, the film is a home movie, featuring snatches of everyday life in Hitler's bunker during the last days of the Third Reich. The discovery of the film's true content undermines the point of the quest, as attested by seedy art dealer Lightborne's dismay: "What do I do with a thing like this? Who needs it?" (*RD*, 268). This is not a product for the erotica industry; it is not a collectible; which means, for Lightborne, that it is as good as garbage (*RD*, 268). By narrating the pursuit of an object that no one has seen, DeLillo explores what it means to assign something the status of a Thompsonian durable as well as the degree to which that assignation has nothing to do with the object itself.

The concerns of DeLillo's project as a whole are articulated in *The Names* (1983), in the protagonist David Keller's meditations on "our piggish habits, our self-indulgence and waste."[19] As the novel's female protagonist Kathryn Axton notes, at issue is:

> the theme of expansionism, of organized criminal infiltration [...] the corporations, the processing plants, the mineral rights. [...] The colonialist theme, the theme of exploitation, of greatest possible utilization [...] contaminants [...] pollutants [...] noxious industrial waste. [...] The theme of power's ignorance and blindness and contempt. (*N*, 266)[20]

The passage brings into sharp focus the degree to which waste, for DeLillo, can never be examined in isolation. Just as the things with which we furnish our existence exist in relation to other things, so, too, do our excretions. This sense of different waste forms' interconnectedness also sets his work apart from other late twentieth-century articulations of consumer culture. Enacted in the montage-like structure of his novels, his view echoes the environmental movement's central trope: that ecological responsibility is merely a way to recognise the effects of our actions on others, our interconnectedness. As H.M. Enzenberger noted in his 1974 essay, "Critique of Political Ecology" (one of the first documented efforts to address the environmental movement within the context of capitalism), one cannot deal with environmental issues singly, or in isolation:

> One is dealing with a series of closed circuits, or rather of interference circuits, that are in many ways linked. Any discussion that attempted to deal

with the alleged "causes" piecemeal and to disprove them simply would miss the core of the ecological debate and would fall below the level that the debate has in the meantime reached.[21]

Like Enzenberger, DeLillo highlights the limits of attempting to "manage" overconsumption rather than putting an end to it. Very simply, our efforts to read what we have excreted will not stop it from subsuming us.

This awareness comes to a head in *White Noise* (1986), in which the preoccupation has shifted to waste's resistance to scrutiny, its coterminous provocative intimations of mystery and cryptic self-contained silence. Contemplating the contents of the family garbage compactor, the novel's protagonist Jack Gladney asks: "[I]s this the dark underside of consumer consciousness?" (*WN*, 259). In so doing, he questions whether garbage belies a "complex relationship" between us and our possessions, or whether we should be scrutinising our *fascination* with it—the capacity of this "shapeless mass" (*WN*, 259) to feed our need for meaningful patterns, and, also, our paranoia and fear.

White Noise is also the first of these novels to render explicit public fears over toxic emissions, emerging as the US garbage crisis was first gaining momentum. As Jennifer Seymour Whitaker notes, the late 1980s saw growing anxieties about the potentially harmful effects of aerosol sprays, chlorofluorocarbons, and emissions from burning fuels.[22] Reflecting these fears, consumerism—embodied in the rituals of shopping and bingeing on junk food—in *White Noise* is presented as both a means of staving off death and as the thing that is killing us. Gladney's family trip to the mall, undertaken as a distraction from the toxic waste cloud that has formed over the city and threatens to annihilate the community, ends with a silent meal in which each member consumes junk food in solitude (*WN*, 13). Exemplifying capitalist excess, junk food functions as the waste matter that circulates through the system "just because"—serving no function other than a kind of inane self-affirmation (i.e. I eat therefore I am), and merely fuelling further desire, in a manner akin to cigarettes, alcohol, or mind-altering drugs. The novel's repeated depictions of the dissatisfaction following junk food binges anticipate Nick Shay's realisation, in *Underworld*, that "Most of our longings go unfulfilled": in this system, we can fill our holes, but filling them just makes them empty again all the more quickly.

In its very explicit engagement with the industrialised world's most prominent waste concerns and mixing of themes touched on in his previous narratives, *Underworld* constitutes, as DeLillo himself has commented, the "book [he]'d been writing all [his] life without knowing it."[23] The following sections focus specifically on what the different recuperative efforts depicted in *Underworld* suggest about the potential, and limits, of historical, aesthetic, and ecological re-use in late capitalism.

"Waste is the Secret History"[24]: Reading the Past

DeLillo's novels suggest that to reclaim meaning from waste is above all to understand it in historiographical terms and to recognise that that understanding will only ever be partial. In *Underworld*, the transnational discourse of consumer and nuclear waste is juxtaposed with the localised history of New York garbage, and, further, of the Bronx of DeLillo's childhood—a Bronx in the process of rapid urban renewal, scarred by crime and arson, and then showing signs of re-birth, thanks to municipal investment, in the 1990s.[25]

Underworld begins on 3 October 1951 at the Polo Grounds in Upper Manhattan on the day the New York Giants won the National League pennant against the Brooklyn Dodgers—which was also the day the Soviet Union announced its successful testing of the atomic bomb. From here, the text a-chronologically charts the interconnected stories of the USA's involvement in the Cold War, the transformation of the Italo-American Bronx after the completion of the Cross-Bronx Expressway, the New York mafia's mobilisation of the city's garbage cartels and heroin trade, and the relentless pursuit, by a series of baseball memorabilia collectors, of the ball that was hit for the home run that won the game. Waste functions as both thematic backdrop and plot element throughout: the protagonist, Nick Shay, is a waste management expert; his brother Matt is a nuclear scientist specialising in the re-routing and effective disposal of atomic waste; and among the sub-plots are the nun Sister Edgar's attempts to engage with orphan children living in the junkyards of the Bronx; J Edgar Hoover's efforts to mount a case against the Mafia underworld via evidence found in their garbage; and a collage artist, Klara Sax, looking to make her mark on the wastelands surrounding a defunct air base in the Nevada desert by re-purposing old fighter planes. Through these interconnected narratives, DeLillo implies that twentieth-century American history is embedded in American waste and that our interpretation of particular forms of American waste illuminates our own ideological biases. Whether we view an old baseball or a used condom as items to be thrown away, or as historical relics, says more about us than it does about the items themselves: and

[handwritten margin notes: "DeLillo: the meaning of waste ≠ Beckett's waste as impediment to meaning and use"]

[handwritten left margin note: "garbological method"]

our efforts to extract meaning from them suggests an effort to put those items to use. To investigate waste for historical clues is thus a recuperative process. While perhaps not legitimising our excesses, such investigations allow us to redeem them, or at least find redemptive aspects in them. To attribute a story to our leavings is to locate them in a broader economy of meaning.

However, *Underworld* is also at pains to show the ease with which re-use can be subsumed by the mainstream or turned into a commercial enterprise, and the perils of viewing the present as past. Shay tells us that he and his wife "s[ee] products as garbage even when they s[it] gleaming on store shelves, yet unbought"—they don't say "What kind of casserole will that make?" but rather "What kind of garbage will that make?" (*U*, 121). Such a perspective exemplifies Jameson's definition of late capitalism's "perception of the present as history," which "de-familiarises it and allows us that distance from immediacy which is at length characterised as a historical perspective." For Jameson, "what is at stake is essentially a process of reification whereby we draw back from our immersion in the here and now (not yet identified as a "present") and grasp it as a kind of thing—not merely a 'present' but a present that can be dated and called the eighties or the fifties" (Jameson, 284).

For DeLillo, this perception of the present as past is tied to the nature of consumerism at the end of the twentieth century, a context characterised by consumers' awareness of their purchases' future obsolescence. He amplifies this concern in his ironic depiction of "garbage guerrilla" Jesse Detweiler, whom scholars have read as a caricature of notorious 1970s garbologist AJ Weberman.[26] A disconnected intellectual who has become enamoured with the very thing he was initially critiquing, Detweiler views waste management as integral to civilization itself: the successful empire is the empire with the most sophisticated disposal methods. No longer a part of the resistance, Detweiler chases book deals and personal accolades while championing the transformation of landfills and nuclear waste sites into cultural heritage sites that will feed a collective "nostalgia for the banned materials of civilization" (*U*, 286). Through this depiction, DeLillo suggests that the capacity for our excretions to subsume us goes beyond the physical—it is not just the physical space taken up by garbage, or what toxic emissions might do to our bodies, that is at stake, but their role in the shaping of individual and cultural identity. Lest we forget, the waste matter Shay and Detweiler are contemplating is the physical remnant of Cold War consumerist ideology, which equated consumerism with patriotism. In weaving waste management into an abstract, immemorial narrative about desire and paranoia, Detweiler glosses over recent history, ignoring the role that the ideology fuelling over-consumption throughout the Cold War played in creating the mountains of discards he is contemplating. The landfill's awe-inspiring magnitude and the prospect of what it might convey to future generations has effectively obscured its origins, in a fashion eerily reminiscent of Marx's theory of com-modity fetishism. Detweiler's championing of the historiographical use of waste negates the actual past and overlooks the fact that he is observing a residue of the USA's efforts to retain global sovereignty.

The problems inherent to reading waste historically are amplified by *Underworld's* inter-layering of past and present, which DeLillo himself has described as an attempt to "wor[k] back" in time and underscore his concern with the enduring qualities of memory.[27] But although the backward gaze reflects an effort to make reparations for past mistakes, DeLillo repeatedly shows us the fraught nature of such an attempt. On the one hand, the repeated depiction of characters searching through piles of antiques, landfills, and their own memories suggests that if any kind of redemption is to be had, it is from the sifting process itself—from the *faith* in our capacity to make meaning from our discards. On the other hand, the framing of these investigations suggests the naïveté of such faith: the investigator will merely find what he is seeking and re-affirm his individual identity within that of the collective.

This critique of historiography is closely related to a broader concern with the construction of national and cultural myths. US involvement in the Cold War was financed largely by a civilian-consumption system. As Maurie J. Cohen notes, military production throughout the Cold War was paid for by tax revenue generated by the conjoined growth of civil-ian incomes and consumption, which were in turn predicated on an ever-expanding production of disposable goods.[28] Emily S. Rosenberg likewise contends that the USA won the Cold War thanks to consumerism's hold not only on the imagination of Russians living in the Soviet Union but that of Americans themselves.[29] *Underworld* is haunted by the repercussions of the Cold War myth that linked consumption with patriotism: figuratively, in the disorientation of its central characters, and physically, by the sheer magnitude of consumer waste the Cold War left behind, and that the coun-try continues to produce, having grown accustomed to mass consumption.

Thus, recycling in the novel is charged with associations of atonement—a palliative to ameliorate the past, and legitimise consumption, as exempli-fied by Shay's meditation on the "redemptive qualities of the things we use and discard" (*U*, 810), and his faith in the redemptive potential of the recycling process. The Shay family's separation of glass from plastics, tin from card, creates a sense of order via ritual, to which Shay self-consciously draws our attention by narrating it repeatedly. A visit to the recycling plant is framed as the closest we can come to undoing our actions, while allowing us to then go home and continue making the same mistakes:

> The tin, the paper, the plastics, the styrofoam. It all flies down the conveyor belts, four hundred tons a day, assembly lines of garbage, sorted, compressed and baled, transformed in the end to square-edged units, products again, wire-bound and smartly stacked and ready to be marketed. [...] Look how [our discards] come back to us, alight with a kind of brave aging. [...] The parents look out the windows through the methane mist and the planes come out of the mountains and align for their approach and the trucks are arrayed [...] bringing in the unsorted slop, the gut squalor of our lives, and taking the baled and bound units out into the world again, the chunky product blocks, pristine, newsprint for newsprint, tin for tin, and we all feel better when we leave. (*U*, 810)

Shay's reverence for the redemptive possibilities of his industry shines through this majestic passage: the recycling plant is where we might all atone for our consumer sins. This is not about making new: it is about making good the old. And yet his comment, "and we all feel better when we leave," is anticlimactic, indicating recognition that this is a flawed faith. As a waste management expert, Shay knows that recycling is not a religion, but an industry that serves the interests of other industries, and the novel reminds us of this in repeated references to its corporate nature and involvement with other concerns, both legal and not. The reverent tone thus amplifies a broader unease regarding what Heather Rogers has termed the "greenwashing" of industry's excesses—the use of recycling to justify production and divert attention away from the need for waste reduction at the source (Rogers, 170–174). DeLillo's narrative suggests the deep connection between the lexicon of green capitalism and that of spiritual cleansing and atonement.

In turn, *Underworld* shows one further facet of capitalism's capacity to subsume both the military industrial, xenophobic, and paranoid discourses of yesterday, and the quasi-religious ones the present deploys to atone for them—as exemplified by the explicit linking of waste and weapons in the novel's last section, *Kapital*. According to the Kazakh nuclear waste capitalist Viktor, whose company vaporises nuclear waste, "Waste is the secret history, the underhistory of weapons," a "dark multiplying by-product" of weapon-making which no one thought about during the Cold War (*U*, 791). Viktor likens his work to "the way archaeologists dig out the history of early cultures, every sort of bone heap and broken tool, literally from under the ground" (U, 791). His job is, essentially, to uncover the past and obliterate it for profit.

Perhaps more ironically, Viktor's story exemplifies a certain entrepreneurial spirit uniquely related to the waste management industry of the late 1970s and early 1980s. As government and industry struggled to deal with where to "put" waste and who was to foot the bill, incineration was posited as a space- and cost-saving alternative to landfills, with, too, money-earning potential for anyone clever enough to find a buyer. Often referred to with the more benign term "waste to energy incineration" in reference to the process's potential capacity to convert organic waste into heat or electricity, the concept of burning waste away implied that waste could be gotten rid of for good. Meanwhile, the notion of converting it into energy appealed to the American entrepreneurial ethos.[30] The process only lost credence after the burning of polymers (the most common plastic found in packaging) was found to produce dioxine, a powerful compound that had gained notoriety during the Vietnam War due to its associations with Agent Orange and DDT (which DeLillo incorporates into the plot of *Underworld*[31]). When burned, ordinary household waste had the potential to be as lethal as the chemical compounds being used in the deforestation of Vietnam. Thus America's anxieties about waste incineration became conflated with a whole host of associations with the Cold War and Vietnam (Miller, 11; 240). The failure of the entrepreneurial ethos, the involvement of gangster capitalism with the waste management industry, and the ultimate recognition of waste's potentially toxic effects were exemplified, in 1987, by the much-cited story of the Mobro 4000, the barge of privately purchased garbage whose owner was unable to find a buyer, and which thus spent the latter half of 1987 drifting around the New York Bay area (Miller, 4–14).

To acknowledge incineration's toxic effects, at this moment in the country's history, was to acknowledge waste's endurance: as Viktor asserts, that "what we excrete comes back to consume us" (U, 791). It will not be moved on. *Underworld's* waste managers are alive to these complexities and they give utterance to the nation's waste fears. Shay and Glassic's Eastern counterpart's project fundamentally parodies the entrepreneurial spirit that simultaneously shaped the course of American sanitation engineering from the 1930s onwards, the country's attempts to commercialise waste removal at the end of the century, and its ongoing modes of shipping waste overseas. Viktor's mythology of waste is thus but a thinly veiled version of late capitalism as we know it and an amplified version of the corporate "greenwashing" discussed by Heather Rogers (Rogers, 170–174).

"Longing on a Large Scale"[32]: Nostalgia, Collecting, and Waste

DeLillo's novels complicate the discussions addressed thus far by exploring very different forms of re-use. Recycling for Nick Shay serves to atone for his criminal youth, as well as the Cold War ethos of overconsumption, while Klara Sax salvages junk to make art. The homeless scavengers in *Underworld* and *Great Jones Street* subsist on others' waste, while a junkie in *Great Jones Street* deliriously suggests transnational "underwear exchange" as a means to reach world peace (*GJS*, 70, 78) and *Running Dog's* Moll Robbins fantasises about how clothing exchange might allow people to "get in touch with other's feelings" (*RD*, 42). Alongside these very disparate acts of practical, aesthetic, and ecological re-use, DeLillo examines the redemptive potential of memorabilia collecting, whose historiographical associations he relates to the enforced nostalgia of the 1970s. In his study of twentieth-century modernity, Marshall Berman ascribes the environmental movement to the decade's renewed interest in home, family, and neighbourhood.[33] The burgeoning green movement, with its attendant grass roots efforts and earth art experimentations, was also an effort to re-connect with the natural landscape of the country's forefathers.[34] Another aspect of this nostalgic thrust was the rehabilitation of ethnic history and ethnic memory (Berman, 333). This is not to say that *Underworld's* nostalgia-ridden characters have ecological sympathies but that their nostalgia forms part of a broader, collective nostalgia—the grand-scale longing that makes history, as DeLillo describes it in the novel's first passage (*U*, 11)—which is in turn incorporated into the act of recycling that is the book itself.

This nostalgic thrust is apparent in the quest for the baseball, to which the novel's central characters attribute commercial and historical value. Transported, at one point, all the way to Russia on a rubbish barge, and riding in the back seat of the Texas Highway Killer's car, the ball ends up in geriatric memorabilia collector Marvin Lundy's basement—a mausoleum to America's past, a quasi-shrine to the Cold War and all of the period's unspoken fears. This underground burial re-enacts the burrowing instinct fostered by the Cold War, as well as further emphasising the novel's concern with the connections between grand narrative and personal. DeLillo himself has highlighted this dualism, acknowledging his interest in the interplay between the story of defunct places and practices and the framework of global events.[35] Most recently, in an interview commemorating the 60th anniversary of the game that inspired the novel, DeLillo commented that the game:

seemed to me wedged between significant world events. [...] Brooklyn's collective memory still bears [its image]. The significance of baseball, more than other sports, lies in the very nature of the game—slow and spread out and rambling. It's a game of history and memory, a kind of living archive.[36]

Marvin Lundy has spent the years following his retirement amassing that living archive in his basement, travelling entire continents in his quest to collect the remnants of the game, including the ball from the Giants-Dodgers game. He eventually retrieves it from a plastic sandwich bag "crammed in a cardboard box filled with junky odds and ends" (U, 180). His collection attracts visits from fellow baseball fans, in whom he identifies a similar nostalgia that goes beyond baseball, relating to the anxieties and paranoia of the Cold War era: they "surrender [themselves] to longing, to listen to [...] anecdotal texts, all the passed-down stories [...] stories that Marvin had been collecting for half a century—the deep eros of memory that separates baseball from other sports" (U, 171). To let go would be to acknowledge the futility of those efforts and the unimportance of the stories found. Marvin notes:

People who save these bats and balls and preserve the old stories through the spoken word and know the nicknames of a thousand players, we're here in our basements with tremendous history on our walls. [...] There's men in the coming years they'll pay fortunes for these objects. They'll pay unbelievable. Because this is desperation speaking. (U, 182)

DeLillo shows us how the assembly of remnants can function as a nostalgic means of retracing individual and collective history, and how waste objects can serve powerful metonymic and symbolic functions that link to both the physical and cultural body, bearing associations of eros and death alike. Lundy's comments also draw attention to the subjective nature of the taxonomic distinctions that distinguish value and waste. By categorising the ball as memorabilia, Lundy situates it within a system of things that, in contrast to other commodities, *accrue* value with time rather than lose it—assigning it to the category of Thompsonian "durable" (Thompson, 7). Lundy's collectibles are the antithesis of the products in the supermarket that Nick Shay cannot help picturing "as garbage, even when they s[it] gleaming on store shelves, yet unbought" (U, 121). The baseball itself is framed as an object that has been *saved* from the path to landfill—its retrieval from a box of "junky odds and ends" is an intervention of sorts into the natural fate of commodities. Like the other seemingly meaningless objects in DeLillo's other novels—*Running Dog's* Hitler film, the mind-altering drug in *Great Jones Street*—the baseball gains subjective meaning when examined through the eyes of the person who has deemed it worth keeping. It is by the grace of subjective valuation that the baseball is salvaged.

Perhaps more importantly, DeLillo shows us the ease with which waste can be deployed in totalising nostalgic discourses. Collecting is a search "for big history" in which the objects collected are often anything but innocuous (*U*, 174). The popularity of Naziana (which Lundy mentions) reminds us that collecting is never politically neutral. DeLillo himself, at the time of the novel's publication, noted that the novel's thematic concern with longing stemmed from his identification of an emergent nostalgic, uncritical, stance towards the Cold War.[37] Lundy embodies that uncritical stance and shows the extent to which nostalgia can neutralise politics—nowhere more so than in his uncritical comparison of the baseball's size to the radioactive core of the atomic bomb (*U*, 172). DeLillo amplifies this problematic dimension of nostalgic collecting by framing Lundy's collecting obsession as pathology: Lundy is less a collector than a hoarder (DeLillo may have even been aware, when he was writing *Underworld*, of Randy O. Frost's and Gail Steketee's efforts throughout the 1980s to have the condition formally diagnosed[38]). Hoarding differs from collecting in its perceived lack of system—to the onlooker, it appears that the hoarder will keep anything and everything they find until they are buried beneath these possessions. It is thus fitting that hoarding is one of Lundy's many pathologies, which include a paranoid aversion towards contamination, dust, and disease, and phobia about his own bodily emissions. Likewise, the insanity of purpose driving his collecting causes his mental faculties to decay. Indeed, while arguing that his collection is "innocuous," the disintegration of his narrative as he attempts to recount it belies the opposite, suggesting that, like the garbologist Jesse Detwiler, he has been subsumed by his passion:

> He forgot some names and mangled others. He lost whole cities, placing them in the wrong time zones. He described how he followed false leads into remote places. He climbed the stairs to raftered upper rooms and looked in old trunks among the grandmother's linen and the photographs of the dead. "I said to myself a thousand times. Why do I want this thing? What does it mean? Who has it?" (*U*, 176)

The quest for the thing, as recounted by Marvin, resists logic and intent; it suggests the incoherence of the paranoid era out of which it sprang. This incoherence in turn is performed within the text, as DeLillo interrupts the third person account of Marvin's narrative with a numbered list of 14 impressions garnered during the quest for the ball, "the whole strewn sense of what they [he, people, the nation] remember and forget" (*U*, 176). The list self-referentially comments upon its inability to tell the story straight. The desperation thus occurs on a dual plane, collective and individual. The process of collecting seeks to dig up history, but it risks both killing and entombing its practitioner in the process. It is the desperation of the collective examining the remains of the Cold War and mourning an ultimately futile national project into which so much effort was invested, and the desperation of the individual who, in the aftermath of the era, perceives himself to be "the lost man of history"—part of a "fraternity of missing men" uncertain of their place in the so-called New World Order (*U*, 182).

Underworld's dealings with longing, then, are fraught: while DeLillo's artists look to make sense of the past on an individual and collective level, the narratives themselves repeatedly underscore memory's capacity to aestheticise—and *anesthetise*—the past, and for traumatic memories to ultimately overwhelm those seeking to make sense of them. However, DeLillo suggests a potentially redeeming aspect to these fraught forms of nostalgia. To examine an old baseball and think about whether it can be thought of as historically or culturally symbolic in any way is to identify the narrative aspect beyond its commercial potential or physical qualities, and to see this narrative as important enough to render it distinct from, say, a banana skin. It is also to recognise that the process of attaching meaning to discards is also in evolution and changes in relation to our own circumstances. The historiography of objects and the narrative(s) we attach to our waste are unstable and ultimately incomplete.

"THE BIGGEST SECRETS"[39]: FRESH KILLS, CONSUMERISM, AND THE COLD WAR

The national and transnational aspects of DeLillo's depictions of waste, their interrogation of the culture of late capitalism during and following the Cold War, and their insight into how national identity and myth are constructed can only be truly understood when examined in conjunction with DeLillo's depiction of Staten Island's Fresh Kills, the presence that underlies *Underworld*'s many different narratives, and which can be seen reflected in the novel's own layered structure. The landfill, the different meanings his characters ascribe to it, and the parallel constructions we find his other characters making throughout the rest of the novel raise important questions about the extent to which one can, in fact, read waste. Strikingly, for all DeLillo's attention to the physical size and scope of Fresh Kills, DeLillo scholars have largely read his depiction of the space metonymically or psychoanalytically, either as a cultural bricolage or a reflection of consumer excess. Ruth Helyer reads waste in the novel as the "unwanted baggage" that "sullies our ability to conform to an acceptable prototype"[40]; for John Duvall, the landfill "figure[s] spiritually wasted lives" (Duvall, 24); while Mark Osteen and David Cowart both read it as an embodiment of the protagonist's personal history.[41] In none of these readings are the actual landfill's geophysical characteristics, or its charged socio-political significance in American history, taken into account (see Figs. 5.1 and 5.2). Moreover, it is surely significant that at the time of the novel's writing, Fresh Kills was (very publicly) scheduled for closure, and thus on its way to becoming, like the other defunct spaces of the novel (the Polo Grounds where the Thompson game took place, the razed streets of the Italian Bronx), an historical relic. Recognising this dimension of Fresh Kills allows

Fig. 5.1   Fresh Kills Landfill, mid-twentieth century. New York City Municipal Archives

Fig. 5.2 Fresh Kills Landfill prior to its closure

us to extend the conservative and positivistic assessments of waste to which scientific or environmental discourses on waste are generally confined (and into which DeLillo criticism does often risk falling) and consider the landfill as an artefact. This more pluralistic examination of waste, which is, I argue, DeLillo's underlying intent, allows us to understand his project in something other than straightforwardly dystopian or redemptive terms.

The effect of Fresh Kills' size and its impending death on its perception by *Underworld*'s characters plays an important role in shaping the novel's landfill passages. The characters' responses to the space aptly reflect the controversies Fresh Kills evinced from its opening, in 1946, by New York's most controversial urban planner Robert Moses, until its much-publicised eventual closure on 11 March 2001, after decades of environmental lobbying (Moses himself had termed it a "temporary" solution).[42] This closure was scheduled several years before *Underworld*'s publication in 1997, and the landfill itself was frequently under scrutiny by the press. Rudolph Giuliani's much-publicised speech to the people of Staten Island in July 1997—four months before the book's US publication—announcing the first stage in phasing out the landfill, provides a useful example of the public's view of the space:

> For Staten Islanders, the landfill has been an unfair burden, an eyesore, impinging on the quality of life for individuals and businesses. As they have seen and smelled the garbage steadily mount over the years, the people of Staten Island have shown remarkable patience. I thank them for that. From here we can see what they have endured.[43]

Elizabeth Royte notes the political dimension of this promise—a Republican, Giuliani's commitment to close the landfill was also an effort to please Staten Island's primarily Republican constituents.[44] By contrast, as DeLillo's character, Brian Glassic, sees it, Fresh Kills has an almost mythological importance:

> It was science fiction and pre-history, garbage arriving 24 hours a day, hundreds of workers. [...] He found the sight inspiring. All this ingenuity and labour, this delicate effort to fit maximum waste into diminishing space. The towers of the World Trade Center were visible in the distance and he sensed a poetic balance between that idea and this one. [...] He looked at all that soaring garbage and knew for the first time what his job was about. Not engineering or transportation or source reduction. He dealt in human behaviour, people's habits and impulses, their uncontrollable needs and innocent wishes, maybe their passions, certainly their excesses and indulgences but their kindness too, their generosity, and the question was how to keep this mass metabolism from overwhelming us. The landfill showed him smack-on how the waste stream ended, where all the appetites and hankerings, the sodden second thoughts came runneling out, the things you wanted ardently and then did not. (*U*, 185)

Glassic emphasises the extent to which Fresh Kills appears to participate in a greater human narrative of needs and wishes, appetites and hankerings (*U*, 185). The landfill is presented as a record of human idiosyncrasies whose immensity dislocates all sense of perspective (*U*, 185). The reference to the World Trade Center in the distance emphasises the landfill's necessity to the maintenance of the capitalist order—a "poetic balance" links this space to the corporations that manufacture things, the banks that circulate money, and the people that buy goods. This is the end point of it all, and we *need* that end point because it *allows us* to keep making things, buying things, and selling things. At the same time, Fresh Kills' depiction as a "mass metabolism" suggests it is a living, pulsating, shape-shifting thing, home for gases and toxins and matter in the process of decomposition—something akin to Bruno Latour's[45] concept of the "quasi-object quasi-subject"—a hybrid material entity that lends itself to both "hard" empirical studies (in relation to its physical appearance) and to "soft" qualitative analysis (in relation to its sociological role).[46] As the repository for objects divested of their commodity value and thus social use, the landfill is defiantly a-social, defiantly "hard"; but as a repository of human possessions and reflective of a larger economic system, it is redolent with social meaning. It is this very hybridity that instigates Glassic's awe.

The second thing to notice here is how Glassic relates the landfill to time. Fresh Kills is both pre-historic and science fiction—the thing that predates humans and that will outlast them. Waste is the thing that endures, but it is also reminiscent of the primordial slime from which we emerged. Glassic's awe is thus directed not only at Fresh Kills, but at himself, as one of the select few who are able to understand the landfill's importance, and who are *shaping its narrative:*

> He saw himself for the first time as a member of an esoteric order, they were adepts and seers, crafting the future, the city planners, the waste managers, the compost technicians, the landscapers who would build hanging gardens here, make a park one day out of every kind of used and lost and eroded object of desire. The biggest secrets are the ones spread open before us. (*U*, 185)

The reference to "the landscapers who would build hanging gardens here" is an explicit reference to the plans for the rehabilitation of the space and its transformation into a state park. This is something of an epitaph—a swan song to the landfill in the face of its imminent closure. It's a very odd thing to be lingering on, the future of a closing landfill, and it plays with our sense of narrative time. Firstly, because landfills are generally regarded as endpoints for things—not places for *beginning* something, and certainly not things worth mourning when they're gone. Secondly, because the closure, in the novel, has yet to occur: this is the present perceiving itself as past, a sanitation engineer imagining future generations' experience of the space following its transformation. And thirdly, because it amounts to a commemoration, or mythology, of post-war consumer culture, envisaged by one of the novel's most self-deluded characters. As his very name suggests, Glassic subscribes to "classic" capitalist notions of achievement and success. His recognition that "the biggest secrets are the ones spread open before us" is darkly humorous, suggesting that Glassic himself is blind to the true meaning of the expanse in front of him. Where Glassic treats the landfill as a legible space—one that only a select few such as he can decode—DeLillo suggests that this is anything but the case.

DeLillo's articulation of the symbolically charged relationship between the landfill and the World Trade Center was uncannily prescient. Elizabeth Royte recounts how Staten Islanders reassessed Fresh Kills when it was re-opened, barely six months after its closure, to house rubble and human remains from Ground Zero: "The landfill had been the shame of the island: now it was hallowed ground upon which a memorial, with federal funds, would soon be built" (Royte, 101). Perhaps referencing DeLillo, Royte adds that "though much has been made by some writers of the majesty of enormous landfills," Fresh Kills' majesty following the attack on the Twin Towers was associated less with its size than with the human remains it now housed. The space's new status as a mass grave effectively confirmed DeLillo's articulation, throughout *Underworld*, of waste's amenability to re-interpretation and its unique capacity to accrue new meaning(s)—although he could not have foreseen what form this would take.

Interestingly, Glassic's self-belief throughout this passage is reminiscent of the self-mythologising tendencies of the waste disposal industry itself and its close association with private industry (Rogers, 70). Since its birth, in the 1890s, from the science of bacteriology, waste management has been figured as a science in order to augment its authority and political sway. The discipline's very culture was founded on and shaped by business interests, and by the principles of free-market development, and has, throughout the last century, been subject to monopolies—first by the Mob, and then by three major firms, WMI, USA Waste, and BFI.[47] Glassic is figured as a senior member of one such monopoly—a deluded emperor with no concept that the landfill's biggest secret is that its contents will outlast everyone, even him. The "sting of enlightenment" Glassic feels in the face of the space is a false epiphany, which DeLillo frames as a small-minded rationalisation on the part of the novel's personification of capitalist ideology.

Nick Shay, tellingly, instead sees the landfill in starkly dystopian terms, as anticipating our undoing. The Jesuits, he tells us early in the novel, "taught [him] to examine things for second meanings and deeper connections. Were they thinking about waste?" (*U*, 88). Having been schooled in the discipline of identifying relationships between things, and the underlying subtext, he recognises not only the immensity of what lies before him but his complicity in its creation. He is not part of an esoteric order, but, rather, of an industry adept at couching their government lobbying in the language of "victims" and at presenting commercial waste management as a right. The greatest secret, he suggests throughout the novel, is that there is much money to be made from the process of dealing with the things the world does not want. Yes, "people look at their garbage differently now, seeing every bottle and crushed carton in a planetary context" (*U*, 88), as he notes, but this awareness has created new markets. Simultaneously rambling and eloquent, Shay's dystopian analysis provides a sharp counter to Glassic's idealised, fervid view of the landfill and his own role as its high priest. The biggest secret, DeLillo suggests, is the inherent semantic fluidity of the landfill and its contents. All things are on their way to land- fill, but the landfill itself can be viewed, variously, as a sublime vision or a sign of our fast-approaching end.

Glassic and Shay's contemplations of Fresh Kills and the rehabilitative role of the waste management industry point to a third issue: the extent to which the recycling industry is complicit in obscuring the effects of consumption. Considered alongside the novel's passages on capitalism in the post-digital age, in which the abstract nature of trading is depicted as severing our ties to the material world, the future rehabilitation of Fresh Kills appears less as an ecological project of redemption than as a further cloaking. "Capital," Shay tells us in the opening of a section in the novel aptly titled "Das Kapital," "burns off the nuance in a culture. Foreign investment, global markets, cor- porate acquisitions, the flow of information through transnational media, the attenuating influence of money that's electronic and sex that's cyber- spaced, untouched money and computer-safe sex" (*U*, 785). The passage points to both the homogenising effect of capitalism as a whole and the particularity of the logic of *late* capitalism—or, perhaps more accurately, what Zygmunt Bauman calls *liquid* capitalism. Bauman defines this as an era defined by virtual commodities, in which capital is able to "travel fast and travel light," while its "lightness and motility" turn into the "paramount source of uncertainty for all the rest."[48] Society itself is viewed as a "matrix of random connections and disconnections and of an essentially infinite volume of possible permutations" (Bauman, 3). DeLillo's depiction of "the flow of information through transnational media" and "the attenuating influence of money that's electronic" encapsulates the ethos of flexible accumulation, in which the very traces of our exchanges are "planed away" (*U*, 786).[49] What happens, *Underworld* asks us, when the evidence of our actions is no longer visible—when the landfill is no longer there, in Glassic's words, to "assault [our] complacency and vague shame"—thus appearing, on the surface at least, to erase the consequences to our consumption? (*U*, 185).

Perhaps it is not only the spectre of Fresh Kills and its potential to "subsume us" that haunts the novel but the prospect of its closure and the effects that might have on "planing away" our consumer guilt. The landfill, DeLillo suggests, has played a similar role in the collective unconscious to that of the Soviet-US threat during the Cold War—haunting and reassuring in equal measure. The biggest secret is perhaps that the country needs Fresh Kills not only practically, but symbolically.

The dark nature of what Glassic terms the great "secrets […] laid open before us" provides much of the subtext to Part Five of *Underworld*, "Better Things For Better Living Through Chemistry" (*U*, 500). A reference to DuPont's advertising slogan from 1935 to 1982, the title draws attention to the involvement of the plastics and synthetic ingredients industries in weapons manufacture, while the section itself interlaces the idyllic description of a sanitised home in 1950s suburbia with fragmented citations from consumer warning labels.[50] DeLillo undermines his pastoral vision by making frequent reference to the Soviet threat. As such, the section not only enacts what Susan Strasser has termed the USA's "cultural reverence for convenience"[51] but suggests a connection between this reverence and efforts to stamp out otherness—a form of localised nationalism. We also find here an unexpected connection between homemaking and protection against nuclear threat, as if in sterilising the home, such threat is kept at bay. As Strasser notes, the cult of convenience was borne out of the application of Taylorist ideologies of industrial efficiency to the marketing of domestic appliances as means to liberate housewives from physical effort (Strasser, 183). Throughout the 1950s, popular magazines were keen to emphasise the "freedom" garnered by the emergence of "miracles in packaging and processing" (Strasser, 269). At the same time, marketers sought to divert attention from the products' toxic ingredients and the companies' involvement in weapons manufacture by promoting the goods themselves as weapons in the fight against communism. These goods became "a vehicle in the political and ideological clash of capitalism and communism" (Strasser, 269).

DeLillo emphasises the dark underside to the 1950s' ideologically charged ethos of domestic efficiency in his montage-like narration of an afternoon in 1957, during which future bomb-head Eric sits in his room, masturbating into a condom, while his suburban housewife mother, Erica, makes "miracles" with that other synthetic wonder of modernity, Jell-O. In another nod to the "better things" achieved by DuPont, DeLillo tells us that "doing things with Jell-O was just about the best way to improve [Erica's] mood" (*U*, 532); in this case, unease over the Russians' recent launching of Sputnik

(*U*, 514, 518). The emphasis on Jell-O in particular is significant. As Erica knows, Jell-O is not one dish: it is many. Initially marketing it as a miracle made possible by the refrigerator, General Electric and Frigidaire were keen to promote Jell-O as a cost-effective means to transform leftovers in a seemingly endless process of recycling and reinvention (Strasser, 210). *Your Frigidaire* (1934) argued that "good things" could be made "out of odds and ends, which would otherwise be wasted," resulting in "a great contribution to better living," a message that posited the domestic economist as a culinary *bricoleur* and indeed anticipated DuPont's marketing angle.[52]

For Erica, Jell-O is miraculous not only for its capacity to give new life to leftovers, but in its semantic fluidity:

> Sometimes she called it her Jell-O chicken mousse and sometimes she called it her chicken mousse Jell-O. This was one of [its] thousand convenient things. [...] The word went anywhere, front or back or in the middle. It was a push-button word, the way so many things were push-button now, the way the whole world opened behind a button that you pushed. (*U*, 517)

Both Jell-O the word and Jell-O as a concept recuperate the old and turn it into something new; they open up the world to the housewife, freeing up time, providing the satisfaction that comes with discovering one's artistic capacities. They underscore the notion, as expressed by Eric in contemplating the contents of the refrigerator with its slots and shelves, of the fundamentally "unspoiled and ever renewable" nature of the world (*U*, 518). But the depiction is ironic, insofar as the entire passage is interspersed with fragments of consumer packaging warning labels such as "If swallowed, induce vomiting at once," that could be found as readily on toxic household cleaning products as on an aerosol food can like whipped cream or canned cheese (*U*, 515–519). The description of technology's capacity to "open up" the world is interrupted by the disclaimer "May cause discolouration of urine or faeces," while the reference to pushing buttons is an implicit reminder of nuclear threat. Erica's obliviousness to these threats amplifies the novel's overarching concern with the unknowable, while her awe for the things her kitchen appliances can do highlights one of the greatest paradoxes of modernity: that our advances merely accelerate the path to our destruction. Just as Glassic intuits that the biggest secrets are the ones spread open before us without knowing what they actually are, Erica imagines a world opening up to her without any knowledge that her son, one day, will be involved in blowing it up. DeLillo's depiction of a circumscribed act of recuperation—the making of Jell-O from leftovers—in the midst of a broader context of horror and dread suggests that the biggest secret is our own naïveté, and our capacity to imagine ourselves as architects, or indeed stewards, of our own destinies. The sanitation engineer overseeing his mound of trash and the domestic housewife immersed in moulding coagulated leftovers show the extent to which we blindly seek to find meanings in our bits and pieces, and to cast ourselves in the role of artist, visionary, or executor.

DeLillo's juxtaposition of technological innovation and financial privilege against the toxicity of the materials used in the name of progress shows us the distancing, almost sterilising effect of our devices, and the antithesis between these effects and our most carnal desires and base bodily functions. In so doing, he suggests that one aspect of our disgust when confronted with the sight or smell of trash, excrement, or rotting food has to do with a more general disconnection from the material world. We have become objectified—or reified—to a new extent, insofar as our disconnectedness from our work is now coupled with a disconnection from lived experience itself. His depictions of artists seeking new means of expression, however, extend the novel beyond a straightforward articulation of consumer desire and disgust. The novel's meditations on art and literature's role in late capitalism amplify our anxieties about mass production's effect on the cultural and geophysical landscape, while suggesting the resistance of these anxieties to coherent analysis, discourse, or representation.

We see this most clearly in the character of Klara Sax, a former painter and junk collagist who developed her craft in New York's Soho district in the 1960s and 1970s. Sax's backstory situates her implicitly alongside the likes of *Nouveau Réalistes* such as César Baldaccini and Arman (who we discussed in Chap. 3), and neo-Dadaists such as Robert Rauschenberg and John Chamberlain. These were artists who pioneered "junk culture," extending the historical avant-garde's preoccupation with commodification, but this time to directly critique consumer culture and planned obsolescence through "the throwaway material of cities, as it collects in drawers, cupboards, attics, dustbins, gutters, waste lots, and city dumps."[53] For Anna Dezeuze, the most interesting aspect of 1960s junk art was its expression not of the binary opposition between parts and whole or criticality and affirmation, but "the movement *between* these oppositions—the dynamic passage between the recognisable object and the transformed artwork or the 'stuff' of junk."[54] Their most salient feature was "not so much the relation between the parts and the whole as the suggestion that this relation remains fluid" (Dezeuze, 58). Junk art was predicated on the transience of commodity flows—the ability of things to move between states, to be either reconfigured into new forms or to become more amorphous, more waste-like. They were expressions of a dialectical approach to waste, which is to say, an effort to understand it both as end point and beginning, as once-commodity and as commodity-potential.[55]

Interestingly, DeLillo does not depict Sax's early junk aesthetic, but introduces her, rather, at the end of her career. Here she is a woman in her seventies, at work on rehabilitating B52s into a "landscape painting [that] use[s] the landscape itself"—a project that, in terms of size at least, competes with Fresh Kills (*U*, 70). It is an immense endeavour, a celebration of the end of the Cold War but also a meditation on its legacy. The introduction of Sax's project at the outset of the novel highlights *Underworld's* preoccupation with posterity. By following a game that coincided with the beginning of the Cold War era with an account of that era's material remainders, DeLillo is making a point about historiography itself. The depiction of a graveyard of bomber planes that never took off signals a stalled modernity, while Sax herself acknowledges her endeavour's belatedness (*U*, 70). Occurring in 1992, her installation art project is but a dim echo of the (real life) sculptor whom she acknowledges to Shay as having "gotten there first" (*U*, 70; 277). Between 1920 and 1950, Sabato Rodia assembled building materials to create the structure of Watts Towers, which he decorated with found objects in a structure meant to represent the diversity of the local community: he called the finished work *Nuestro Pueblo*, Spanish for "our town" (see Figs. 5.3 and 5.4).[56]

Sax's project differs from Rodia's, however, in that it is concerned with collective experience rather than familial. DeLillo draws our attention to this contrast in his depiction of Shay's very different response to Sabato Rodia, later in the novel. In contemplating the towers on a visit to Los Angeles, Shay imagines Rodia to be his father—another Italian American who went out one day to buy a pack of Lucky Strikes and never came back. Shay intuitively recognises that to recuperate materials is also to draw attention to the individual pieces within the collective whole, the personal within the grand narrative. In a pamphlet produced in 1961 to produce the Towers from levelling, the real Rodia described his project as an effort to do something for the people of the USA.[57] This approach—not included in the novel but well documented in accounts of Rodia's work—exemplifies Shay's understanding of the interiorised narrative embedded in the

Fig. 5.3 Sabato Rodia, Watts Towers/Nuestro Pueblo, detail

100-foot tall construction, the self-enclosed, private story to be found in the collective exteriority of public life.

We see this same interplay in Sax's own articulation of the evolution of her aesthetic. From documenting the marginal and the everyday—one of the central preoccupations of the first collagists, and, also, of 1960s murals and mosaics—Sax's junk aesthetic has come to encompass *Underworld*'s ethos of grand-scale longing. In so doing it evidences how a "local yearning" can grow into an "assembling crowd," turning into shock or mesmerised awe with a potentially ambiguous politics of its own. Waste, like history, like narrative, is subject to interpretation: hence the military's amenability to the project despite its pacifist strains. "Longing on a large scale is what makes history" but the texture of that longing is subject to circumstance (*U*, 11). As Marvin Lundy knows all too well, time's passage will change the public perception and valuation of the assembled objects, often in grotesque ways—a sentiment that echoes Murray Suskind's recognition, in *White Noise*, that "nostalgia is a product of dissatisfaction. [...] It's a settling of grievances between the present and the past. [...] War is the form nostalgia takes when men are hard-pressed to say something good about their country"

Fig. 5.4   Sabato Rodia,
Watts   Towers/Nuestro
Pueblo, detail

(*WN*, 258). Thus Sax, once derided for her junk assemblages, now receives congressional approval, donations of materials from plane manufacturers, art foundation grants, and international media coverage.

As an aesthetic project, Sax's strategy of re-painting the planes offers multiple readings. On one level, it is a project of renewal, an almost eco-logical vision. Out of the remains of a war that never actually started, she is creating a new use-value. But it also has a more ambiguous role, which scholars aside from David Evans have largely neglected.[58] Visible from the sky, this larger-than-life assemblage in the middle of the desert can be seen as the counterpart to that other, soon-to-be-rehabilitated space in the novel, Fresh Kills. Existing on the other side of the country, Sax's fighter plane-graveyard-turned-installation work suggests itself as an aesthetic counter-point, the "other," to the soon-to-be state park. The airplane project is less an ecological or pacifist attempt at reconciling land with technology or the mistakes of the past with the future, than a commemorative act. Crucially, the complexity of Sax's vision lies in her consciousness of the capacity for it to be misunderstood: "We may want to place this whole business in some bottom pit of nostalgia but in fact the men who flew these planes, and we are talking about high alert and distant early warning, we are talking about the edge of everything—well, I think they lived in a closed world with its particular omens and symbols and they were very young and horny to boot" (*U*, 77). And again: "Not that I want to bring it back. It's gone, good riddance. But the fact is" (*U*, 76). The unfinished sentence—while typical of the speech of DeLillo's characters—also suggests that discourse on waste and its recuperation is also bound to remain unfinished. Waste, like history itself, lives in time, and even the aesthetic of re-use has the capacity to be used towards violent or universalising ends—ones that obliterate the anxieties of the past left behind. Misinterpretation is as dangerous as erasure. By interlacing his depiction of the historico-politically charged site of Fresh Kills with larger ontological and metaphysical enquiries into the recuperation of warplanes, DeLillo demonstrates not only the fear of mortality that underlies our awe of landfills and recuperative art but also the complexities inherent to such subjective readings.

"[A] FORM OF COUNTERHISTORY"[59]: WASTE AND LANGUAGE

While critiquing the risk his characters' historical readings of waste run of rationalising or legitimising overconsumption, DeLillo reveals the ambiguous role that language itself plays in constructing and propagating these myths. His novels suggest that just as all objects have the potential to become waste, they also carry the potential to be re-integrated into human narrative. Through this re-integration, waste has the capacity to reveal the hidden affinities between condom manufacturing and the military industrial complex, a toxic cloud and a housewife's efforts to lose weight.

While the means DeLillo's characters adopt in their quests vary greatly, they all share a common fascination between the physical aspect of waste, its narrative import, and its affinities with the workings of language itself. In *White Noise*, Murray Suskind expresses his love for the "bold new form" of consumer packaging, terming it "the last avant-garde" (*WN*, 18); in *Underworld*, Shay contemplates the etymology of waste, and the word's "funding [of] such derivatives as empty, void, vanish and devastate" (*U*, 120). In *Great Jones Street*, Bucky Wunderlich regains the power of speech after having renounced the excesses of his celebrity lifestyle and experienced life on the street. His temporary speechlessness, here, has implications for his art (singing) but is more specifically related to the metaphorical lack of voice of the Bowery bums and vagrants he has encountered throughout the novel: the city's marginalia have no voice in the socio-political sense, and the words they speak might as well be babble. In *Running Dog*, Glen Slevy and his boss, Lomax, argue over the terms for erotica and porn, and whether these should be termed "art" or "smut" (*RD*, 31). One man's trash is another man's art, but more importantly, the words we use to define them as such are what make the difference.

For DeLillo, the whole question of where garbage should go and who should buy it and who should be responsible for it when it proves toxic, and the whole (interrelated) question of nuclear waste and where *that* should go, is inextricable from the words used to articulate it. That the sheer space taken *up* by consumer waste and the horrific effects of nuclear fallout should inspire wordless awe in the characters themselves reflects an important tension. DeLillo's project not only posits the twentieth century as a story of humankind and its leavings: it also posits that story as one resistant to coherent expression. This tension is amplified by DeLillo's understanding of the very ideas, beyond the environmental, which recycling connotes.

DeLillo's narrative style, which intersperses time periods and makes frequent use of montage, has inspired a rich array of critical responses. David Cowart argues that "the recycling theme of *Underworld* subsumes a vision of art that lends itself to conclusions about the entire DeLillo oeuvre."[60] Mark Osteen has identified the use of montage as a means of emphasising social alienation.[61] Perhaps most compellingly, David Evans has argued against the conflation of authorial vision and represented figuration, contending, instead, that to relate the two is to fall into the very trap that avant-gardism seeks to fight. "The final triumph of late capitalism," he argues, is "to turn the merely useless into raw material for future output, and to transform the resistantly non-identical into a convertible commodity" (Evans, 109–110).

Evans' argument reveals the inherent difficulty of binary readings of DeLillo's waste and complicates our understanding of his *oeuvre*, but it falls short in neglecting to consider the linguistic and semantic component of these narratives. Ira Nadel's articulation of the DeLillo *oeuvre* as systematically reclaiming language from waste—and in turn wresting meaning from it—is more accurate, as it takes into account the explicit reference, in his novels, between waste and the words used to describe it.[62] These novels, and *Underworld* above all, rely on the premise that consumerism and war, terrorist plots and organised sports, depend upon homogeneity and a totalising narrative: what Dave Bell terms the "universal third person" that is advertising's greatest success (*A*, 270). DeLillo's novels seek to peel away the universal third person and reveal the particular underneath. By articulating the narrative that connects producers, consumers, and the different kinds of waste to which our consumption practices give form, DeLillo shows the ripple effects of Western consumerism and its broader relationship with global politics.

DeLillo's explicit fascination with language's signifying capacity forms an important aspect of his figuration of the composition of history. As DeLillo himself noted in "The Power of History," an essay published just prior to *Underworld*, the excavation of defunct languages is intrinsic to the process of historiography: "In *Underworld* I searched out the word-related pleasures of memory, the smatter of old street games and the rhythms of a thousand street-corner conversations, adolescent and raw" (*TPOH*). Language is posited as a means to recall the past—the closest approximation to re-living it—not in a nostalgic sense, but as a means to rehabilitate it. DeLillo's use of non-iterative narration recalls Bill Brown's conceptualisation of repetition as "the mode of becoming historical."[63] Brown terms non-iterative narration a historiographical tool that foregrounds the inexactness of historiography as a form (Brown, 73). This reading suggests that historiography's failure to fully disclose the true nature of an event merely amplifies language's own limitations.

DeLillo signals language and waste's relationship throughout *Underworld*, including at the very basic level of plot: Nick Shay recalls that his switch from teaching English to working in waste management was driven by a sense of the affinities between studying linguistic discards and studying material effluvia (*U*, 742). Beyond this, however, DeLillo relates waste to the defunct language of erased communities. This is particularly apparent in *Underworld*'s Bronx passages, which immortalise a now extinct district via the Sicilian dialect of its inhabitants and call attention to waste as the stuff unassimilated by history. As Nadel notes, the Sicilian dialect of Shay's Bronx subverts the dominant discourse (Nadel, 188). To speak (of) dialect is to reveal the marginal and particularised and to recognise, as DeLillo articulates it, that "language can be a form of counterhistory […] allow[ing] us to find an unconstraining otherness" (*TPOH*, 4).

Language's capacity to disclose and rectify past ills is exemplified in *Underworld* by the Italian word "dietrologia," which means "the science of what is behind something. A suspicious event" (*U*, 280). Language contains within it the capacity to suggest and solicit as much as the material waste the culture itself excretes. DeLillo's project has cultivated this ethos from as early as *Great Jones Street*, in the drug-dealing Doctor Pepper's articulation of "latent history"—the history of the unsaid, the unrecorded, or the misunderstood, "events that almost took place, events that definitely took place but remain unseen and unremarked upon [...] and events that probably took place but were definitely not chronicled" (*GJS*, 72). He notes: "Latent history never tells us where we stand in the sweep of events but rather how we can get out of the way" (*GJS*, 72–73). The language of latent history is the language of waste, insofar as it is the language of the (historiographically) undervalued. *Underworld* itself seeks to narrate America's own latent history and to suggest the underside to all narrative. The challenge is to study our culture's effluvia without becoming inured to its import or lulled into complacency.

DeLillo's investigations of language and form wrest order and signification from waste, in an aesthetic that owes much to the historical avant-garde practices we examined in the second chapter. His narratives are as concerned with the politics of waste management and consumer culture and their connection with the mass production of weapons as they are with art's ability to speak out against these seemingly unstoppable processes, and language's capacity to express them coherently. His explorations of the etymology of waste and the history of dying dialects connect the trans-historical to the contemporary, the universal to the particular, and the transnational to the local. In relating urban argot and domestic particulars to global economic crises and ecological disasters, DeLillo's work shows us the links between landfill waste and national ideology, and the paranoid discourses in between.

NOTES

1. Don DeLillo. "Human Moments in World War III" (1983). *"The Angel Esmeralda" and Other Stories* (London and New York: Picador, 2011), 25–46. Henceforth, *HM*.
2. Alexandra Alter. "Author Q&A: Don DeLillo Deconstructed," *Wall Street Journal*, 29 January 2010, accessed 5 February 2016: http://www.wsj.com/articles/SB10001424052748703906204575027094208914032.

3. David Harvey. *The Condition of Postmodernity* (Oxford: Blackwell, 1991 [1989]).
4. David Harvey. *Spaces of Global Capitalism: Towards a Theory of Uneven Geographic Development* (London: Verso, 2006), 17 and 25. George Monbiot provides an excellent account of the development of the term "neoliberalism" in *How Did We Get Into This Mess? Politics, Equality, Nature* (London: Verso, 2016), dating its emergence to the early 1940s and the work of Ludwig von Mises and Friedrich Hayek.
5. David Harvey, *A Brief History of Neoliberalism* (Oxford, 2005), 23.
6. Fredric Jameson, *Postmodernism, or, the Cultural Logic of Late Capitalism* (Durham, NC: Duke University Press, 1991).
7. Diane Osen, *The Book That Changed My Life* (New York: Random House, 2002), 18.
8. Don DeLillo, *Americana* (London: Penguin, 1971), 349. Henceforth, *A*.
9. Marguerite Duras, "Madame Dodin" in *Whole Days in the Trees and Other Stories*, 105.
10. William Rathje and Cullen Murphy, *Rubbish! The Archaeology of Garbage* (New York: Harper Collins, 1992), 24.
11. See Elizabeth Fee and Steven H. Corey, *Garbage!: The history and politics of trash in New York City* (New York: New York Public Library, 1994).
12. "The Paris of the Second Empire in Baudelaire." *The Writer of Modern Life*. Ed. Michael W. Jennings (Cambridge, MA: Belknap, 2006), 46–133. Henceforth, *PSEB*.
13. Baudelaire, *Ouevres Vol. I*, fn 249. As cited in *PSEB*, 109.
14. Morrison provides an excellent reading of the poet-as-rag-picker in the last chapter of *The Literature of Waste*. Building on the "long tradition of seeing poetry as a kind of alchemy," she proposes different ways one might see the poet as participating in the circulation of waste (Morrison, 179–199).
15. Don DeLillo, *End Zone* (London: Picador, 2011 [1972]), 69. Henceforth, *EZ*. For an analysis of the desert wasteland's role in *End Zone* see David Cowart. 'Football and *Unsaglichkeit*.' *The Physics of Language* (Athens, GA: University of Giorgia Press, 2002), 17–32.
16. Anya Taylor, "Words, War and Meditation in Don DeLillo's *Endzone*," *International Fiction Review* (January 1977): 68–70. See also Peter Boxall, "There's no lack of void: Waste and abundance in Beckett and DeLillo," *SubStance* 37. 2(2008): 56–70.
17. Don DeLillo, *Running Dog* (London: Picador, 2011 [1978]). Henceforth, *RD*.
18. See *Conversations with Don DeLillo*, ed. Thomas DePietro (University Press of Mississippi, Mississippi, 2005), 52.
19. Don DeLillo, *The Names* (London: Picador, 1987 [1983]), 193–194. Henceforth, *N*.

20. For a nuanced analysis of the language of environmental wreckage in *The Names*, see Elise Martucci, *The Environmental Unconscious in the Fiction of Don DeLillo* (New York: Routledge, 2007), 49–74.
21. H.M. Enzenberger, "A Critique of Political Ecology" (1974) in *The Greening of Marxism*, 17–49. Citation on 25.
22. Jennifer Seymour Whitaker, *Salvaging the Land of Plenty*, 24.
23. Richard Williams, "Everything Under the Bomb: Interview with Don DeLillo," *The Guardian*, 10 January 1998.
24. *Underworld*, 791.
25. See Evelyn Diaz Gonzalez, "The Road Back" in *The Bronx* (New York: Columbia University Press, 2004), 130–143.
26. See Robert McMinn, "*Underworld:* Sin and Atonement" in *Underwords: Perspectives on Don DeLillo's Underworld*, ed. Joseph Dewey, Steven G. Kellman and Irving Malin (Newark: University of Delaware Press, 2002), 37–49. Citation on 47; John Scanlan, *On Garbage* (London: Reaktion, 2005), fn. 59.
27. Adam Begley, "Don DeLillo, The Art of Fiction No. 135," *The Paris Review* 128 (Fall 1993). Accessed 6 April 2014.
28. Maurie J. Cohen, "Bringing Consumerism in from the Cold War," *Sustainability: Science, Practice & Policy Blog*, 22 May 2012. http://sspp-journal.blogspot.co.uk/2012/05/bringing-consumerism-in-from-cold-war.html. Accessed 7 June 2015.
29. Emily S. Rosenberg, "Consumer Capitalism and the end of the Cold War," *The Cambridge History of the Cold War, Vol 3: Endings*, ed. Melvyn P. Leffler and Odd Arne Westad (Cambridge University Press: 2010).
30. Benjamin Miller, *Fat of the land: Garbage in New York* (New York: Four Walls Eight Windows, 2000), 11.
31. *Underworld*, 465; 599.
32. *Underworld*, 11.
33. See Marshall Berman, *All That is Solid Melts into Air* (London: Verso, 2010 [1981]), 332.
34. Jane Jacobs, *The Death and Life of Great American Cities* (New York: Random House, 1961).
35. Don DeLillo, "The Power of History," *The New York Times Book Review*, 7 September 1997, 6.
36. Rafe Bartholomew, "Director's Cut: Q&A With Don DeLillo," *Grantland* (3 October 2011). http://www.grantland.com/story/_/id/7032210/qa-don-delillo. Accessed 28 July 2012.
37. Don DeLillo, as cited in Diane Rosen, *The Book That Changed My Life* (New York: Random House, 2002), 18.
38. Randy O. Frost and Rachel C. Gross, "The hoarding of possessions," 367–382.

39. *Underworld*, 185.

40. Ruth Heyler, "'Refuse Heaped Many Stories High': DeLillo, Dirt and Disorder," *Modern Fiction Studies* 45 (1999): 987–1006.

41. See Mark Osteen, *American Magic and Dread* (Philadelphia, PA: University of Pennsylvania Press, 2000); David Cowart. "Shall These Bones Live?" in *Underwords*, 50–67.

42. Marshall Berman. *All That is Solid Melts into Air*, 290–311.

43. Rudolph Giuliani, "Fresh Kills Exportation Announcement," 1 July 1997, Archives of Rudolph W. Giuliani, http://www.nyc.gov/html/records/rwg/html/97/freshkls.html.

44. Elizabeth Royte, *Garbage Land: On the Secret Trail of Trash* (New York: Little, Brown, 2005), 13.

45. Christine Temko has also explored the "vibrant" qualities of waste in *Underworld*, although from the perspective of queer ecology and ecological postmodernism, relating DeLillo's waste to what Andrew Pickering has termed human actors' "inextricabl[e] entangle[ment] with the nonhuman" and Serenella Iovino's summary of New Materialism as concerned with how the world "makes us in one and the same process in which we make the world." See Christine Temko, "Regulation and Refuse Matter in Don DeLillo's Underworld and Eugene Marten's Waste,"Interdisciplinary Studies in Literature and Environment 20.3 (2013): 494–512.

46. Bruno Latour, *We have never been modern*, 55.

47. Carl A. Zimring and William L Rathje, eds. *Encyclopedia of Consumption and Waste: The Social Science of Garbage* (London: Sage, 2012), 81; 978.

48. Zygmunt Bauman, *Liquid Times: Living in an Age of Uncertainty* (Cambridge: Polity, 2007), 121. David Evans also provides a very useful— and perceptive—reading of *Underworld* through a Baumian lens in "Taking Out the Trash: Don DeLillo's *Underworld*, Liquid Modernity, and the End of Garbage," *The Cambridge Quarterly* 35.2 (2006): 103–132.

49. For a compelling ecocritical reading of this passage, see Jennifer Ladino, *Reclaiming Nostalgia: Longing for Nature in American Literature* (Charlottesville: University of Virginia Press, 2012), 180–210.

50. Ann McCarthy, *The Citizen Machine: Governing by Television in 1950s America* (New York: New Press, 2010), 50.

51. Susan Strasser, *Waste and Want*, 12.

52. Alice Bradley, *Electric Refrigerator Menus and Recipes* (Cleveland: General Electric, 1929), 11, 36; "Left-Overs," *Frigidaire Recipes* (Dayton: Frigidaire, 1928), 55–62, as cited in Strasser, 209–211.

53. Lawrence Alloway, "Junk Culture as a Tradition," *New Forms—New Media* (New York: Martha Jackson Gallery, 1960).

54. Anna Dezeuze, "Neo-Dada, Junk Aesthetic and Spectator Participation," 49–71. Citation on 54.

55. This reading is informed by Brandon Joseph's analysis of Rauschenberg's combines in *Random Order: Robert Rauschenberg and the Neo-Avant-Garde* (Cambridge, Mass and London: MIT Press, 2003), 157.

56. A complete account of the construction of the Watts Towers can be found in Bud Goldstone and Arloa Paquin Goldstone, *The Los Angeles Watts Towers* (Los Angeles: the Getty Conservation Institute and J. Paul Getty Museum, 1997).

57. http://www.pbs.org/independentlens/offthemap/html/level2_byp.html?6. Accessed 28 August 2012.

58. Evans argues against conflating Sax and Rodia with DeLillo, and contends that Sax's project is designed to *prevent* the recycling of the decommissioned warplanes, and their reprocessing for other purposes: "What ties art and garbage is a common resistance to utility" (Evans, 122).

59. Don DeLillo, "The Power of History" 4. http://www.nytimes.com/books/images_br/toolbar_br.map, Accessed 10 August 2012. Henceforth, *TPOH.*

60. David Cowart, *Don DeLillo: The Physics of Language* (Athens, GA: University of Giorgia Press, 2002), 198.

61. Mark Osteen. *American Magic and Dread,* 230–231.

62. Ira Nadel, "The Baltimore Catechism; or Comedy in *Underworld*" in *Underwords,* 176–198.

63. See Bill Brown, *A Sense of Things: The Object Culture of American Literature* (Chicago: University of Chicago Press, 2003), 74.

CHAPTER 6

Conclusion

The environmental crisis is the combined result of a long-standing Western
anthropocentric tradition, the modern mechanistic worldview predicated on
violent opposition to nature and the capitalist economic system that requires
endless growth, expansion and accumulation.[1]

We cannot predict what the overall climatic results will be of our using
the atmosphere as a garbage dump.[2]

[P]lanetwide, more every day, the payback keeps gathering.[3]

The central aim of this book has been to examine how a selection of novelists influenced by the historical avant-garde has harnessed waste over the
course of the twentieth century to critique capitalist commodity culture,
to interrogate capitalist ascriptions of value, and to consider how these
affect artistic production, culture, and the popular imagination. This has
been an investigation into how novelists have sought, through representations of waste, to liven us to the danger of being "subsumed," to para-
phrase DeLillo, by our excretions—to make us think about the extent to
which capitalism governs how we ascribe value to people and things—and,
via different enactments of this ecological process, to test the limits of the
novel form.

This concluding chapter extends the ideas discussed thus far to consider
literary depictions of waste since the turn of the millennium and how they
engage with capitalism today. We have of course only recently crossed the
threshold into the new millennium, but even at this early stage, certain
differences in the literary depiction of waste are evident. These features

© The Editor(s) (if applicable) and The Author(s) 2016   181
R. Dini, *Consumerism, Waste, and Re-Use in Twentieth-Century Fiction*,
DOI 10.1057/978-1-137-58165-5_6

lend themselves to a proto-theory about waste in postmillennial literature as something simultaneously all pervasive and ineffable, which in
turn reflects the all pervasiveness of neoliberalism and the ineffability of
global warming. In what follows, I explore the efforts of three recent
novels—Jonathan Miles' *Want Not* (2013), Thomas Pynchon's *Bleeding
Edge* (2013), and Tom McCarthy's *Satin Island* (2015)—to depict the
intangible aspects of waste. These three works break from resorting to
visual characteristics and reflect upon the relationship between the unseen
effects of waste (which are invisible to the naked eye, and whose direct
negative effect on people is so far removed as to make it difficult for them
to engage with the issue), and an unknowable global economic model.
Although it is perhaps premature to assume a rupture between twentieth-
century fiction's approach to waste and twenty-first century's, it is worth
considering the extent to which contemporary novelists are approaching
waste differently from their late twentieth-century forebears, and what this
might say about our understanding of the present.

A proliferation of literature following the global economic crisis of 2007–
2008 has sought to understand how the neoliberal model has evolved since
the 1990s.[4] Of particular note are David Harvey's *The Enigma of Capital:
And the Crises of Capitalism* (2010), David Graeber's *Debt: The Last 5,000
Years* (2011), and Thomas Piketty's *Capital in the Twenty-first Century*
(2013).[5] Harvey, Graeber, and Piketty dissect neoliberalism's role in promoting income inequality and its complicity in what Graeber terms the
"militarization of capitalism" (Graeber, 382). These address neoliberalism's refusal to acknowledge the limits to growth imposed by—among
other things—soil depletion, water pollution, scarce resources, and climate
change, as well as its reliance on debt. Where Keynesianism sought to promote consumerism through wage inflation, and Fordism sought to culti-
vate the ethos of the worker-consumer, neoliberalism cultivated an ethos of
speculation that relies on the concept of credit to counter the gap between
what labour earns and what it wants to spend (Harvey, 17–20; 22).

This—admittedly very simplified—account highlights the central
dynamics to which Marxist economists ascribe the global financial crisis:
the banking system's reliance on fictitious capital and the opaque marketing of unregulated financial products targeted specifically at lower-income
households.[6] The roots of the global financial crisis, according to this
view, are to be found in the very *tenets* of neoliberalism, which cloaks
the concentration of wealth in few hands under the rhetoric of individual
freedom, sees the volatility of markets as a necessary evil, and makes the
state the protector of financial institutions rather than of its citizens.[7] That
very same market-oriented mentality was harnessed by the American right

throughout the 1990s, to champion the growth of the Internet as "the latest triumph of American enterprise"—further evidence that capitalism was necessary to both democracy and the fostering of technological innovation.[8] The speculative bubble that resulted—and the ensuing crash—can be seen as symptomatic of an economistic view of the Internet, reducing a space that, for others, should have been governed by altruism and collaboration to a series of use-values.[9]

Most importantly for our purposes, these readings indicate how the speculative dimension of neoliberalism has insinuated itself into all areas of life and altered the very texture of culture. As Wendy Brown explains it in *Undoing the Demos* (2015), the difference between neoliberal ideology and traditional capitalism on a cultural level is that neoliberalism sees the individual as nothing more than "financialised human capital."[10] This economisation of subjects differs from classic economic liberalism in its specific view of leisure, consumption, and reproduction as strategic decisions capable of increasing one's future value (Brown, 34). Brown elaborated on these ideas in a recent interview with *Dissent* magazine:

> This is not simply a matter of extending commodification and monetization everywhere—that's the old Marxist depiction of capital's transformation of everyday life. Neoliberalism construes even non-wealth generating spheres—such as learning, dating, or exercising—in market terms, submits them to market metrics, and governs them with market techniques and practices. Above all, it casts people as human capital who must constantly tend to their own present and future value.[11]

This speculative dimension has transformed us from a society that monetises everything and everyone to a society that speculates on the future value of everything and everyone. Based on these different readings, we might term the present moment "advanced neoliberalism"—an intensified, speculative free market ideology that is fundamentally at odds with the basic values upheld by the novelists examined in this book.

Where, then, does that leave a radical politics? For Graeber, "There is very good reason to believe that, in a generation or so, capitalism itself will no longer exist—most obviously, as ecologists keep reminding us, because it's impossible to maintain an engine of perpetual growth forever on a finite planet" (Graeber, 382). In a similar vein, citing similarities between the revival of environmentalism today and its first emergence during the economic recession of the 1970s, Harvey sees "times of economic turmoil" as the perfect opportunity to address the interrelation of economy and ecology. These views are encapsulated in what one of *appraisal of an economic and historical context in which to situate post-2000 examples.*

Thomas Pynchon's characters, in his most recent novel, *Bleeding Edge* (2013), terms neoliberalism's predisposition to:

> liv[e] on borrowed time. Never caring about who's paying for it, who's starving somewhere else all jammed together so we can have cheap food, a house, a yard in the burbs ... planetwide, more every day, the payback keeps gathering. (*BE*, 340)

However, the passage is tempered—or perhaps undermined—by the fact that the novel itself takes place in 2001 and is thus framed as an omen (and a warning to the reader) rather than as a reflection of public sentiment. Similarly, Graeber, Harvey, and Brown's analyses are markedly at odds with the narrative that has dominated discussions about the economic crisis and its causes since 2010. "How Neoliberalism Survived the Financial Meltdown," the subtitle of Philip Mirowski's *Never Let a Serious Crisis Go to Waste*, pithily conveys the way the crisis has been in fact deployed as "evidence" of an overstretched state rather than of an unsustainable economic model, thus strengthening neoliberal rhetoric and providing the groundwork for further privatisation and austerity policies. In the face of such developments, it is difficult to assert that we are at the endpoint of capitalism or on the verge of revolution, and it would appear that the social and ecological effects of our current economic model are only being questioned by some (most notably, movements such as Syriza in Greece and Podemos in Spain, and figures such as Jeremy Corbyn in the UK and Bernie Sanders in the US). The corporate sector certainly remains reluctant to accept environmental policy and continues to find ways to pressure governments into relaxing it when it suits business interests, while discussion of the environment both at a government and industry level remains centred on its economic ramifications.[12] Environmental regulation since the 1970s has focussed on taxation as the main method to deter use of particular pollutants, effectively allowing companies to pollute as long as they are willing to pay for it.[13] Similarly, the rhetoric of corporations that acknowledge global warming frames the issue as an economic challenge (as exemplified by former chief economist of the World Bank Nicholas Stern's description of climate change's potential to cut annual Global Domestic Product by the end of the twenty-first century as "the greatest market failure the world has ever seen" [Weart, 195]). Such an economistic view ignores the role that the culture of capitalism has played in the environmental crisis, and, in particular, the ramifications of equating individual rights and freedoms with the "right" to unfettered consumption and disposal.[14] Thus, criticism of capitalism's conflation of consumption with fulfilment and desires with needs remains largely confined to environmentalist and Marxist discourse.

From the perspective of waste theory, what is perhaps most interesting about this moment is its depiction in recent fiction, and particularly the way that fiction has assumed the threat posed by the environmental crisis and the financial crisis to be inextricably connected as well as defying expression. As alluded to earlier, if we were to formulate a proto-theory about the postmillennial novel's approach to waste thus far, the most noteworthy aspect to emerge would surely be waste's depiction as something simultaneously all pervasive and inapprehensible. This approach is significantly at odds with the markedly visible, tangible waste representations we have discussed thus far. The writers we have examined engage with waste as a sensory thing whose amenability or resistance to interpretation reassures us that we still retain some kind of agency—if only the agency to say we do not know what to do with it. This understanding is reflective of the cultural contexts in which the novels reviewed were written. We might argue that the twentieth century is interested above all in the *image* of waste, and that it conceives of waste's hold on (or hiddenness from) the public imagination as something palpable. Taking our cue from Strasser's historical analysis of rag picking, we might further argue that the very different literary approaches discussed seek to make literature a steward of human waste, and through that stewardship, to point out capitalism's wrongs.

Postmillennial literature's approaches to waste differ in their implication that such stewardship is no longer possible. There is simply *no language*, now, with which to articulate something so culturally embedded. Elaine Scarry puts forth a very similar argument to this in her analysis of our incapacity to properly conceive of, let alone confront, issues such as anthropogenic climate change.[15] In interview, Scarry describes this incapacity to fully comprehend climate change as its resistance to "aesthetic imagining," which she likens to the notion of aesthetic distance in the theatre:

> It was often said [...] that in the theatre you have to be at the right aesthetic distance to experience the play. If you're too close, you see the safety pins on the costumes and it ruins the effect, and if you're too far away everything is miniaturized and you can't accept it. And I think that this question may well be right, that apocalypse is what happens for all those things that are happening at a distance—it incapacitates us because they're outside our own sensory horizon, either by being much too long or much too short. (Hiltner-Scarry, 273)

Michel Faber makes that resistance to "aesthetic imagining" the central focus of *The Book of Strange New Things* (2014), in which a Christian missionary sent to another planet hears (via e-mails from his wife) about the ecological and financial disasters occurring on planet earth, but is unable or unwilling to truly assimilate the news.[16] His wife's daily updates about the latest economic collapse, earthquake, or flood and the garbage piling up outside of their house "don't feel real" as they are "just so alien to [his] life" on his planet (*BSNT*, 359). Faber frames this incomprehension as a "failure of compassion"—an inability to empathise with anything beyond our immediate context, recalling Fredric Jameson's identification of the absence of "sympathetic participation" in subject–object relations under late capitalism (Jameson, 371). That "failure of compassion," we discover, has been cultivated by the corporation for which the missionary works (*BSNT*, 532; 542). It is precisely the inability to comprehend the annihilation of planet Earth, and the capacity to forget their own past, that renders the missionary and his fellow employees suitable to their tasks.

A similar obscuring of these ecological effects plays out in one of the sub-strands of Jonathan Franzen's *The Corrections* (2001)—a text that reads, in its preoccupation with financial capital and entropic disarray on the one hand, and the rehabilitation of memory on the other, as a conceptual sequel to both Gaddis' *JR* and DeLillo's *Underworld*.[17] Mid-way through *The Corrections*, the geriatric protagonists, Alfred and Enid, are on a cruise through Northern Europe, where they converse, at dinner, with a Norwegian and Swedish couple:

> 'Once we burn up all the coal and oil and gas,' said Dr Roth, 'we'll have an antique atmosphere. A hot, nasty atmosphere that no one's seen for three hundred million years. Once we've let the carbon genie out of its lithic bottle.'
>
> We own a great many stocks. I can't remember every name. At the same time, too, the print in the newspaper is very tiny.'
>
> 'Norway has superb retirement benefits, hm, but I also supplement my national coverage with a private fund […]'
> 'The moral of the story is don't recycle plastic. Send your plastic to a landfill. Get that carbon underground.'
>
> 'If it had been up to Al, we'd still have every penny in passbook savings.'
> 'Bury it, bury it. Stopper the genie in the bottle.' (376-378)

The interlaced fragments of these different conversations about stock market trading, retirement planning, and environmental pollution—reminiscent, in their absurdity, of the dialogues about money and waste in *JR*—beautifully capture the competing interests of finance and ecology. More importantly, they convey the tone-deafness of those for whom the earth is merely an instrument of capital, and the tone-deafness of a decade enthralled to the seemingly limitless possibilites of financial speculation. Environmental degradation in the novel is repeatedly sidelined by characters whom Franzen depicts as collectively choosing to ignore the (ecological, financial, ethical) ramifications of unchecked growth.

From a very different standpoint, DeLillo's most recent novel, *Zero K* (2016), is a long meditation on the distance between what we know and what we can imagine.[18] Where *Underworld* examined America's garbage to piece together its history, *Zero K* traces the work of "geneticists, and climatologists, and neuroscientists, and psychologists, and ethicists, if that's the right word" intent on "design[ing] a response to whatever eventual calamity may strike the planet" (*ZK*, 33; 66). Where Nick Shay looks at products in the supermarket and sees only the garbage they will become, the scientists in *Zero K* are preoccupied with eschatology as a whole, and the reclamation of cryogenically preserved bodies in particular. Most importantly, *Zero K*'s central conceit is that the world its characters are shaping defies articulation: we lack the language, the ability, to imagine the reclaimed bodies and ruins that will constitute our future.[19]

One way of understanding the novelists reviewed in the previous chapters—particularly Ballard, Barthelme, Gaddis, and DeLillo, but also, to an extent, the historical avant-garde and Beckett—is as projects that still assume the possibility of broaching something conceptually out of reach, and whose long-term implications are frankly unfathomable. They attempt, in other words, to materialise that which cannot be, or has yet to, materialise(d). Read in this light, the mannequin figures in de Chirico's *Hebdomeros* are efforts to imagine what human reification *looks* like—to put a face, so to speak, to the dehumanising tendencies of capitalist production. Such a figuration is of course self-contradictory, since depersonalisation is not something visible. It is the mannequin figure that allows us to believe that the issue is containable, and even reversible. In a similar way, we find waste deployed in the other novelists' work as a way to visualise particular forms of "wrongs" and to imagine their reversibility. Loy's junk collages are attempts to reveal the social inequality of the Bowery from which their scraps were taken. The depiction of objects cast off by humans, and humans deemed superfluous in the works of these different writer-artists, allows us to *see* the stultifying effects of commodification on art, the homogenising effects of Fordist rationalisation, and the ecologically devastating effects of overconsumption. By contrast, Jennifer Egan's *A Visit from the Goon Squad* (2010) suggests the archaism of such efforts. The novel's last chapters imagine the USA in the 2020s as a desert, in which lawns and gardens are scarce commodities, and the landscape is dotted with wind turbines and solar panels.[20] The central protagonist Sasha, a kleptomaniac in youth, has taken to making sculptures out of trash and her children's old toys (*AVFTGS*, 250; 272). Where the first chapter of the novel introduced Sasha as a collector of "found objects" (her term for the things she stole), the penultimate chapter presents her as a steward of the things no one wants—a shift that Egan frames as at once redemptive and belated. That this chapter is narrated entirely through the Microsoft PowerPoint-style slides of her daughter's diary (paper, too, having become a scarce commodity) renders Sasha's transformation all the more poignant. The digital form of the slide show presentation exemplifies what another character in the novel calls the "aesthetic holocaust" of digitization (*AVFTGS*, 24)—and it is entirely at odds with the physicality of those quintessentially twentieth-century forms, collage and assemblage. The juxtaposition of PowerPoint and collage is a study in contrasts. Egan's figuration of scavenging and assemblage as on their way to becoming archaic practices, and bound to befuddle future generations unfamiliar with "stuff," effectively historicises the experimentations of the last century—while simultaneously drawing attention to their significance.[21]

The investigation into effluvia's unseen characteristics in the texts discussed above suggests that we are moving towards a conceptualisation of waste as matter that can neither be apprehended visually nor sifted through or treated as a relic. And each of these texts treats that transition as fundamentally terrifying. This is perhaps best embodied in the recuperative practices at the heart of Brenda Coultas's collection of prose poems, *A Handmade Museum* (2002).[22] Indeed, the collection's longest prose poem, "The Bowery Project," in which Coultas kept inventories of detritus littering the streets of New York City's Bowery prior to its redevelopment, was effectively an effort to re-house, in language, remnants of Mina Loy's old neighbourhood displaced by the erection of luxury apartments. The texts in this collection—which read as elements in a collage-novel more than discrete poems—echo Virginia Woolf's famed surrealistic short story, "Solid Objects" (1920), in their depiction of refuse collecting. But where the refuse-collecting in Woolf's story is generally read (following Douglas Mao) as reflecting anxieties about the abandonment of

Victorian values, in Coultas's text, like in the ones discussed above, they point to the concerns of a postmillennial, digitized, and hyper-capitalist, space. Here, the perception of all that is solid (object) melting into air—to conflate Woolf and Marx—is on the one hand literal (with regards to the advancement of digitization) and grossly naïve (insofar as the effects of capitalist modernity are all too palpable, embodied in landfill-cities such as Mumbai).[23]

This is not to say, however, that the concerns with the ephemeral reflected in postmillennial fiction's approach to waste—as exemplified by the Miles, Pynchon, and McCarthy texts we are about to discuss—result in complete abstention from visual description, nor indeed from addressing historical questions. Rather, my contention is that these texts repeatedly gesture towards something just outside the visual frame—towards another dimension to waste, and to the capitalist economy, that eludes us. I read Miles', Pynchon's, and McCarthy's novels as indicative of a new approach to waste that relates the unseen to the logic of neoliberalism and to specific cultural anxieties about climate change. The works discussed in this last section extend the critiques of the historical avant-garde and its descendants, but they indicate the untenability of subverting the productivist paradigm through a discourse on waste in a landscape that is suffused with it.

"THERE LIES A DARKER NARRATIVE"[24]: SILICON ALLEY, FRESH KILLS, AND THE DEEP WEB IN THOMAS PYNCHON'S BLEEDING EDGE

Thomas Pynchon's *Bleeding Edge* (2013) frames this postmillennial dimension of waste as a mystery—a thriller, in fact. Published in 2013 but set in the midst of the 2000–2002 dot-com crash and the months just prior to and immediately following 9/11, the novel effectively takes up where DeLillo's *Underworld* leaves off. But where DeLillo examines waste as a metaphor for the Cold War's legacy and its complicity in promoting overconsumption, Pynchon considers it in relation to the burgeoning online world, and "late fuckin' capitalism" (*BE*, 308). This is a novel in which everything relates back to the "holy fucking market" (*BE*, 338)—people's lives, the built environment, and the national consciousness are all products of the neoliberal context, in which waste symbolises the soon-to-be re-commodified, as well as the radical (if not *anarchic*) potential of the online sphere. The novel's very title draws attention to these concerns, referring to the term for technology with "no proven use, high risk, something only early-adoption addicts feel comfortable with" (*BE*, 78). Where the term "cutting-edge" refers to the latest development of a product or idea, "bleeding-edge" refers to an earlier phase, in which the product's future is undetermined and largely reliant on the willingness of investors to finance its development.

The novel's plot is likewise acutely concerned with the shape of things to come. Very briefly, *Bleeding Edge* traces the quest of an unlicensed fraud detective, Maxine Tarnow, as she investigates a series of sums being paid out from a leading computer security firm to a defunct online company, hwgaahwgh.com (short for "Hey, We've Got Awesome And Hip Web Graphix, Here!"). Pynchon interlaces this narrative with that of a number of hackers, cyberpunks, and digital entrepreneurs. These include two of Maxine's acquaintances, who are developing a virtually animated guide to the Deep Web[25] called DeepArcher (a pun on "departure"), which is designed to enable individuals to escape the constraints of the real world. The novel's plot is self-consciously set against the backdrop of a New York in transition (a city recovering from the shocks of the dot-com boom that transformed Manhattan in the 1990s, the ensuing crash, and the subsequent attacks on the Twin Towers), while the transitional nature of the yet-to-be colonised Deep Web is repeatedly likened to an urban neighbourhood vulnerable to speculators. As one of Pynchon's characters terms it, what we are dealing with is "post–late capitalism run amok" (*BE*, 138).

In some cases, the anxieties expressed in Pynchon's figuration of waste itself are not new, but merely amplifications of long-standing concerns about the pace of change under capitalism. The extensive passages he dedicates to describing the trendy bars and office spaces once housed by the now-empty buildings of "Silicon Alley"[26] recall Walter Benjamin's descriptions of the Paris Arcades—defunct spaces Benjamin viewed as exemplifying the transience of capitalist modernity.[27] For instance, we follow Maxine into the empty office spaces of hwgaahwgh.com:

> another failed dot-com joining the officescape of the time—tarnished metallic surfaces, shaggy gray soundproofing, Steelcase screens and Herman Miller workpods—already beginning to decompose, littered, dust gathering. (*BE*, 43)

This depiction of the newly-made obsolete recalls Walter Benjamin's understanding of the empty spaces of the Paris Arcades as a way to rethink—in fact, to *awaken* from—the nineteenth century's dream-myth of its own modernity. Benjamin described his project as a literary montage of "the rags, the refuse" of the nineteenth century (*AP*, 460; [N1a,8]). As Esther Leslie frames it,

> The *Arcades Project* asks how a mythic dream consciousness, such as the longing for dream fulfilment in the commodity or the idea of love satisfied in prostitution or the desire for human union through imperialism, can be rattled, forced to wake up from the wishful thinking it indulges. Perhaps assertion simply of the actuality of commercial brutality would suffice.[28]

Maxine's perambulations through the vacant spaces of what was once Silicon Alley are similarly imbued with a somnambulant quality, leaving the reader frequently unclear as to whether what is being narrated is past or present, lived or dreamed. The recent past is framed as a nightmare whose legacy the characters cannot yet fully grasp and from which they have yet to awaken. This impression is amplified by Maxine's disorientation in hearing the sound of a clicking keyboard in one of the rooms of the empty office, which leads her to wonder whether she has "entered some supernatural time-warp where the shades of office layabouts continue to waste uncountable person-hours playing Tetris"—a depiction that spectacularly relates the notion of time-wasting to the capitalist valuation of labour-time (*BE*, 43). The source of the sound is soon attributed to mundane causes—it is merely a lingering ex-employee making use of the Wi-Fi—but it heightens the sense of colliding temporalities that pervades the entire novel.

However, what sets the text apart from Benjamin's (and the Surrealists') articulations of obsolescence is that it views obsolescence to be a *temporary* condition. Pynchon repeatedly reminds us that at the dawn of the new century, nothing remains uncommodified for long. Each visit Maxine makes to a different area of the city sparks a reflection regarding its likely redevelopment and gentrification, and even the disembowelled space of Ground Zero, after 9/11, is recognised as "future real estate" (*BE*, 42; 328). And this spirit of redevelopment is explicitly framed throughout the novel as a putting-to-use of waste. For example, Maxine attends her children's eighth-grade graduation, where the commencement speech is given by a radical septuagenarian, March Kelleher, who, in lieu of a speech tells a parable about a powerful ruler who travels the world in disguise in order to spy on his subjects (*BE*, 112). The ruler meets an old lady-scavenger who "kn[ows] everything and is the guardian of whatever the city thr[ows] away" (*BE*, 113). When she refuses his offer of money to forget having seen him, claiming that, "Remembering is the essence of what I am," he offers her a job, which she also refuses (*BE*, 114). To the baffled audience, March asks:

> Who is this old lady? What does she think she's been finding out all these years? Who is this "ruler" she's refusing to be bought off by? And what's this "work" he was "doing in secret?" Suppose "the ruler" isn't a person at

all but a soulless force so powerful that though it cannot ennoble, it does entitle, which, in the city-nation we speak of, is always more than enough? The answers are left to you. (*BE*, 113–114)

For a reader of novels about waste, the old lady of the parable, like March Kelleher herself, recalls DeLillo's Klara Sax, who also deals in waste and speaks in parables, or Beckett's bums, who wade through waste but refuse to make it profitable. And as the novel unspools, it becomes evident that the soulless force in the parable is late capitalism and its underlying logic—what Harvey terms "a process in which money is perpetually sent in search of more money" (*BE*, 108; Harvey, 40). As March tells Maxine, "every building you love, someday it'll either be a stack of high-end chain stores or condos for yups with more money than brains" (*BE*, 115). We are reminded of Wendy Brown's understanding of the pervasiveness of neoliberalisation:

> Neoliberalization is generally more termite-like than lionlike … its mode of reason boring in capillary fashion into the trunks and branches of workplaces, schools, public agencies, social and political discourse, and, above all, the subject. Even the termite metaphor is not quite apt: Foucault would remind us that any ascendant political rationality is not only destructive, but brings new subjects, conduct, relations, and worlds into being. (Brown, 36)

What is truly terrifying here is the *hiddenness* of that productive force. Like the ruler in the parable, neoliberalisation produces its subjects without their even realising it. The scavenging old lady is a figure of resistance who is alive to the aspects of the system that no one else notices. She who never forgets embodies what Maxine later describes as "the landfill of failing memory"—she is a repository for everything that this economic model razes (*BE*, 267).

Pynchon juxtaposes these impressions of the city space as a victim to the whims of capital against depictions of the hinterland of the Deep Web—and it is in this juxtaposition that we find the crux of the narrative, which in turn both echoes and modifies the ideas put forth by the historical avant-garde and its twentieth-century descendants. For Pynchon depicts the Deep Web as an anarchic counterforce to the endless expansion of global capital. The Deep Web, in *Bleeding Edge,* is a space where "advertising is still in its infancy" (*BD*, 35), while the very structures through which users move—the links and nodes that connect different pieces of content—are the product of anonymous hackers who uphold the "hacker ethic [of] doing their piece of it, then just vanishing uncredited" (*BE*, 69). The portal to the Deep Web, DeepArcher, is in turn posited as a "virtual sanctuary"—a place "way down'" in the deep recesses of the Internet's underbelly, where one might lose hours, even days, in a kind of cyber-flânerie:

limitation of resistance to waste as a neoliberal ideology

Before long, Maxine finds herself wandering around clicking on everything, faces, litter on the floor, labels on bottles behind the bar, after a while interested not so much in where she might get to than the texture of the search itself. (*BE*, 76)

DeepArcher combines the poetic dimension of urban wandering and scavenging, and the radical dimension of the first avant-gardists. It is a place safely out of view from commercial enterprises, a place where the whole point is to waste time and to "get lost" in something akin to the Surrealist tradition (*BE*, 76). Again, however, what distinguishes this postmillennial depiction of subversion from the early twentieth-century figurations of a Breton, Loy, or de Chirico is the pervasive awareness of its short-lived nature, the knowledge of the space's vulnerability to development and commodification. Pynchon repeatedly reminds us of the extent to which the dissemination of the Internet was perceived, in the nineties and early 2000s, to symbolise "the victory of (US-led) neo-liberal free market capitalism."[29] Much of the novel's discussions about the Internet reflect upon its co-option, in the mid-nineties, by the right wing-libertarian "New Economy" movement, which was intent on harnessing the Internet to overturn the regulatory market intervention policies of the nation states (Lovink, 8).

Pynchon relates this awareness of the incipient commodification of the Deep Web to a postmillennial nostalgia about garbage. In the novel's most melancholy passage, Maxine and March drive past Fresh Kills landfill— which is in the process of being closed—and the rehabilitated space at its heart, known (also in real life) as the Island of Meadows. In the ensuing two pages, Pynchon masterfully weaves the soon-to-be closed landfill into a meditation on the economic forces of global capital, the industrialised world's "addiction" to oil, the landfill's coterminous marginality and centrality to the city's economy, and the paradoxes implicit in its rehabilitation. The landfill, Maxine meditates, gathers "everything the city has rejected so it can keep on pretending to be itself," but it also functions as a repository for the city's collective unconscious:

Every Fairway bag full of potato peels, coffee grounds, uneaten Chinese food, used tissues and tampons and paper napkins and disposable diapers, fruit gone bad, yogurt past its sell-by date that Maxine has ever thrown away is up in there someplace, multiplied by everybody in the city she knows, multiplied by everybody she doesn't know, since 1948, before she was even born, and what she thought was lost and out of her life has only entered a collective history. (*BE*, 170)

The landfill is perhaps the only place where, in the era of individualism, a collective history can even occur. The fact that it is soon to be closed—and the uncertainty regarding whether it will indeed be rehabilitated or simply sold off to the highest vendor—endows the passage with added poignancy. Maxine has previously noted that the future of "100 acres of untouched marshland" of the Island of Meadows is precarious: "given the real-estate imperatives running this town," it is only a matter of time before the space becomes another victim of the market (*BE*, 167). But her sudden recognition of the affinities between Fresh Kills and the Deep Web, and between the Island of Meadows and DeepArcher, complicates this discussion:

> As if you could reach into the looming and prophetic landfill, that perfect negative of the city in its seething foul incoherence, and find a set of invisible links to click on and be crossfaded at last to unexpected refuge, a piece of the ancient estuary exempt from what happened, what has gone on happening, to the rest of it. Like the Island of Meadows, DeepArcher also has developers after it. Whatever migratory visitors are still down there trusting in its inviolability will some morning all too soon be rudely surprised by the whispering descent of corporate Web crawlers itching to index and corrupt another patch of sanctuary for their own far-from-selfless ends. (*BE*, 168)

The "unexpected refuge" of the Island of Meadows—a place "exempt from what happened" and "what has gone on happening"—is akin to the uncommodified space of DeepArcher. Just as the rehabilitation of the landfill into a marshland threatens to be but a temporary moment of respite before the land gets sold off to real estate developers, the anonymous sprawl of DeepArcher risks falling prey to the indexing and speculative logic of late capitalism. As Phil Mirowski notes, while promoted as a form of anarchic production, open source content eventually makes its way into the market. Thus, work originally cherished by its producers "as a direct expression of their individuality" amounts to voluntary unpaid labour and has in fact "become so prevalent in the current neoliberal era that some have suggested it actually constitutes a novel form of economic organization, or incipient mode of production, if they indulge in Marxist terminology" (Mirowski, 142). A hacker acquaintance of Maxine reiterates this same sentiment later in the novel, noting that:

> once they get down here, everything'll be suburbanized faster than you can say "late capitalism." Then it'll be just like up there in the shallows. Link by link, they'll bring it all under control, safe and respectable. (*BE*, 241)

It is a startling analogy, not only in its figuration of DeepArcher as an ecosystem vulnerable to the digital equivalent of industrial development but also in its figuration of the Deep Web itself as a kind of digital scrapheap from which one might potentially derive meaningful, as-yet-uncommodified, fragments of experience. Pynchon elaborates on this vision of the Deep Web as a landfill elsewhere in the novel, as the same computer hacker explains to Maxine that the Deep Web was initially meant to be "mostly obsolete sites and broken links, an endless junkyard" where "adventurers will come [...] someday to dig up relics of remote and exotic dynasties" (*BE*, 226). Moreover, Maxine draws explicit parallels to the Deep Web's resistance to development in her reference to Robert Moses, the engineer responsible for Fresh Kills as well as for the Cross-Bronx Expressway that displaced thousands of families in the 1960s, noting that "If there were a Robert Moses of the Deep Web, he'd be screaming, Condemn it already!" (*BE*, 241). Likewise, Maxine's night-time exploration of Deep Web videogames is a foray into aesthetic materials "one way or another deemed too violent or offensive or intensely beautiful for the market as currently defined" (*BE*, 240). Such a figuration of the hinterland of the online world as a "dump, with structure" (*BE*, 226) is startling to a waste theorist accustomed to dealing with the effluvia of industrial production. Pynchon takes us, here, into an entirely new realm, inviting us to consider how our understanding of novelty, obsolescence, regeneration, and resistance might translate in the virtual sphere, where waste is not a material aftermath or visible entity, but a series of defunct links.

Pynchon expands this discussion to suggest another dimension to the Deep Web—something akin, perhaps, to the reproachful nature of actual landfills, with their potential to harbour uncomfortable secrets, and to remind us of sins that, like the ruler in March's parable, we would prefer to forget. This becomes apparent when Maxine explores the Cold War sites of the Deep Web:

> Broken remnants of old military installations, commands long deactivated, as if transmission towers for ghost traffic are still poised out on promontories far away in the secular dark, corroded, untended trusswork threaded in and out with vines and leaves of faded poison green, using abandoned tactical frequencies for operations long defunded into silence. ... Missiles meant for shooting down Russian prop-driven bombers, never deployed, lying around in pieces, as if picked over by some desperately poor population that comes out only in the deepest watches of the night. Gigantic vacuum-tube computers with half-acre footprints, gutted, all empty sockets and strewn wiring. Littered situation rooms, high-sixties plastic detailing gone brittle and yellow, radar consoles with hooded circular screens, desks still occupied by avatars

of senior officers in front of flickering sector maps, upright and weaving like hypnotized snakes, images corrupted, paralyzed, passing to dust. (*BE*, 241)

As much as the Deep Web suggests the marginal and uncontained, it is also testament to the nation's secrets—to all the things that get left out of official histories. Maxine's father reminds her that the Internet itself was conceived during the Cold War, by men tasked with "imagin[ing] all the ways the world was going to end" (*BE*, 418). The result of these endeavours, DARPAnet, was a product of the "pure terror" that underlay the apparent idyll of the Eisenhower years (*BE*, 419). The Deep Web is a graveyard for the nightmares of the Cold War era—the broken remnants of terror, a digital equivalent to DeLillo's basements of Cold War memorabilia where the "lost men to history" go to relive the past, and the dystopian futures imagined in the 1970s by Ballard, where a few survivors pick over the remains of past civilizations.

Where, then, lies redemption? One place, Pynchon suggests, is in the world of online gaming—a form that he repeatedly frames as an aesthetic on par with the realist novel, allowing players to visit, among other places, exact replicas of their city in a previous era (in this case, New York before the most recent wave of gentrification). Here objects are re-imbued with their nineteenth-century realist function, the only difference being that the reader-gamer is allowed to intervene and manipulate them in a way that the bourgeois readership of Dickens or Zola could only have dreamed. Another place is in a state of mind that embraces the ambiguity of life in the post-digital world, as evidenced in a disorientating passage towards the end of the novel:

> Out of the ashes and oxidation of this postmagical winter, counterfactual elements have started popping up like li'l goombas. Early one windy morning Maxine's walking down Broadway when here comes a plastic top from a nine-inch aluminum [*sic*] take-out container, rolling down the block in the wind, on its edge, an edge thin as a predawn dream, keeps trying to fall over but the airflow or something—unless it's some nerd at a keyboard—keeps it upright for an implausible distance, half a block, a block, waits for the light, then half a block more till it finally rolls off the curb under the wheels of a truck that's pulling out and gets flattened. Real? Computer-animated? (*BE*, 431)

It is one of many passages in the novel in which Pynchon adopts a Surrealist tone to imbue waste with something approximating a life force and hidden radicalism. That vibrancy is amplified by our uncertainty regarding where the waste-dance is occurring. Are we in the real world, or online? Is the container a material entity, or an agglomeration of pixels, the work of "some nerd at a keyboard?" Are we witnessing something happening, or the *representation* of something happening? The questions remain unanswered (and of course, one could argue that either way, we are witnessing a representation, since the waste-dance is occurring in a novel), but perhaps they are beside the point. For what Pynchon draws our attention to in this depiction is not the physicality of waste, but its connotation of liminality. As in the other passages mentioned thus far, the emphasis is on waste's in-betweenness. Pynchon conceptualises waste as an object or space *on the verge*—of being interpreted, put to use, or of no longer making sense. This is a novel about aftermaths and forebodings—about what it is to be aware of change as it happens, and to wonder about, and fear, its implications. It little matters whether the phantasmagoric things one sees—or thinks one has seen—are occurring in the material world, online, or in a dream. What matters is that one is there to experience them.

Pynchon's postmillennial novel asks us to read the effluvia of the digital world both as historical relics and subversive tools in an as-yet-unwritten future. His twinning of landfill waste with the dark matter of the Deep Web broadens our "sense" of what waste is, where it resides, and what form it can take, suggesting that waste can be an invisible, intangible entity as much as a seen thing. His conceptualisation of the Deep Web as a space for cyber-flânerie and creative acts of subversive resistance as well as rumination over the recent past combines the ideas of the historical avant-garde and its descendants in new and important ways. His comparison of the vulnerability of the rehabilitated marshlands of Fresh Kills to that of the uncommercialised spaces of the Deep Web draws our attention to the fragility of *any* attribution of value outside and apart from the logic of capitalism—reminding us that, as March Kelleher tells Maxine, "there's always a way to monetise anything" (*BE*, 349).

Scavenging for "The Only *Truthful* Thing Civilisation Produced": Jonathan Miles' *Want Not*

Jonathan Miles' *Want Not* (2013) extends the ideas discussed thus far, but focuses in particular on the redemptive possibilities of scavenging. Miles' novel juxtaposes the narratives of two dumpster-divers, a millionaire debt collector, and an obese linguist concerned with developing a semiotic system to warn future civilizations from approaching our radioactive leftovers.[30] Set in New York in the immediate aftermath of the global financial crisis, the novel deploys waste to examine what it means to live in a world that runs on desire and speculation. However, it does so retroactively: the anxieties of the recession's aftermath are narrated via flashbacks that, like the scavenged items collected by Miles' central, dumpster-diving protagonists, promise to shed light on the present. Waste offers the potential to redress past wrongs, but—and this is where Miles departs from DeLillo, and recalls, in fact, Beckett or Gaddis—the attempt to interpret it proves to be too late. The novel is shaped by the tension between waste's redemptive capacity and its intransigence.

For Miles' dumpster-divers, Micah and Talmadge, waste is:

> like some barely known wormhole into another dimension of society, the flip side, the ass end, where everything is genuine and raw because it's not meant to be seen [...] the only *truthful* thing civilisation produced. (*WN*, 222)

To live off society's discards is to not only be morally righteous but privy to "the secret files of mankind, dragged weekly to the curb" (*WN*, 222). For Micah, scavenging provides the closest approximation to abstention from participation in the capitalist economy, since garbage itself remains the "only pure crop" civilisation has ever produced: while "land, air, water, people, animals [have] been commodified," garbage is "free, in every sense of the word [for] no one [...] ever launched a war to claim it" (*WN*, 349). Her view encapsulates the ethos of freeganism, a lifestyle born in the 1990s as part of the environmental and anti-globalisation movements, whose basis was—and is—to abstain from participation in the market economy by living off discards.[31] Freeganism for Micah is a way to appreciate waste's radical potential—reminding us of the scavenging practices of Beckett's bums. What she eventually realises, however, is that even those who live off the waste stream are to an extent complicit with the economic system they are intent on resisting. It is impossible to live entirely outside of the system, for the grid is everywhere:

> Go out into the middle of the Pacific Ocean. The very middle, as far from any land as you can get. And you know what's there? A floating garbage patch that's nearly the size of Africa. One hundred million tons of debris. So tell me where the grid ends. Show me the 'city limits' sign of civilisation. (*WN*, 76)

Such a realisation is very different to Beckett's bums' implicit faith in waste as a space of respite, and where Beckett questions the epiphanic potential of waste, here we are led to consider waste's toxicity and potential for corruption. The latter is made apparent when Micah and Talmadge's friend, Matty, is tempted by a dumpster full of steaks in the back lot of a local supermarket. Disregarding the DANGER signs surrounding it,

Matty jumps into the dumpster and begins filling his rucksack with enormous steaks. A self-proclaimed sceptic, Matty contemplates the mounds of steaks and suddenly realises freeganism's benefits:

> It was *free*, man, it was like wheeling your cart past the cashier and right out the fucking door, it was just like discovering back in college that every song you wanted was free for the downloading on bit.torrent networks. When he'd stuffed his backpack to the point of unzippability, he tried cramming the meat down harder, which didn't do the trick, then knelt there agonizing over what to leave behind. (*WN*, 228)

Matty's epiphany is not a political awakening, but rather a realisation of the profitability—or at the very least, cost-saving capacity—of dumpster-diving. This is not a critique of capitalist excess, but rather a realisation of just how easily freeganism might be manipulated for personal gain. Miles' emphasis on the frantic quality of Matty's scavenging, and on the paralysis of choosing between different items, highlights the resemblance between his approach to dumpster-diving and ordinary bargain-hunting. It is desire, and ultimately greed, that drives this search. Thus, in an almost Dickensian vein, Miles punishes Matty: the sound of a "click" triggers the realisation that the dumpster through which he is rifling is actually a trash compactor. We watch as the heavy backpack stuffed with scavenged steaks impedes Matty's efforts to climb out, and the individual bags of trash bear down upon him as the compactor churns:

> He felt [...] a single bag rolling onto his head as another one flattened itself on his face, then an intensified pressure as the air in the bags welled and then with deafening gassy bangs the bags blew [...] he could feel the backpack growing harder and tighter against his ribcage and the sharp corner of something in a bag behind him being drilled into his ass cheek. [...] He needed air, but his nostrils were goo-clogged [...] an instinctual inhale brought a film of polypropylene into his mouth, and his lungs began thrashing. (*WN*, 232–233)

The trash compactor's activation also sets in motion Matty's subsuming by his own desires. The compactor takes on an almost lively or agentic quality, wreaking vengeance on Matty's greed. Miles stops just short of a tragic ending—Matty is saved by one of the supermarket employees, who switches the machine off just as it is about to vacuum-pack him to death—but he has nevertheless made his point. This is the thing that will ultimately kill us: greed, and its residues. Waste is not something that can be managed, or in which one can dwell and thus remain outside the constraints of the system. As Matty dumbfoundedly staggers out of the compactor, "stripped of thoughts, a reasonless zombie operating on purely sensory consciousness," we are livened to the stultifying nature of the capitalist machine, and its by-products' very literal capacity to quash us (*WN*, 233).

Miles also posits waste as exceeding articulation. One of the novel's protagonists, the linguist Elwin Cross Junior, is invited by the management of the New Mexico Waste Isolation Pilot Plant (WIPP), a nuclear waste repository, to take part in an interdisciplinary panel tasked with preventing future civilisations from settling in the vicinity. The challenge is that no language has ever lasted more than a millennium, while nuclear waste has the capacity to last 24,000 years. The WIPP is not Miles's invention, but a real site, and the project the novel depicts is based on a number of real-life interdisciplinary endeavours that took place between 1970 and 1990 to ameliorate the public's resistance to the construction of nuclear waste depositories in the western states.[32] The view of the project expressed by Elwin's father, an octogenarian historian in the late stages of Alzheimer's, echoes the response of (real-life) environmentalists who opposed the project: "All the terrible effort of human civilisation, the great big arc of it. And in ten thousand years the only intelligible trace of it might be your 'keep out' sign in the desert, stuck in a big heap of trash" (*WN*, 96). It is the ultimate irony that the thing we expend so much energy looking to remove or hide is ultimately that by which we will be remembered, and that those remains will outlast any of our sign systems. Waste, here, very literally defies articulation.

Miles elaborates on this point by subtly referencing one of the solutions proposed by two (real-life) linguists involved in one such project, which consisted of breeding a species of cat that would change colour in the presence of radiation. By disseminating a mythology of fear and dread around the "ray cats" through songs and folklore, governments would be able to propagate a message that might "morph over time" but still "get pulled through over millennia," and endure as myth. Miles' awareness of the ray cats can be inferred by his inclusion, in the novel's Acknowledgements page, of Gregory Benford's book, *Deep Time: How Millennia Communicates Across Millennia* (1999), which provides an in-depth account of the ray cat proposal (*WN*, 387). And he references this proposed mythology in his depiction of a rumour among residents in Elwin Senior's nursing home, that a visit to a resident's room by the nursing home's cat is a death omen. The Alzheimer-plagued Elwin Senior does not even remember the rumour. He only remembers his distaste for the cat—a sharp, inexplicable dread that mirrors that which the WIPP scholars (both in the novel and in real life) sought to evince from future civilisa- tions. Elwin Senior's fear gives us a glimpse of the effects of the WIPP and highlights its absurdity. By interlacing references to the Nevada project's proposal to foster a collective fear in his depiction of Elwin Senior's own instinctual fear, Miles reveals a hidden pathos in the project itself. What does it say about civilisation, if we have to actively foster fear and dread around the things we have produced in order to co-exist with their rem- nants? Ann Larrabbee's analysis of the (real-life) WIPP is especially telling, in this regard. She notes that such spaces are:

> layered with cultural meanings that are so contradictory that their messages all have a certain inherent irony. These monuments to safety are built around a continuing disaster that will unfold for thousands and thousands of years, barring some miraculous technological fix. And they stand in demarcated territories now considered experimental zones, where assertions of certainty are undermined by incomplete understandings of polluted ecological sys- tems and unfolding social changes.[33]

The discussion between Elwin Junior and Elwin Senior implies the absurdity of codifying the danger of our emissions while continuing to produce them. In contrast to DeLillo's view of waste as something that can, ultimately, be read historically and reclaimed through language, Miles posits it as an entity that defies expression and that will likely annihilate future civilisations.

Miles' novel complicates Beckett's figuration of scavenging and waste- dwelling, and DeLillo's understanding of waste's legibility, and asks whether recuperation of the vanguardist variety is even possible in the twenty-first century. The capitalist grid having swallowed everything, even the oceans, it is unclear where the margins are anymore from which a countercultural voice might speak.

"THERE'S ALWAYS [AN OIL SPILL] HAPPENING"[34]: UBIQUITOUS WASTE AND PATTERN SEEKING IN TOM MCCARTHY'S *SATIN ISLAND*

Like *Bleeding Edge* and *Want Not*, Tom McCarthy's *Satin Island* is a quest for meaning in the chaos of postmillennial capitalism, and it makes the inap- prehensibility of manufactured waste a central part of that search. Where Pynchon's search is embodied in a detective and Miles' in dumpster-divers,

McCarthy's is embodied in "U," an in-house anthropologist for a global consultancy firm based in London, whose work entails "purveying cultural insight" to extract "some kind of inner social logic" from people's consumption habits. Structured in 164 numbered paragraphs, the novel's plot is driven by various loosely interlinked Internet searches that, in their combination, resemble the project spearheaded by his company:

> It was a project formed of many other projects, linked to many other projects—which rendered it well nigh impossible to say where it began and ended, to discern its "content," bulk or outline. Perhaps all projects nowadays are like that—equally boring, equally inscrutable. (*SI*, 13)

From this description, one would not immediately assume that U's company is a market research firm, and that U himself is a glorified market researcher. But that is perhaps what renders the novel's premise so eerie. McCarthy intuits that it is the people who juxtapose consumer data against large-scale sociological trends in order to "divin[e], for the benefit of a breakfast-cereal manufacturer, the social or symbolic role of breakfast" who are ultimately in control of shaping civilization (*SI*, 31). This eeriness is amplified by the fact that U's approach to market research incorporates concepts lifted from classic anthropology and French poststructuralist theory. Over the decades, he has perfected the science of "feeding vanguard theory, almost always from the left side of the spectrum, back into the corporate machine" (*SI*, 31). Gilles Deleuze and Alain Badiou, in this context, are tools for understanding the primordial desires that drive consumption—an analytical process he justifies by claiming that what he is enabling is "not simply better-tasting cereal or bigger profits for the manufacturer, but rather *meaning*, amplified and sharpened, for the millions of risers lifting cereal boxes over breakfast tables, tipping out and ingesting their contents" (*SI*, 32). Thus throughout the novel, we follow U in his work as he:

> unpicks the fibre of a culture (ours), its weft and warp—the situations it throws up, the beliefs that underpin and nourish it—and let a client in on how they can best get traction on this fibre so that they can introduce into the weave their own fine, silken thread, strategically embroider or detail it with a mini-narrative (a convoluted way of saying: sell their product). (*SI*, 21)

It is a frightening thought, for the production of cultural meaning to be in the hands of breakfast-cereal manufacturers and their marketing teams—and yet as twenty-first-century readers we cannot fail to recognise its accuracy. As the explanation in parentheses indicates, U's work is a product of the knowledge economy under neoliberalism: the semantics in which he cloaks his work obscures its underlying intent—the use of behavioural analysis to estimate the market potential of products (a practice known, in real life, as "future scoping" or "trend analysis," which evolved in the early 2000s from traditional market research). U's searches for the hidden logic that ties together the collection of news clippings and inventoried lists he has hung on his office wall are likewise aimed at helping others make a sale. Where Beckett's characters make lists that defy any logic or intent, and Barthelme's dwarfs acknowledge the futility of consumer surveys, U expresses faith in the methods of corporate anthropology. His rhetorical question, early in the novel, "who's to say what is, or might turn out to be, related to what else?" (*SI*, 34) signifies not only the interconnectivity of all things but a recognition of their economic interdependence. The search for patterns that drives both his anthropological report on "the First and Last Word on our age" (*SI*, 56), and his company's project, is inextricable from the commercialisation of those patterns and their capacity to shape the future.

McCarthy puts waste at the heart of this pattern making. We in fact meet U as he sits in a waiting room at Torino-Caselle airport, watching news coverage of an oil spill on his laptop screen. He soon notices the images reflected in the nearby glass display cases of luxury goods: "oil flows and re-flows on a watch's face," creating a "collage-effect" that expands as the news channels on the airport television screens begin to carry the story (*SI*, 9). Slowly, U is surrounded by these mediated images of oil. While the oil spill itself is most likely a reference to the BP spill of 2010 in the Gulf of Mexico (U never mentions its exact location), the vision of oil reflected on the various surfaces is an evident reference to the embeddedness of oil in everything we consume.

We are reminded of the spill again when U describes his company ethos, which is based on his boss' conceptualisation of the Tower of Babel as a relic rather than an embodiment of hubris. "What actually matters isn't the attempt to reach the heavens, or to speak God's language. No: what matters is what's left when that attempt has failed" (*SI*, 43). The tower "becomes of interest only once it has flunked its allotted task"—once it becomes waste (*SI*, 44). Cultural production, for U's boss, consists of putting the defunct to use: it is an object's uselessness that "sets it to work: as symbol, cipher, spur to the imagination, to productiveness. [...] The first move for any strategy of cultural production [...] must be to liberate things—objects, situations, systems—into uselessness" (*SI*, 44). According to such a view, it is in effluvia that companies should be looking for insight into how to grow their market share—corporations have much to learn from Surrealism and de Chirico's Scuola Metafisica.

For this same reason, U becomes obsessed with the oil spill—a perfect example if ever there was one of something that has "flunked its allotted task" (*SI*, 44). Even more disquieting is the link between U's concern with the spill and his anthropological sensibilities, as expressed in his recollection of Claude Lévi-Strauss' view of civilisation's destructive effects. Paraphrasing Lévi-Strauss' *Tristes Tropiques* (1955), U notes that

> What the anthropologist encounters when he ventures beyond civilization's perimeter-fence is no more than its effluvia, its toxic fallout. The first thing we see as we travel round the world is our own filth, thrown into mankind's face. (*SI*, 130)

Anthropology—a tradition borne out of Western imperialist thought—only serves to accelerate the cataclysmic effects of culture. What we find, upon visiting other cultures, is not the exotic other but evidence of the outcome of our industrial processes—the "other side" of our culture. In the context of the novel, the passage takes on an amplified meaning, appearing as a judgement of both U's own corporate anthropology (which seeks to shape culture itself) and of globalisation's ecologically devastating effects. Lévi-Strauss' sentiment casts new light on the reflection of the images of the oil spill on the luxury items in the airport, reminding us not only of the ubiquity of oil in so much of what capital produces but also its ecological effects. Situated alongside U's growing doubts regarding his complicity in his company's ambiguous but far-reaching project, the passage appears as an omen, warning against the direction in which he and his fellow participants in the information economy are headed.

The following section corroborates this impression: following these ruminations on Lévi-Strauss, U has a vivid dream about Fresh Kills landfill. In the dream, he flies over a series of cities before alighting on an island lit up by the glow of an immense, "regal" trash-incinerating plant (*U*, 131). The island is called "Satin Island"—a mangling, he assumes upon waking, of the real-life "Staten Island" (*SI*, 132). He recognises during the dream that if the city he has flown over is "the capital, the seat of empire," then the island is:

> the exact opposite, the inverse—the *other* place, the feeder, filterer, overflow-manager, the dirty, secreted-away appendix without which the body-proper

couldn't function; yet it seem[s], in its very degradation, more weirdly opulent than the capital it serve[s]. (*SI*, 131)

The landfill is posited as a necessary component to the body of civilisation, an unsavoury entity that is ultimately more important than the thing it helps sustain. For the reader who has read Ballard and Barthelme, DeLillo and Pynchon, or Sharp and Miles, such a depiction is perhaps not so compelling, appearing merely to echo their conceptualisation of waste as the uncanny other to capitalist expansion. However, McCarthy's passage departs from these prior depictions in its framing. Note, firstly, that the landfill occurs in a dream—it is an *imagined* space. Secondly, its source, Fresh Kills, no longer exists: as U frantically searches the Internet for insight into the dream's meaning, he discovers that Fresh Kills the landfill has been closed since 2001 (see Fig. 6.1), and that in its place are miles and miles of parkland (see Figs. 6.2 and 6.3). Thus as well as a dream, this is a memory that pulls us back into the last century. Thirdly, U only visits the landfill virtually, through online research, as he downloads images of the landfill when it was still open, and seeks an etymological connection

Fig. 6.1 Fresh Kills Landfill, early 2000s, Alamy

Fig. 6.2   Fresh Kills Park (c. 2008). Reproduced with the permission of The City of New York, NYC Parks, Freshkills Park

between the words "satin," "statin" and "Staten" (*U*, 133). This aesthetic distance is reinforced by U's recognition that the landfill resists interpretation. In contemplating the photographs of Fresh Kills he has taped to his wall, U notes that in contrast to other subjects over which he has obsessed, *"These* images—the piles of rubbish, barges, seagulls—see[m] to resist all incorporation into any useful or productive screed" (*SI*, 134). There is no connection between the words "Satin" and "Staten" or between the landfill in his dream and the images of it on the web—nor can he find a link between the landfill and the oil spill he has been following in the news. Waste is presented as something that resists our efforts to "strategically embroider" it into a narrative, commercial or otherwise.

McCarthy continues to redefine our sense of waste's tangibility in the novel's final passages, as, in the spirit of "who's to say what is, or might turn out to be, related to what else," U decides, during a work trip to New York, to take the ferry from the city's mainland to Staten Island and visit the rehabilitated landfill. Again, McCarthy takes a different approach to that of the waste novelists we have discussed so far: for U never actually reaches, or in

Fig. 6.3 Fresh Kills Park (c. 2015). Reproduced with the permission of The City of New York, NYC Parks, Freshkills Park

fact *sees*, the rehabilitated landfill. Instead, while riding the ferry, he watches a filmed montage sequence of the island—a "compilation of vague and generic scenes" showcasing its attractions—followed by an image of it from above, in which it appears "out of time, past all statutes and limits, to some other place where everything, even our crimes, have been composted down, mulched over, transformed into moss, pasture and wetland" (*SI*, 167).

Following this viewing of a mediated image of the landfill redeemed, made over, and returned to nature, the ferry arrives at the island, and U decides not to dismount, for:

> [t]o go to Staten Island—*actually* go there—would have been profoundly meaningless. What would it, in reality, have solved, or resolved? Nothing. [...] Not to go there was, of course, profoundly meaningless as well. And so I found myself, struggling just to stay in the same place, suspended between two types of meaninglessness. Did I choose the right one? I don't know. (*SI*, 171)

Where the dream-image of Fresh Kills appears as a mere repetition of previous depictions of landfill waste and its reproach to consumerism,

McCarthy's deferral of U's visit to Fresh Kills, and refusal to make it visible, takes us into entirely new narrative territory. We have been given a dream of a landfill, a sequence of online and filmed images, and, finally, a decision to abstain from viewing the real thing, and a critical judgement that this is not where the story lies. The passage's ethos is entirely at odds with the historical avant-garde's aesthetic of reparation, Beckett's jubilant descriptions of junk-dwelling and DeLillo's historiographical approach, although it does recall Ballard's quasi-scientific meditations on waste. The fact that a character obsessed with making connections voices this judgment endows the moment with a further anticlimactic dimension: if *he* can't find the connection, there is most likely no connection to be found.

One way of reading this non-visit to Fresh Kills and its alleged meaninglessness is as a refutation of narrative's capacity to make meaning, a wilful subversion of the narrative arc that would have the protagonist visit Fresh Kills, experience catharsis, and then return home, humbled into buying biodegradable items, leaving his job, committing to the woman he has been sleeping with (who, herself, has abandoned a life of anti-capitalist activism), and, in short, doing upstanding things that restore our faith in humankind. By "preferring not," in Melvillean fashion, to complete the trip to Staten Island, U challenges our assumptions about what realism should or can do—a reading substantiated by McCarthy's own criticism of contemporary realism's alleged failures. In a recent essay in the *London Review of Books* that begins with a discussion of Ballard's articulation of realism in the 1995 introduction to *Crash* (discussed in this study in Ch. 4),[35] McCarthy suggests we consider the concept of realism in relation to different definitions of the "real." The first of these is Michel Leiris' conceptualisation of the "real" as the tip of the bull's horn in a bullfight, where the bullfight stands for literature itself (McCarthy, 21). The "real," in this scenario, has nothing to do with "the empirically understood world" and "certainly nothing to do with authenticity" (McCarthy, 21). Rather, it recalls the Lacanian definition of the "real," as that which is "unassimilable by any system of representation" (McCarthy, 22). This in turn shifts the author's aim from "depicting [the] real realistically, or even well" to approaching the "real" in the full awareness that, "like some roving black hole, it represents (though that's not the right word anymore) the point at which the writing's entire project crumples and implodes" (McCarthy, 22). The real is always threatening to sabotage the writing project itself, its very presence reminding us of the work's own tenuousness. U's ascription of meaninglessness to Fresh Kills, which the reader intuitively associates with the anthropological work he has failed to complete, can be seen to comment on *Satin Island*'s constructed quality, but also—

and relatedly—to openly reflect upon writing's limitations. To not look at the landfill is a means to undermine narrative's capacity to make the world legible and explain the inexplicable. This attendance to the meaninglessness of the landfill—and the meaninglessness of that meaninglessness—directly counters the artifice of realism: rather than a moral or a climactic discovery, McCarthy offers an honest acknowledgement, not unlike that of a Ballardian or Beckettian protagonist, that not all lived experience is meaningful.

But McCarthy's second reference in his exploration of the real is perhaps even more revealing. Here, McCarthy draws on the concept of "form-lessness" Georges Bataille delineated in an essay in the magazine *Critical Dictionary*, to suggest that we read the "real" as the material dimension of an object. For Bataille, McCarthy notes, "existence is a relentless and ongoing process of deformation" that "releases objects, and the world, the entire universe, from all categories of the knowable and denotable until they 'resemble nothing." Viewed from this perspective,

> a thing's real would consist in its materiality: a sticky, messy and above all base materiality that overflows all boundaries defining the thing's—and everything's—identity. It thus threatens ontology itself. "Matter," Bataille writes elsewhere, "represents in relation to the economy of the universe what crime represents in relation to the law." (McCarthy, 22)

To capture the "real," the writer must contend with the stickiness and messiness of matter, and recognise, too, the limits of its legibility. It would run counter to this understanding of the "real" for U to decode Fresh Kills, or introduce it into his writing. The point of Fresh Kills—and, indeed, the point of the oil spill—is to defy our efforts to read it. If we consider U's boss' view that "any strategy of cultural production" must first "liberate things—objects, situations, systems—into uselessness" (*SI*, 44), it becomes obvious that the landfill must be stripped of all other functions before it is put to epistemological use. It must be divested of its imaginative capacity to threaten the economy of the narrative, and recognised as something that has "flunked its allotted task" (*SI*, 44). To ascribe the landfill meaning would be to impede its incorporation into U's company's grand project.

Beyond self-consciously commenting on the limits of representation, U's non-visit to Fresh Kills, like his obsession with other forms of waste, speaks to a specific set of postmillennial anxieties relating to the environment and the economy. McCarthy's text suggests one need not visit Fresh Kills, today, to comprehend the extent of our consumer ills—one need only open a browser window and scroll through the day's news to see "our own filth, thrown into mankind's face" (*SI*, 130). Such a view is borne out by other passages in McCarthy's novel, in which, as mentioned earlier, we find repeated references to the pervasiveness of waste and ecological disasters. References to the oil spill that occurred in the novel's opening pages are made on nearly every page: it permeates U's dreams as he sleeps and colours his perception of the world around him when he is awake. This seeping of the oil spill into his thoughts, he suggests, is a direct result of what he calls its "generic" nature. U summarises anthropology as the extrapolation of larger ideas from the apparent particular (*SI*, 35). Oil spills are an ideal subject for such pattern seeking since "there's always one happening, one that's recently transpired or, it can be said with confidence, one that's on the verge of happening" (*SI*, 35). In a similar vein, pollution, fallout, and wreckage are part of the very texture of capitalist civilisation. Understand that and you understand civilisation itself. The pervasiveness of oil imagery in this sense is a counterpart, or at the very least metaphorical equivalent, of the anthropological project "formed of many other projects" in which U's company is involved, which, he explicitly tells us,

> will have had direct effects on you; in fact, there's probably not a single area of your daily life that it hasn't, in some way or another, touched on, penetrated, changed; although you probably don't know this. (*SI*, 13)

Just as there is always an oil spill happening or about to happen, the corporate anthropology of U's company pervades every sphere of culture. U's assertion of the pointlessness of visiting Fresh Kills is indicative of a broader message. It is unnecessary to look at *any* discrete instance of waste, be it a landfill site or an individual item of trash—for the landfill (the oil spill, the fallout) is all around us. Waste is no longer the underside of culture, as U first perceived it in his dream—it has *become* culture. As Micah in *Want Not* intuited, the capitalist grid is everywhere, and so, too, are its effluvia. U's own complicity in a system that not only investigates social behaviour but *engineers* it highlights the source of the issue. What we are dealing with is not where to put waste, or how to offset its ecologically damaging effects, but with the embedded nature of consumerism and the speculative quality of neoliberal ideology.

However, the pervasiveness of which U speaks also has an aesthetic dimension. We have been repeatedly reminded throughout the novel that anthropology deals in fiction—in the narrative underlying things and the patterns that connect them. Mid-way through the novel, U expands on this idea in a daydream. Obsessing over the poor reception to a presentation he recently gave at a conference, U mentally re-writes the event, envisaging himself developing an anthropological theory based on "*the* Oil Spill — an ongoing event whose discrete parts and moments [...] have run together, merged into a continuum in which all plurals drown" (*SI*, 103). The daydream grows more animated, as he imagines himself seducing his audience:

> "You might say that what we're observing is ecological catastrophe, or an indictment of industrial society, or a parable of mankind's hubris. Or you might say, more dispassionately, that we're observing a demonstration of chemical propensities. But the truth is that. [...] Beneath all these dramas, I'd say, and before them, we're observing, simply (gentlemen), differentiation. Differentiation in its purest form: the very *principle* of differentiation. [...] Behind all behaviour, issuing instructions, sending in the plays—just as behind life itself, its endless sequencing of polymers—there lies a source code. This is the base premise of all anthropology." (*SI*, 104)

The imagined speech effectively rephrases U's boss' concept of the Tower of Babel: like the ruined tower, the oil spill is not a "parable of mankind's hubris" but a subject of enquiry in its own right, deserving of attention due to its difference from the matter it stains. The oil spill is aesthetically transformative and deserving of awe. It augments the animals whose fur and feathers it tars, turning them into "Living Pompeians! Victims of the Oil Gorgon!" and re-casts the rocks on which it sticks, "mak[ing] them rockier" (*SI*, 106). *It enhances their realism.* There is no shame in stating such admiration, since it merely counters the arguments of environmentalists, which are also rooted in aesthetics: "They dislike the oil spill for the way it makes the coastline look 'not right,' prevents it from illustrating the vision of nature [...] as sublime, virginal and pure" (*SI*, 107). Admiration for an oil spill is not misplaced, "for what is oil *but* nature?" (*SI*, 108).

As with the rest of U's musings, we are not to take this interpretation of the aesthetics of oil seriously—these are not McCarthy's views, nor are we expected to be convinced. Spanning six of the novel's 164 numbered paragraphs, U's oil daydream takes on the shape of a spill, spreading on and on until U runs out of ideas. The daydream is intended to convey the extent of U's abstraction from the actual politics of oil—recalling the self-centredness of Ian McEwan's protagonist in *Solar* (2010), who has built his reputation on climate change research he has stolen from a deceased colleague, and who similarly weaves the topic of energy renewal into a grand narrative about (particularly his own) human enterprise.[36] But for a reader of literary representations of waste and the forms it can take, there is a different dimension to this section. Like the non-visit to Fresh Kills, U's daydream-speech is an exercise in futility, an experience of waste at a

Fig. 6.4 Cover of *Concrete Island* (2008), Fourth Estate/Harper Collins/Lebrecht Music and Arts Photo Library/ Alamy

remove—mediated, imagined, and indeed, since he doesn't actually give the speech, not even articulated. The oil spill of the daydream, like the other waste forms in the novel, is depicted as all pervasive and imbued with the promise of some deeper (ontological or aesthetic) meaning, which it ultimately withholds. The cover art of the book, which transforms the colour swatch design of Ballard's Fourth Estate editions into a swatch-qua-Internet buffering sign stained by pools of oil, conveys this visually as well as making explicit McCarthy's debt to Ballard's hyperrealism (see Figs. 6.4 and 6.5). The transformation of the colour swatch of Ballard's cover into a buffering symbol alludes to the shift from material to digital, just as the ephemeral "satin" of the title invites comparisons not only to the novel's mediated visions of "Staten Island," but to Ballard's "concrete" wasteland. Internet, visual representation, and the obfuscating quality of waste are brought together, implying an aesthetic credo that extends the twentieth century's countercultural literary representations of waste to explore virtual, as opposed to concrete, wastelands.

Fig. 6.5 Cover of *Satin Island* (2014), Jonathan Cape/Random House and Suzanne Dean

Satin Island links the pervasiveness of ecological disasters and waste to the tentacular quality of the information economy under neoliberalism. McCarthy weaves together the market economy and waste through surrealistic representations of oil spills and landfills, but he suggests that this relationship is too embedded to be changed, and that the spirit of avant-gardism has become part of the productivist paradigm.

The Future of Waste

The texts discussed in this conclusion use waste to challenge neoliberalism's cultural and ecological effects, while suggesting that waste in this phase of capitalism is something that can be neither contained nor represented in the ways deployed by novelists in the twentieth century. Jonathan Miles' *Want Not* livens us to the fact that in the twenty-first century, there are few—if any—ways in which one can truly live outside the capitalist grid: even a Beckettian style of living in and off of waste is a tacit form of participation. The attention both Pynchon and McCarthy's novels give to the (now closed) Fresh Kills Landfill on Staten Island implies a longing for the days when the major problem waste posed us was the expense (and space) taken up in housing it, and it casts a new light on their twentieth-century forebears. However, the apparent defeatism manifest in these aesthetic responses—and the implication that a radical aesthetics, in the early postmillennial neoliberal economy, is not possible—is also a call to arms that extends the efforts of the historical avant-garde and its descendants, and allows us to read them in a new light. Pynchon, Miles, and McCarthy harness waste to identify free market capitalism's role in spiralling class inequality, civil unrest, and ecological devastation in order to explode popular conceptions about that model. The story they tell provides a counter to the rhetoric that equates laissez-faire economics with democracy and consumerism with happiness, and that sees nature as purely a resource for producing goods.

Each of the texts examined in this book has introduced us to very different responses to capitalism, to the culture(s) that capitalism fosters, and to the roles of countercultural art within these contexts. They have invited us to consider waste from myriad perspectives: metaphorically, as a sign of a system gone awry, or literally, as an obstacle to production; as a reproach to our compulsion to consume, or as a means to shock and arrest us into thinking otherwise; as something produced and expelled by humans, or as a category to which humans themselves are relegated. And, also, we have seen waste posited in redemptive terms. Surrealism envisages the discard as material for aesthetic production and as a source of epiphanic discovery; Beckett's vagrants show how one might resist commercialisation through a kind of dwelling in waste and a poetics of immersion; and DeLillo's garbologists, archivists, and waste managers show how waste might be investigated as an artefact, allowing us to find, in and among the brand names and advertising slogans, a glimpse of our common humanity. Similarly, we have seen recuperation cast alternately as a means to radically alter the course of artistic production and challenge consumerism's obsession with novelty, and as a means to further squeeze out profits and extract use. Indeed, we have seen how the radical potential of both waste *and* recuperation are always at risk of being neutralised, or assimilated.

Perhaps the most salient reason we have addressed these literary depictions of manufactured waste and recuperation is the relevance they have for us today, as twenty-first-century readers and (however unwitting) participants in the global(ised) market economy, which has, since the 1980s, been modelled on neoliberal ideology. The paths traversed by the historical avant-garde's junk artists, Beckett's gloriously unproductive vagrants, Barthelme's dwarfs, Ballard's instigators of car crashes, Gaddis' failed artists and imbecilic speculators, and DeLillo's philosophical waste managers remain acutely relevant to contemporary discussions about capitalism's effects on culture, on social well-being, and on the environment. Moreover, reading these works today, at a time when awareness of the ecological crisis has never been higher, and at a time of acute doubt regarding the future of capitalism itself, gives us a new perspective on them, and on the contexts from which they emerged. de Chirico, Loy, and Breton's haunting depictions of waste were not borne out of an ecological sensibility, and yet they uncannily anticipate the ideology of re-use that has governed environmentalist thought over the last 40 years, as well as the ethos of environmentalist art that has emerged from that discourse.[37] Beckett's narratives remain relevant to contemporary discussions about social inequality under capitalism—an aspect of his work that remains regrettably under-discussed. Finally, the evolution of both contemporary environmental discourse and neoliberal ideology since the publication of the post-1960s novels discussed allows us to effectively historicise them as critiques of specific moments in late capitalism rather than as broadly representative of contemporary culture. Indeed, as I have proposed elsewhere, DeLillo's more recent engagement with global warming, a play titled *The Word For Snow* (2007/2014), suggests the author's own recognition that we have moved beyond the problem of where to put waste, and must now face how to manage its *effects*.[38] The approach he takes in this play, depicting a dystopian future in which the material world has been obliterated and replaced by the words used to describe it, can be seen as indicative of a broader shift in the aesthetics of waste.

My contention, throughout this book, has been that the literary depictions of waste of the last century still have much to teach us. Loy and de Chirico, Breton and Beckett, Ballard and Barthelme, Gaddis and DeLillo, and Pynchon, McCarthy and Miles illuminate capitalist ideology in important ways while reaffirming art's capacity to critique the status quo. In their very different interpretations of waste—as a magical cipher, a sign of marginality, a moral reproach to capitalist excess, or an artefact—these authors throw into relief the extent to which the economic system under which we live influences our engagement with the material world and our fellow humans. The novels we have discussed invite us to reflect upon the ways in which capitalism shapes our perception of objects and people and, relatedly, our aesthetic and moral judgments. The depictions of manufactured waste in these narratives enjoin us to relate to inanimate matter and to each other in other ways; to look at that world and at each other at a slant; and to see them for something other than their use-value.

NOTES

1. Steven Best and Ian Kellner, *The Postmodern Turn* (Guilford Press, 1997), 269.
2. Paul R. Elhrich, *The Population Bomb* (Buccaneer Books, 1968), 39.
3. Thomas Pynchon, *Bleeding Edge* (London: Jonathan Cape, 2013), 340. Henceforth, *BE*.
4. It is especially worth flagging Philip Mirowski, *Never Let a Serious Crisis Go to Waste: How Neoliberalism Survived the Financial Meltdown* (London: Verso, 2013) and Jennifer Wingard, *Branded Bodies, Rhetoric and the Neoliberal Nation State* (New York and Plymouth: Lexington Books, 2013).
5. David Harvey, *The Enigma of Capital: And the Crises of Capitalism* (Oxford and New York: Oxford University Press, 2010); David Graeber, *Debt: The Last 5,000 Years* (New York: Melvill House Publishing, 2011); Thomas Piketty. *Capital in the Twenty-First Century* (Harvard University Press, 2013).
6. See Harvey, *Enigma of Capital*, 20. Philip Mirowski provides an excellent account of this in Chapter Three of *Never Let a Serious Crisis Go to Waste*.
7. Other important contributions to this discussion include Lisa Duggan, *The Twilight of Equality? Neoliberalism, Cultural Politics, and the End of Democracy* (Boston: Beacon Press, 2003); and Nick Couldry, *Why Voice Matters: Culture and Politics After Neoliberalism* (London: Sage, 2010).
8. John Cassidy, *Dot.Con: The Greatest Story Ever Sold* (New York: HarperCollins, 2002), 26.
9. It is beyond the scope of this study to examine the discourse around the open source movement—and its arguable cooption, over the last two decades, by commercial interests—but it is worth noting the wealth of publications that have sought to do so. Of particular note are: Gabriella Coleman, "The political agnosticism of free and open source software and the inadvertent politics of contrast,' *Anthropological Quarterly* 77. 3 (Summer 2004): 507–519; Sara Schoonmaker, "Globalization from Below: Free Software and Alternatives to Neoliberalism," *Development and Change* (2007): 999–1020; and Bart Cammaerts, "Disruptive Sharing in a Digital Age: Rejecting Neoliberalism?" *Continuum: Journal of Media & Cultural Studies* (2011), 47–62.
10. Wendy Brown, *Undoing the Demos: Neoliberalism's Stealth Revolution* (Cambridge, MA and London: MIT Press, 2015).
11. Timothy Shenk, "Booked #3: What Exactly is Neoliberalism?—Q&A with Wendy Brown," *Dissent*, 2 April 2015.
12. Naomi Klein provides a useful—and harrowing—account of this in *This Changes Everything: Capitalism versus the Climate*, 19–20; 83.
13. See for instance England and Bluestone, "Ecology and social conflict" in *Toward a Steady-State Economy*, ed. Herman E. Daly (San Francisco:

Freemanc, 1973), 190–214; André Gorz, *Ecology as Politics*, transl. Patsy Vigderman and Jonathon Cloud (Boston: South End Press, 1980 [1975]); Arran E. Gare, *Postmodernism and the Environmental Crisis* (London and New York: Routledge, 1995).

14. There have, however, been a few encouraging moves that counter this ideology. For example, in an effort to counter the environmental effects of built-in obsolescence, the French government has rolled out regulations obliging manufacturers to explicitly state how long their appliances will last, and how long spare parts will be available, in what could be the first step towards rendering obsolescence itself obsolete. Homa Khaleeli, "End of the Line for Stuff that's Bound to Die?" *The Guardian* (3 March 2015). Accessed 2 March 2016: http://www.theguardian.com/technology/shortcuts/2015/mar/03/has-planned-obsolesence-had-its-day-design.

15. Ken Hiltner, "Interview with Elaine Scarry," *Environmental Criticism for the Twenty-First Century*, eds. Stephanie LeMenager et al. (London and New York: Routledge, 2011), 273.

16. Michel Faber, *The Book of Strange New Things* (London: Canongate, 2014). Henceforth, *BSNT*.

17. Jonathan Franzen, *The Corrections* (London: Fourth Estate, 2002 [2001]).

18. Don DeLillo, *Zero K* (New York: Simon & Schuster, 2016). Henceforth, *ZK*.

19. Rachele Dini, "Don DeLillo's *Zero K*," *European Journal of American Studies* (April 2016).

20. Jennifer Egan, *A Visit From the Good Squad* (London: Corsair, 2011 [2010]). Henceforth, *AVFTGS*.

21. Egan's vision of our future relationship to material goods may not be entirely speculative. Journalist James Wallman makes a similar case in his book, *Stuffocation: Living More with Less* (London: Crux, 2013), relating digitization to a broader shift away from material possessions. The idea that we have reached "peak stuff" has been posited by a number of prominent figures including IKEA's head of sustainability, who explained the company's plans to become "increasingly circular," investing in products that allow consumers to mend their purchases rather than replace them with new ones. See Stuart Jeffries and Paola Cocozza, "Goodbye to Curtains and Clutter: How we Learned to Buy Less Stuff," *The Guardian* (1 March 2016). Accessed 2 March 2016: http://www.theguardian.com/society/2016/mar/01/goodbye-curtains-clutter-learned-to-buy-less-stuff-shopping.

22. Brenda Coultas, "The Bowery Project," in *A Handmade Museum* (Saint Paul (MN): Coffeehouse Press, 2003), 11–54.

23. Virginia Woolf, "Solid Objects" (1920) in *A Haunted House, and Other Short Stories* (London: Mariner Books, 2002).

24. Thomas Pynchon, *Bleeding Edge*, 137.

25. The term "Deep Web" was coined by BrightPlanet founder Mike Bergman, who likened a standard Internet search to the act of dragging a net across the ocean's surface: a proliferation of content remains outside the scope of

a surface search, but can be accessed by non-traditional search engines. "The Deep Web: Surfacing Hidden Value," BrightPlanet (September 2001). Accessed 15 July 2015: http://brightplanet.com/wp-content/uploads/2012/03/12550176481-deepwebwhitepaper1.pdf.

26. Silicon Alley was the name given to the area of Manhattan where the tech industry grew in the 1990s; it has since become a metonym for the New York City tech industry as a whole.

27. Walter Benjamin, *The Arcades Project* (Cambridge, MA: Bellknapp University Press, 1999), Henceforth, *AP*.

28. Esther Leslie, "Walter Benjamin's *Arcades Project*," *Benjamin Papers/militantesthetix.html*, accessed 1 May 2015. http://www.militantesthetix.co.uk/waltbenj/yarcades.html.

29. Geert Lovink, *Dynamics of Critical Internet Culture: 1994–2001* (Amsterdam: Institute of Network Cultures, 2009), 7.

30. Jonathan Miles, *Want Not* (New York: Mariner, 2014 [2013]). Henceforth, *WN*.

31. Tristram Stuart, *Waste: Uncovering the Global Food Scandal* (New York: Penguin, 2009), 220–231.

32. The original report of these investigations is freely available online: Kathleen M. Trauth, Stephen C. Hora and Robert V. Guzowski, "Expert Judgment on Markers to Deter Inadvertent Human Intrusion into the Waste Isolation Pilot Plant," Printed November 1993 by Sandia National Laboratories.

33. Anna Larabee, *Decade of Disaster* (Chicago: University of Illinois Press, 2000), 53.

34. Tom McCarthy, *Satin Island* (London: Jonathan Cape, 2015), 38. Henceforth, *SI*.

35. Tom McCarthy, "Writing Machines," *London Review of Books* 36. 24 (18 December 2014), 21–22.

36. Ian McKewan, *Solar* (London and New York: Jonathan Cape, 2010), 152–154.

37. For an exhaustive account of environmentalist visual art from the 1970s to the present day see Linda Weintraub, *To Life: Eco Art in Pursuit of a Sustainable Planet* (Berkeley, CA: University of California Press, 2012).

38. Commissioned by the 2007 Chicago Humanities Festival, whose theme was climate change, DeLillo's play premiered on 27 October 2007 in a production by the Steppenwolf Theatre Company. It was published in 2014 by Karma and Glenn Horowitz, New York, with illustrations by Richard Prince. Its central conceit is reminiscent of "Human Moments in World War III." See Rachele Dini, "On aftermaths, language and silence: Don DeLillo's *The Word for Snow*," *Bookmunch* (4 March 2016). Accessed 5 March 2016: https://bookmunch.wordpress.com/2016/03/04/on-aftermaths-language-and-silence-the-word-for-snow-by-don-delillo/.

BIBLIOGRAPHY

1960: Les Nouveaux Réalistes. Paris: MAM/Musée d'Art Moderne de la Ville de Paris, 15 May–7 September 1986.

AbÃ¡di-Nagy, ZoltÃ¡n. William Gaddis, The Art of Fiction No. 101. *The Paris Review* 105 (Winter 1987). http://www.theparisreview.org/interviews/2577/the-art-of-fiction-no-101-william-gaddis. Accessed 31 Aug 2015.

Abadie, Daniel. 1977. *Arman: L'âge de fer et ses monuments*. Paris: Galerie Beaubourg.

Ackerly, Chris and Stan E. Gontarski 2009. A Sense of Unending: Samuel Becket's Eschatological Turn. In *Where Never Before: Beckett's Poetics of Elsewhere*, ed. Sjef Houppermans and Marius Buning, 135–150. Amsterdam: Rodopi.

Adams, Robert Martin. 1976, Spring. Rags, Garbage, and Fantasy. *The Hudson Review*: 54–68. http://www.jstor.org/stable/3850320. Accessed 11 Feb 2013.

Adamson, Walter L. 2007. *Embattled Avant-Gardes: Modernism's Resistance to Commodity Culture in Europe*. Berkeley: University of California Press.

Alexander, Catherine, and Joshua Reno, eds. 2012. *Economies of Recycling: Global Transformation of Materials, Values and Social Relations*. London: Zed Books.

Allen, Michelle Elizabeth. 2007. *Cleansing the City: Sanitary Geographies in Victorian London*. Athens, GA: Ohio University Press.

Alloway, Laurence. 1960. Junk Culture as a Tradition. In *New Forms—New Media*. Exhibition Catalogue. New York: Martha Jackson Gallery.

Alter, Alexandra. 2010, 29 January. Author Q&A: Don DeLillo Deconstructed. *Wall Street Journal*. http://www.wsj.com/articles/SB10001424052748703906204575027094208914032. Accessed 5 Feb 2016.

© The Editor(s) (if applicable) and The Author(s) 2016   219
R. Dini, *Consumerism, Waste, and Re-Use in Twentieth-Century Fiction*, DOI 10.1057/978-1-137-58165-5

Appadurai, Arjun, ed. 1986. *The Social Life of Things: Commodities in Cultural Perspective*, 3–63. Cambridge: Cambridge University Press.

Apollonio, Umbro, ed. 2009. *Futurist Manifestos*. London: Tate Publishing.

Ardvisson, Adam. 2003. On the 'Pre-History of the Panoptic Sort': Mobility in Market Research. *Surveillance and Society* 1(4): 1–19. www.surveillance-and-society.org/articles1(4)/prehistory.pdf. Accessed 5 Jan 2016.

Arman. 1999. *Le Nouveau Réalisme*. Paris: Editions du feu de Paume.

Armstrong, Tim. 1998. *Modernism, Technology and the Body: A Cultural Study*. Cambridge: Cambridge University Press.

Arnold, Elizabeth. 1990. *Mina Loy and the Avant Garde*. Chicago, IL: University of Chicago Press.

Arp, Hans. 1958. Looking. In *Arp*, ed. James Thrall Soby, 12–16. New York: Museum of Modern Art.

Ballard, J.G. 1966, July. The Coming of the Unconscious. *New Worlds*. http://www.jgballard.ca/non_fiction/jgb_reviews_surrealism.html. Accessed 17 Nov 2015

——— 1968. *Unspeakable Practices, Unnatural Acts*. New York: Farrar, Straus and Giroux.

——— 1969. *Crash*. London: Fourth Estate, 2011.

——— 1970, 9. *Books and Bookmen* 15(10): 6.

——— 1974. *Guilty Pleasures*. New York: Farrar, Straus and Giroux.

——— 1975a [1993]. *High-Rise*. London: Flamingo.

——— 1975b. Interview by David Pringle and Jim Goddard. *Science Fiction Monthly* 4: 30–31.

——— 1976. *Low-Flying Aircraft and Other Stories*. London: Cape.

——— 1981. *Sixty Stories*. New York: Putnam.

——— 1994 [1974]. *Concrete Island*. New York: Noonday Press.

——— 1996. *A User's Guide to the Millennium*. New York: Picador.

——— 1997. *Not Knowing: The Essays and Interviews of Donald Barthelme*. In ed. Kim Herzinger. New York: Random House.

——— 2001a. "The Subliminal Man" (1963). *The Complete Short Stories. London: Fourth Estate* 2014: 559–577.

——— 2001b. "The Ultimate City" (1975). In *The Complete Short Stories*. London: Flamingo.

——— 2006 [1969]. *The Atrocity Exhibition*. London: Fourth Estate.

Barthelme, Donald. 1967. *Snow White*. New York: Scribner.

Barthes, Roland. 1986. "The Reality Effect" (1967). In *The Rustle of Language*, 141–148. Trans. RichardHoward. Oxford: Blackwell.

Bartolini, Gérard. 2011. *Montre-moi tes déchets: L'art de faire parler les restes*, 9–13. Paris: L'Harmattan.

Bartholomew, Rafe. 2011, 3 October. Director's Cut: Q&A With Don DeLillo. In *Grantland*. http://www.grantland.com/story/_/id/7032210/qa-don-delillo. Accessed 28 July 2012.

Bataille, Georges. 1991. *The Accursed Share: An Essay in General Economy*, vol 1. New York: Zone Books.

Baudrillard, Jean. The System of Collecting. In *The Cultures of Collecting*, 7–24, ed. John Elsner and Roger Cardinal. London: Reaktion Books.

Bauman, Zygmunt. 2004. *Wasted Lives: Modernity and Its Outcasts*. Cambridge: Polity.

———. 2007. *Liquid Times: Living in an Age of Uncertainty*. Cambridge: Polity.

———. 2008. Radical Surrealism: Re-reading Photography and History in J.G. Ballard's *Crash*. *Textual Practice* 22(3): 507–528.

Baxter, Jeanette, ed. 2008. *JG Ballard: Contemporary Critical Perspectives*. London: Continuum.

———. 2009. *J.G. Ballard's Surrealist Imagination: Spectacular Authorship*. Farnham: Ashgate.

Beaumont, Matthew, and Gregory Dart, eds. 2010. *Restless Cities*. London: Verso.

Beckett, Chris. 2015. J.G. Ballard's 'Elaborately Signalled Landscape': The Drafting of *Concrete Island*. *eBLJ*: 1–21. http://www.bl.uk/eblj/2015articles/pdf/ebljarticle52015.pdf. Accessed 30 Oct 2015.

Beckett, Samuel. 1958. *Endgame* (1957) and *Act Without Words II and II* (1957). London: Faber. Originally published in French as *Fin de partie suivi de Acte sans paroles I et II*. Paris: Minuit, 1956.

———. 1964. *How It Is*. New York: Grove. Originally published in French as *Comment c'est*. Paris: Minuit, 1961.

———. 1967 [1974]. *Stories and Texts for Nothing*. New York: Grove; London: Calder & Boyars. Originally published in French as *Nouvelles et textes pour rien*. Paris: Minuit, 1955.

———. 1973 [1938]. *Murphy*. London: Picador.

Beckett, Samuel. *Molloy* (1955); *Malone Dies* (1956); *The Unnameable* (1958) in *Trilogy*. London: John Calder, 1959. Originally published individually in French as *Molloy*. Paris: Minuit, 1951; *Malone Meurt*. Paris: Minuit, 1951; *L'innomable*. Paris: Minuit, 1953.

Beck, John. 2009. *Dirty Wars: Landscape, Power and Waste in American Literature*. Lincoln: University of Nebraska Press.

Begley, Adam. 1993. Don DeLillo: The Art of Fiction. *Paris Review* 35(Autumn): 274–306.

———. 1997, 15 September. In DeLillo's Hands, Waste is a Beautiful Thing. *New York Observer*, 38.

Benford, Gregory. 1999. *Deep Time: How Millennia Communicates Across Millennia*. New York: Harper Perennial.

Benjamin, Walter. 1983. *Charles Baudelaire: A Lyric Poet in the Era of High Capitalism*. Trans. Harry Zohn. London: Verso.

———. 2006. *The Writer of Modern Life: Essays on Charles Baudelaire*. Cambridge, MA: Harvard/Belknapp.

Bennett, Jane. 2010. *Vibrant Matter: Toward a Political Ecology of Things*. Durham, NC: Duke University Press.

Benton, Ted, ed. 1996. *The Greening of Marxism*. London: Guilford Press.

Berg, Anne. 2015. The Nazi Rag-Pickers and their Wine: The Politics of Waste and Recycling in Nazi Germany. *Social History* 40(4): 446–472.

Bergman, Michael K. 2001, September. The Deep Web: Surfacing Hidden Value. BrightPlanet LLC White Paper.

Bernstein, Jessica. 2013. *Cold Modernism: Literature, Fashion, Art*. University Park: Penn State University Press.

Berman, Marshall. 1981. *All That is Solid Melts into Air: The Experience of Modernity*. London: Verso, 2010.

Borges, Jorge Luis. The Analytical Language of John Wilkins. Trans. Lilia Graciela Vásquez (Alamut: Bastion of Peace and Information). https://ccrma.stanford.edu/courses/155/assignment/ex1/Borges.pdf. Accessed 10 Feb 2016.

Boscagli, Maurizia. 2014. *Stuff Theory: Everyday Objects, Radical Materialism*. London: Bloomsbury.

Boxall, Peter. 2002. *Don DeLillo: The Possibility of Fiction*. London: Routledge.

———. 2008. 'There's No Lack of Void': Waste and Abundance in Beckett and DeLillo. *Substance* 37(2): 56–70.

———. 2015. *The Value of the Novel*. Cambridge: Cambridge University Press.

Bragard, Véronique. 2013. Introduction: Languages of Waste: Matter and Form in our Garbage. *Interdisciplinary Studies in Literature and Environment* 20(3): 459–463.

Brater, Enoch. 2011. *Ten Ways of Thinking About Samuel Beckett*. London: Bloomsbury.

Braverman, Harry. 1998 [1974]. *Labor and Monopoly Capitalism: The Degradation of Work in the Twentieth Century*. New York: Monthly Review Press.

Breton, André. 1960 [1928]. *Nadja*. Trans. Richard Howard. New York: Grove Weidenfeld.

———. 1965 [1928]. *Le Surrealisme et la peinture*. Paris: Gaillmard.

———. 1969. *Manifestoes of Surrealism*. Trans. Richard Seaver and Helen R. Lane. Ann Arbor: University of Michigan Press.

———. 1987 [1937]. *Mad Love*. Trans. Mary Ann Caws. University of Nebraska Press.

———. 2002 [1972]. *Surrealism and Painting*. Trans. Simon Watson. New York: MFA Publications.

Brienza, Susan. 1987. *Samuel Beckett's New Worlds: Style in Metafiction*. Norman: University of Oklahoma Press.

Brigg, Peter. 1985. *J.G. Ballard*. Washington, DC: Starmont House.

Brown, Bill. 2001. Thing Theory. *Critical Inquiry* 28(1): 1–22.

———. 2004. *A Sense of Things: The Object Matter of American Literature*. Chicago, IL: University of Chicago Press.

———. 2006. Reification, Reanimation and the American Uncanny. *Critical Inquiry* 32(Winter): 175–207.

Bukatman, Scott. 1993. JG Ballard and the Mediascape. In *Terminal Identity: The Virtual Subject in Postmodern Science Fiction*, 41–45. Durham, NC and London: Duke University Press.

Bürger, Peter. 1984 [1974]. *Theory of the Avant-Garde*. Trans. Michael Shaw. Minneapolis: University of Minnesota Press.

Burke, Carolyn. 1996. *Becoming Modern: The Life of Mina Loy*. Berkeley: University of California Press.

———. 2011. Recollecting Dada: Juliette Roche. In *Women in Dada: Essays on Sex, Gender and Identity*, ed. Naomi Sawelson-Gorse, 571–575. Cambridge, MA: MIT Press.

Burnett, John. 1994. *Idle Hands: The Experience of Unemployment, 1790–1990*. London: Routledge.

Calder. 1956. *Waiting for Godot*. London: Faber (1954).

Calinescu, Matei. 1995 [1977]. *Five Faces of Modernity: Modernism, Avant-garde, Decadence, Kitsch, Postmodernism*. Durham, NC: Duke University Press.

Calvino, Italo. 1974 [1972]. *Invisible Cities*. Trans. William Weaver. New York: Harcourt Brace Jovanovich.

Cammaerts, Bart. 2011. Disruptive Sharing in a Digital Age: Rejecting Neoliberalism? *Continuum: Journal of Media & Cultural Studies* 25(1): 47–62.

Carrick, Jill. 2010. *Nouveau Réalisme, 1960s France, and the Neo-Avant-garde: Topographies of CHANCE and Return*. Farnham: Ashgate.

Carver, Beci. 2014. Waste Management in Beckett's. In *Watt. Granular Modernism*, 142–170. Oxford: Oxford University Press.

de Certeau, Michel. 1988. *The Practice of Everyday Life*. Trans. Steven Randall. Berkeley: University of California Press.

Chaplin, Charlie. *Modern Times* (1936). Directed by Charlie Chaplin. Film. USA: United Artists Corporation.

Chappell, Peter. 2013. Paper Routes: Bleak House, Rubbish Theory, and the Character Economy of Realism. *ELH: A Journal of English literary history* 80(3): 783–810.

Chipp, Hershel B., ed. 1992. *Theories of Modern Art: A Source Book by Artists and Critics*. Berkeley: University of California Press.

de Chirico, Giorgio. 1964 [1929]. *Hebdomeros*. Paris: Flammarion.

———. 1992. *Hebdomeros*. Trans. John Ashberry. London: Peter Owen Publishers.

———. 2008 [1962]. *Memorie della Mia Vita*. Bologna: Bompiani.

Clare, Ralph. 2013. Family Incorporated: William Gaddis's *JR* and the Embodiment of Capitalism. *Studies in the Novel* 45(1): 102–122.

Clune, Michael W. 2010. *American Literature and the Free Market, 1945–2000*. Cambridge: Cambridge University Press.

Cohen, Maurie J. 2012, 22 May. Bringing Consumerism in from the Cold War. *Sustainability: Science, Practice & Policy Blog*. http://ssppjournal.blogspot. co.uk/2012/05/bringing-consumerism-in-from-cold-war.html. Accessed 7 June 2015

Cohen, William, and Ryan Johnson, eds. 2005. *Filth: Dirt, Disgust, and Modern Life*. Minneapolis: University of Minnesota Press.

Coleman, Gabriella. Summer 2004. The Political Agnosticism of Free and Open Source Software and the Inadvertent Politics of Contrast. *Anthropological Quarterly*. 77(3): 507–519.

Comnes, Gregory. 1989. Fragments of Redemption: Reading William Gaddis' JR. *Twentieth Century Literature* 35: 161–182.

Connor, Steve. 2008, 25 August. Thinking Things. Plenary presented at the European Society for the Study of English, Aarhus, Denmark. http://www.stevenconnor.com/thinkingthings/

Couldry, Nick. 2010. *Why Voice Matters: Culture and Politics After Neoliberalism*. London: Sage.

Coultas, Brenda. 2003. *A Handmade Museum*. Saint Paul, MN: Coffeehouse Press.

Cowart, David. 2003. *Don DeLillo: The Physics of Language*. Athens: University of Georgia Press.

Cran, Rona. 2014. *Collage in Twentieth-Century Art, Literature and Culture*. London: Routledge.

Crangle, Sara. 2015. Mina Loy. In *A History of Modernist Poetry*, eds. Alex Davis, and Lee M. Jenkins, 275–302. Cambridge: Cambridge University Press.

Crosland, Margaret. 1999. *The Enigma of Giorgio de Chirico*. London: Peter Owen.

Daugherty, Tracy. 2009. *Hiding Man: A Biography of Donald Barthelme*. New York: St Martin's Press.

Deleuze, Félix, and Gilles Guattari. 1983 [1972]. *Anti-Oedipus: Capitalism and Schizophrenia*, vol. 1. Trans. Robert Hurley, Mark Seem and Helen R. Lane. Minneapolis: University of Minnesota Press.

DeLillo, Don. 1971. *Americana*. London: Penguin.

———. 1986. *White Noise*. New York: Penguin.

———. 1987 [1983]. *The Names*. London: Picador.

———. 1997, 7 September. The Power of History. *The New York Times Book Review*, 60–63. http://www.nytimes.com/books/images_br/toolbar_br.map. Accessed 10 Aug 2012.

———. 2011a. *The Angel Esmeralda and Other Stories*. London and New York: Picador.

———. 2011b, 1972. *End Zone*. London: Picador.

———. 2011c, 1973. *Great Jones Street*. London: Picador.

———. 2011d, 1978. *Running Dog*. London: Picador.

———. 2011e, 1997. *Underworld*. London: Picador.

———. 2014 [2007]. *The Word for Snow*. New York: Karma and Glenn Horowitz.

———. 2016. *Zero K*. New York: Simon & Schuster.

DePietro, Thomas, ed. 2005. *Conversations with Don DeLillo*. Jackson: University Press of Mississippi.

Derrida, Jacques. 1996. *Archive Fever: A Freudian Impression*. Trans. Eric Prenowitz. Chicago, IL: University of Chicago Press.

Dewey, Joseph. 2006. *Beyond Grief and Nothing: A Reading of Don DeLillo*. Columbia, SC: University of South Carolina Press.

Dewey, Joseph, Steven G. Kellman, and Irving Malin, eds. 2002. *Underwords: Perspectives on Don DeLillo's Underworld*. Newark: University of Delaware Press.

Dezeuze, Anna. 2006. Neo-Dada, Junk Aesthetic and Spectator Participation. In: *Avant-Garde Critical Studies*, ed. David Hopkins, 49–71. Amsterdam: Rodopi.

Dini, Rachele. 2016a, 4 March. On aftermaths, language and silence: Don DeLillo's *The Word for Snow*. *Bookmunch*. https://bookmunch.wordpress.com/2016/03/04/on-aftermaths-language-and-silence-the-word-for-snow-by-don-delillo/. Accessed 5 Mar 2016.

———. 2016b, April. Don DeLillo's *Zero K*. *European Journal of American Studies*.

Doctorow, E.L. 2009. *Homer and Langley*. London: Abacus.

Douglas, Mary. 2002 [1966]. *Purity and Danger: An Analysis of Concepts of Pollution and Taboo*. London: Routledge.

Dugdale, J.S. 1996. *Entropy and Its Physical Meaning*. London and New York: Taylor and Francis.

Duggan, Lisa. 2003. *The Twilight of Equality? Neoliberalism, Cultural Politics, and the End of Democracy*. Boston, MA: Beacon Press.

Duras, Marguerite. 1984 [1954]. Madame Dodin. In *Whole Days in the Trees and Other Stories*, 83–126. Trans. Anita Barrows. London: John Calder.

Duvall, John. 2002. *Don DeLillo's Underworld*. New York: Continuum.

Egan, Jennifer. 2011 [2010]. *A Visit from the Goon Squad*. London: Corsair.

Ekstrom, Karin M., ed. 2015. *Waste Management and Sustainable Consumption: Reflections on Consumer Waste*. London: Routledge.

Elam, Keir. 1986. Not I: Beckett's Mouth and the Ars(e) Rhetorica. In *Beckett and/Beckett in Context*, ed. Enoch Brater, 124–148. New York: Oxford University Press.

Ellmann, Maude. 2008. Ulysses: The Epic of the Human Body. In *A Companion to James Joyce*, ed. Richard Brown, 54–70. Oxford: Blackwell.

Ernst, Max. 1970. *Écritures*. Paris: Gallimard "Le Point du Jour".

Evans, Franklin B. 1959. Psychological and Objective Factors in the Prediction of Brand Choice: Ford Versus Chevrolet. *Journal of Business* 32: 340–369.

Evans, David H. 2006. Taking Out the Trash: Don DeLillo's *Underworld*, Liquid Modernity, and the End of Garbage. *The Cambridge Quarterly* 35(2): 103–132.

Faber, Michel. 2014. *The Book of Strange New Things*. London: Canongate.

Fee, Elizabeth, and Steven H. Corey. 1994. *Garbage!: The History and Politics of Trash in New York City*. New York: New York Public Library.

Fifield, Peter, Samuel Beckett, and the Interwar Avant-Garde. 2014. *The Edinburgh Companion to Samuel Beckett and the Arts*, ed. Stan E. Gontarski, 170–184. Edinburgh: Edinburgh University Press.

Fónagy, Ivan. 1983. *La vive voix: Essais de psycho-phonétique*. Paris: Payot.

Ford, Simon. 2005, November. A Psychopathic Hymn: J.G. Ballard's 'Crashed Cars' Exhibition of 1970. *Slash Seconds 1*. http://slashseconds.org/issues/001/001/articles/13_sford/index.php#3. Accessed 30 Oct 2015.

Foucault, Michel. 1989 [1966]. *The Order of Things: An Archaeology of the Human Sciences*. London: Routledge.

Franzen, Jonathan. 2002 [2001]. *The Corrections*. London: Fourth Estate.

Freedgood, Elaine. 2006. *The Ideas in Things: Fugitive Meaning in the Victorian Novel*. Chicago, IL and London: Chicago University Press.

Freud, Sigmund. 1955. "The 'Uncanny'" (1919). In *The Standard Edition of the Complete Psychological Works of Sigmund Freud*: Vol. XVII, ed. James Strachey. London: Hogarth Press.

Frick, Thomas. 1984, Winter. J.G. Ballard, The Art of Fiction No. 85. *The Paris Review* 94. http://www.theparisreview.org/interviews/2929/the-art-of-fiction-no-85-j-g-ballard. Accessed 23 Nov 2015.

Frost, Andrew. 2013, 22 October. *Crash* and the Aesthetics of Disappearance. *Ballardian*. http://www.ballardian.com/crash-and-the-aesthetics-of-disappearance. Accessed 31 Oct 2015.

Frost, Randy O., and Rachel C. Gross. 1993. The Hoarding of Possessions. *Behaviour Research and Therapy* 31(4): 367–382.

Fry, Edward. 1966. *Cubism*. London: Thames & Hudson.

Fullerton, Donald A. 2013. The Birth of Consumer Behavior: Motivation Research in the 1940s and 1950s. *Journal of Historical Research in Marketing* 5(2): 212–222.

Gaddis, William. 2012 [1975]. *JR*. London: Dalkey Archive.

Gasoriek, Andrzej. 2005. *J.G. Ballard*. Manchester: Manchester University Press.

Gass, William. 1971. The Leading Edge of the Trash Phenomenon. In *Fiction and the Figures of Life*, 97–103. New York: Nonpareil Books.

Gordon, Lois. 1981. *Donald Barthelme*. Boston, MA: Twayne.

Gauthier, Marnie. 2001. *Moving Stories: Migration and the American West, 1850–2000*, ed. Scott E. Casper. Reno: University of Nevada Press.

Gifford, James. 2010. Anarchist Transformations of English Surrealism: The Villa Seurat Network. *Journal of Modern Literature* 33(4): 57–71.

Goddard, James, and David Pringle. 1975, 4 January. Interview with J.G. Ballard. *Science Fiction Monthly*.

———, eds. 1976. *J.G. Ballard, the First Twenty Years*. Hayes: Bran's Head Books.

Goody, Alex. 2007. *Modernist Articulations: A Cultural Study of Djuna Barnes, Mina Loy, and Gertrude Stein*. Basingstoke: Palgrave Macmillan.

————. 2013. *Technology, Literature, and Culture*. Oxford: Wiley.

Goldstone, Bud, Arloa Goldstone, and Paquin Goldstone. 1997. *The Loss Angeles Watts Towers*. Los Angeles: Getty Conservation Institute and the J. Paul Getty Museaum.

Gonzalez, Evelyn Diaz. 2004. *The Bronx*. New York: Columbia University Press.

Gordon, Leslie. 1981. *Donald Barthelme*. Boston, MA: Twayne.

Graeber, David. 2011. *Debt: The Last 5,000 Years*. New York: Melville House Publishing.

Greenberg, Clement. 1986. *The Collected Essays and Criticism Volume Four*, ed. John O'Brien. Chicago, IL: Chicago University Press.

Groes, Sebastian. 2011. The Texture of Modernity in J.G. Ballard's *Crash, Concrete Island* and *High Rise*. In *J.G. Ballard: Visions and Revisions*, eds. Jeanette Baxter and Rowland Wymer, 123–141. London: Palgrave Macmillan.

Guggenheim, Peggy. 1979. *Out of this Century: Confessions of an Art Addict*. New York: Universe.

Hawkins, Gay, and Stephen Muecke, eds. 2003. *Culture and Waste: The Creation and Destruction of Value*. New York and Oxford: Rowman & Littlefield Publishers.

Harvey, David. 1991. *The Condition of Postmodernity: An Enquiry into the Origins of Cultural Exchange*. Oxford: Blackwell.

————. 2005. *A Brief History of Neoliberalism*. Oxford: Oxford University Press.

————. 2006. *Spaces of Global Capitalism*. London: Verso.

————. 2010. *The Enigma of Capital: And the Crises of Capitalism*. Oxford: Oxford University Press.

Harvey, Penny, et al. 2014. *Objects and Materials: A Routledge Companion*. London: Routledge.

Hauser, Susanne. 2002. Waste into Heritage: Remarks on Materials in the Arts, on Memories and the Museum. In *Waste-Site Stories: The Recycling of Memory*, eds. Brian Neville, and Johanne Villeneuve, 39–54. Albany: State University of New York Press.

Hayden, Sarah. 2014. Introduction. In *Insel*, 3–12. New York and London: Melville House.

Herring, Scott. 2011a. Material Deviance: Theorizing Queer Objecthood. *Postmodern Culture* 21(2): 45 pars.

————. 2011b. Collyer Curiosa: A Brief History of Hoarding. *Criticisms* 53(2): 159–188.

————. 2014. *The Hoarders: Material Deviance in Modern American Culture*. Chicago, IL: University of Chicago Press.

Heyler, Ruth. 1999. 'Refuse Heaped Many Stories High': DeLillo, Dirt and Disorder. *Modern Fiction Studies* 45: 987–1006.

Highmore, Ben. 2002. Benjamin's Trash Aesthetics. In *Everyday Life and Cultural Theory: An Introduction*, 60–75. London: Routledge.

Howard, Vicki. 2006. Rings and the Birth of a Tradition. In *Brides, Inc: American Weddings and the Business of Tradition*, 33–70. Philadelphia: University of Pennsylvania Press.

Hubert, Renée Riese. 1972, Autumn. The Fabulous Fiction of Two Surrealist Artists. *New Literary History* 4(1): 151–166. http://www.jstor.org/stable/468498. Accessed 4 Jan 2012.

Huyssen, Andreas. 1986. *After the Great Divide: Modernism, Mass Culture, Postmodernism*. Bloomington: Indiana University Press.

Jacobs, Jane. 1961. *The Death and Life of Great American Cities*. New York: Random House.

Jeffries, Stuart and Paola Cocozza. 2016, 1 March. Goodbye to Curtains and Clutter: How we Learned to Buy Less Stuff. *The Guardian*. http://www.theguardian.com/society/2016/mar/01/goodbye-curtains-clutter-learned-to-buy-less-stuff-shopping. Accessed 2 Mar 2016.

Johnston, John. 1990. JR and the Flux of Capital. *Revue Française d'Études Américaine* 45: 161–171.

Joyce, James. 2000. *Ulysses*. London: Penguin.

Khaleeli, Homa. 2015, 3 March. End of the Line for Stuff that's Bound to Die? *The Guardian*. http://www.theguardian.com/technology/shortcuts/2015/mar/03/has-planned-obsolesence-had-its-day-design. Accessed 2 Mar 2016.

Kennedy, Greg. 2007. *An Ontology of Trash: The Disposable and its Problematic Nature*. Albany: State University of New York Press.

Kenner, Hugh. 1961. *Samuel Beckett: A Critical Study*. New York: Grove Press.

Kindleberger, Charles P., and Robert Z. Aliber. 2005. *Manias, Panics and Crashes: A History of Financial Crises*, 5th edn. London: Palgrave Macmillan.

Kinnucan, Michael, 2011, 5 June. Beckett and Failure. In *The Hypocrite Reader*. http://www.hypocritereader.com/5/beckett-and-failure. Accessed 10 May 2015.

Klinkowitz, Jerome. 1991. *Donald Barthelme: An Exhibition*. Durham: North Carolina University Press.

Knowlson, James, and John Pilling. 1979. *Frescoes of the Skull*. London: Calder.

Koponen, Arthur. 1960. Personality Characteristics of Purchasers. *Journal of Advertising Research* 1: 6–12.

Kroll, Jack. 1968, 6 May. The Comanches Are Here. *Newsweek*, 112.

Ladino, Jennifer. 2010, January. 'Local Yearnings': Re-Placing Nostalgia in DeLillo's *Underworld*. *The Journal of Ecocriticism* 2(1): 1–18. http://ojs.unbc.ca. Accessed 28 Aug 2012.

———. 2012. Don DeLillo's Postmodern Homesickness: Nostalgia after the End of Nature. In *Reclaiming Nostalgia: Longing for Nature in American Literature*. Charlottesville: University of Virginia Press.

Larabee, Ann. 2000. *Decade of Disaster*. Chicago: University of Illinois Press.

Latour, Bruno. 1993. *We Have Never Been Modern*. Trans. Catherin Porter. Cambridge, MA: Harvard University Press.

Lautréamont, Comte. 1965 [1869]. *Maldoror.* Trans. Guy Wernham. New York: New Directions.

LeClair, Tom. 1989. William Gaddis's *JR.* In *The Art of Excess: Mastery in Contemporary American Fiction*, 87–105. Urbana and Chicago: University of Illinois Press.

LeMenager, Stephanie, Teresa Shewry, and Ken Hiltner, eds. 2011. *Environmental Criticism for the Twenty- First Century.* London: Routledge.

Leslie, Esther. Walter Benjamin's *Arcades Project.* Benjamin Papers/militantes-thetix.html. http://www.militantesthetix.co.uk/waltbenj/yarcades.html. Accessed 1 May 2015.

Leslie, Esther. 2010. Recycling. In *Matthew Beaumont and Gregory Dart*, ed. Restless Cities, 233–253. London: Verso.

Lévi-Strauss, Claude, 1992 [1955]. *Tristes Tropiques.* Trans. John and Doreen Weightman. London: Penguin.

Lindenlauf, Astrid. 2000. Waste Management in Ancient Greece, from the Homeric to the Classical Period: Concepts and Practices of Waste, Dirt, Disposal and Recycling. Doctoral thesis. http://discovery.ucl.ac.uk/1317693/1/271246_Vol_1.pdf. Accessed 14 May 2013.

Lista, Giovanni. 1983. *De Chirico et l'Avant-Garde.* Lausanne: L'Age d'Homme.

Lovink, Geert. 2009. *Dynamics of Critical Internet Culture: 1994–2001.* Amsterdam: Institute of Network Cultures.

Loy, Mina. 1991. In *Insel*, ed. Elizabeth Arnold. Santa Rosa: Black Sparrow Press.

———. 1997. *The Lost Lunar Baedeker.* London: Carcanet.

Lukács, Georg. 1967 [1968]. *History and Class Consciousness.* London: Merlin.

Maltby, Paul. 1991. Donald Barthelme. In *Dissident Postmodernists: Barthelme, Coover, Pynchon*, 43–81. Philadelphia: University of Pennsylvania Press.

Manalansan, Martin F. IV. 2014. The 'Stuff' of Archives: Mess, Migration and Queer Lives. *Radical History Review* 120(Fall): 94–107.

Mandel, Ernest. 1998 [1972]. *Late Capitalism.* Trans. Joris De Bres. London: Verso.

Mao, Douglas. 1998. *Solid Objects: Modernism and the Test of Production.* Princeton University Press.

Mars, Roman. 2014, 12 May. Episode 114: Ten Thousand Years. In *99% Invisible: A Tiny Radio Show About Design with Roman Mars.* http://99percentinvisible.org/episode/ten-thousand-years/. Accessed 30 May 2014.

Martucci, Elise. 2007. *The Environmental Unconscious in the Fiction of Don DeLillo.* London: Routledge.

Marx, Karl and Friedrich Engels. 2015 [1848]. *The Communist Manifesto.* London: Penguin.

Marx, Karl. 1983 [1867–1883]. *Capital: A Critique of Political Economy* Volume I. Trans. Samuel Moore and Edward Aveling. London: Lawrence & Wishart.

———. 2008 [1867–1883]. *Capital.* Trans. Samuel Moore and Edward Aveling. Oxford: Oxford University Press.

Maude, Ulrika. 2009. *Beckett, Technology and the Body*. Cambridge: Cambridge University Press.

McCaffery, Larry. 1982. Donald Barthelme: the Aesthetics of Trash. In *The Metafictional Muse: The Works of Robert Coover, Donald Barthelme, and William H. Gass*, 99–150. Pittsburgh: University of Pittsburgh Press.

McCarthy, Ann. 2010. *The Citizen Machine: Governing by Television in 1950s America*. New York: The New Press.

McCarthy, Tom. 2014. Writing Machines. *London Review of Books* 36(24): 21–22.

———. 2015. *Satin Island*. London: Jonathan Cape.

McHale, Brian. 2015. *The Cambridge Introduction to Postmodernism*. Cambridge: Cambridge University Press.

McKendrik, Neil, John Brewer, and J.H. Plumb. 1982. *The Birth of a Consumer Society: The Commercialisation of Eighteenth-Century England*. Bloomington: Indiana University Press.

McKewan, Ian. 2010. *Solar*. London: Jonathan Cape.

Metz, Nancy. 1979. The Artistic Reclamation of Waste in *Our Mutual Friend*. *Nineteenth-Century Fiction* 34: 59–72.

Miller, Tyrus. 1999. More or Less Silent: Mina Loy's Novel *Insel*. In *Late Modernism: Politics, Fiction, and Art Between the World Wars*, 207–221. Berkeley: University of California Press.

Miller, Benjamin. 2000. *Fat of the Land: Garbage in New York: The Last Two Hundred Years*. New York: Four Walls Eight Windows.

Miller, Cristanne. 2005. *Cultures of Modernism: Marianne Moore, Mina Loy and Else Lasker Schüler*. Ann Arbor: University of Michigan Press.

Miller, Caroline Georgianna. 2011. *Abstract Concrete: Experimental Poetry in Post-WWII New York*. Doctoral thesis, University of Michigan.

Millman, Esmera. 2004. Pop, Junk Culture, Assemblage, and the New Vulgarians. In *An American Odyssey, 1945–1980*, ed. by Stephen C. Foster Madrid. Spain: Circulo de Belles Artes.

Mirowski, Philip. 2013. *Never Let a Serious Crisis Go to Waste: How Neoliberalism Survived the Financial Meltdown*. London: Verso.

Molesworth, Charles. 1982. *Donald Barthelme's Fiction: The Ironist Saved from Drowning*. Columbia, MI: University of Missouri Press.

Monbiot, George. 2016. *How Did We Get Into This Mess? Politics, Equality, Nature*. London: Verso.

Montresor, Jaye Berman. 1989. Sanitization and its discontents: Refuse and Refusal in Donald Barthelme's *Snow White*. *Studies in American Humor*, 74–84. http://www.jstor.org/stable/42573293. Accessed 9 Dec 2015

Moran, Joe. 2009. *On Roads: A Hidden History*. London: Profile Books.

Morrison, Susan Signe. 2015. *The Literature of Waste: Material Ecopoetics and Ethical Matter*. London: Palgrave Macmillan.

Moretti, Franco. 2006. Serious Century. In *The Novel, Volume I: History, Geography and Culture*, ed. Franco Moretti, 364–399. Princeton and Oxford: Princeton University Press.

Moser, Walter. 2007, May. Garbage and Recycling: From Literary Theme to Mode of Production. *Other Voices* 3.1. http://www.othervoices.org/3.1/wmoser/index.php. Accessed 9 Dec 2015.

Nel, Philip. 1999. 'A Small Incisive Shock': Modern Forms, Postmodern Politics, and the Role of the Avant-Garde in *Underworld*. *Modern Fiction Studies* 45: 724–752.

———. 2002. Some of Us Had Been Threatening Our Friend Postmodernism: Donald Barthelme and the Historical Avant-Garde. In *The Avant-Garde and American Postmodernity: Small Incisive Shocks*, 73–95. Jackson: University Press of Mississippi.

Nicol, Brian. 2009. *The Cambridge Introduction to Postmodern Fiction*. Cambridge: Cambridge University Press.

O'Brien, Martin. 2008. Rubbish Literatures. In *A Crisis of Waste?: Understanding the Rubbish Society*, 35–56. London and New York: Routledge.

O'Hara, J.D. 1981, Summer. Donald Barthelme, The Art of Fiction No. 66. *The Paris Review* 80. http://www.theparisreview.org/interviews/3228/the-art-of-fiction-no-66-donald-barthelme. Accessed 8 Dec 2015

Olster, Stacey. 2003. *The Trash Phenomenon: Contemporary Literature, Popular Culture, and the Making of the American Century*. Athens: University of Georgia Press.

Orlando, Francesco. 2006. *Obsolete Objects in the Literary Imagination: Ruins, Relics, Rarities, Rubbish, Uninhabited Places and Hidden Treasures*. Trans. Garbiel Phias, Daniel Seidel and Alessandra Grego. New Haven, CT: Yale University Press.

Osen, Diane. 2002. *The Book That Changed My Life*. New York: Random House.

Osteen, Mark. 2000. *American Magic and Dread: Don DeLillo's Dialogue With Culture*. Philadelphia: University of Pennsylvania Press.

Paddy, David Ian. 2015. *The Empires of J.G. Ballard: An Imagined Geography*. Canterbury: Gylphi.

Parmar, Sandeep. 2011. *Reading Mina Loy's Autobiographies: Myth of the Modern Woman*. London: Bloomsbury.

Parsons, Liz. 2008. Thompson's *Rubbish Theory*: Exploring the Practices of Value Creation. *European Advances in Consumer Research* 8: 390–393.

Patteson, Richard F., ed. 1992. *Critical Essays on Donald Barthelme. New York*: G.K. Macmillan: Hall.

Penzel, Fred. 2015. Hoarding in History. *The Oxford Handbook of Hoarding and Acquiring*, ed. Randy O. Frost and Gail Steketee, 1–13. Oxford: Oxford University Press.

Phillips, Dana, and Heather Sullivan. 2013. Material Ecocriticism: Dirt, Waste, Bodies, Food, and Other Matter. *Interdisciplinary Studies in Literature and the Environment* 19(3): 445–447.

Piketty, Thomas. 2013. *Capital in the Twenty-First Century*. Cambridge: Harvard University Press.

Pilling, John, ed. 1994. *The Cambridge Companion to Beckett*. Cambridge: Cambridge University Press.

du Plessis, Michael. 1988. The Postmodern Object: Commodities, Fetishes and Signifiers in Donald Barthelme's writing. *Journal of Literary Studies*, 4(4): 443–458. doi:10.1080/02564718808529888. Accessed 31 Aug 2015.

Polizzotti, Mark. 1995. *Revolution of the Mind: The Life of André Breton*. London: Bloomsbury.

Polloczek, Dieter Paul. 1996. Recycling Semiotic Junk in William Gaddis's J R. *Compar(a)ison* 1: 203–29.

Potter, Rachel, and Suzanne Hobson, eds. 2010. *The Salt Companion to Mina Loy*. London: Salt.

Punter, David. 1985. Alone Among the Murder Machines. In *The Hidden Script: Writing and the Unconscious*, 9–17. London: Routledge.

Pynchon, Thomas. 1995 [1963]. *V.* London: Jonathan Cape and Vintage.

———. 2000 [1966]. *The Crying of Lot 49*. London: Jonathan Cape and Vintage.

———. 2013. *Bleeding Edge*. London: Jonathan Cape.

Rathje, William, and Cullen Murphy. 1992. *Rubbish: The Archaeology of Garbage*. New York: HarperCollins Publishers.

Reno, Joshua Ozias. 2014. Toward a New Theory of Waste: From Matter Out of Place to Signs of Life. *Theory, Culture and Society* 31(6): 3–27.

Restany, Pierre. 1988. *Nouveau Réalistes*. Trans. Editha Carpenter. New York: Zabriskie.

Richards, Thomas. 1991. *The Commodity Culture of Victorian England: Advertising and Spectacle, 1851–1914*. Stanford, CA: Stanford University Press.

Roe, Barbara L. 1992. *Donald Barthelme: A Study of His Short Fiction*. New York: Twayne.

Rogers, Heather. 2005. *Gone Tomorrow: The Hidden Life of Garbage*. New York: The New Press.

Rosenberg, Emily S. 2010. Consumer Capitalism and the End of the Cold War. In *The Cambridge History of the Cold War, Volume 3: Endings*, eds. Melvyn P. Leffler and Odd Arne Westad. Cambridge: Cambridge University Press.

Ross, Kristin. 1995. *Fast Cars, Clean Bodies: Decolonization and the Re-Ordering of French Culture*. Cambridge, MA: MIT Press.

Royte, Elizabeth. 2005. *Garbage Land: On the Secret Trail of Trash*. New York: Little, Brown.

Ruhrberg, Karl, et al. 2000. *Art of the 20th Century, Part II*. Köln: Taschen.

Salisbury, Laura. 2012. *Samuel Beckett: Laughing Matters, Comic Timing*. Edinburgh: Edinburgh University Press.

Sardin, Pascale, and Karine Germoni. 2011. Scarcely Disfigured: Beckett's Surrealist Translations. *Modernism/Modernity* 18(4): 739–753.

Sayeau, Michael. 2013. *Against the Event: The Everyday and Evolution of Modernist Narrative*. Oxford: Oxford University Press.

Schaffner, Anna Katharina, and Shane Weller. 2012. *Modernist Eroticism: European Literature After Sexology*. New York and London: Palgrave Macmillan.

Scanlan, John. 2005. *On Garbage*. London: Reaktion Books.

Sellars, Simon. 2009. Stereoscopic Urbanism: J.G. Ballard and the Built Environment. *Architectural Design* 79(5): 82–87.

Sellars, Simon. 2012. 'Zones of Transition': Micronationalism in the Work of J.G. Ballard. In *J.G. Ballard: Visions and Revisions*, 230–248.

Schmied, Wieland. 1980. L'histoire d'une influence: 'Pittura Metafisica' et 'nouvelle objectivité.' *Les Realismes: 1919–1939*, 20–25. Paris: Centre Pompidou.

Schoonmaker, Sara. 2007. Globalization from Below: Free Software and Alternatives to Neoliberalism. *Development and Change*, 999–1020.

Schroeder, David O. 1999. *Mozart in Revolt: Strategies of Resistance, Mischief, and Deception*. New Haven, CT: Yale University Press.

Shenk, Timothy. 2015, 2 April. Booked #3: What Exactly is Neoliberalism?—Q&A with Wendy Brown. *Dissent*.

Sierra, Nicole. 2013. Surrealist Histories of Language, Image, Media: Donald Barthelme's 'Collage Stories'. *European Journal of American Culture* 32(2): 153–171.

Sloboda, Nicholas. 1997. Heteroglossia and Collage: Donald Barthelme's *Snow White*. *Mosaic* 30(4): 109–123.

Soby, James Thrall. 1966. *Giorgio de Chirico*. New York: Museum of Modern Art and Arno Press.

1968, 24 May. Social Science Fiction. *Time*, 106.

Spaethling, Robert. 2000. *Mozart's Letters, Mozart's Life: Selected Letters*. New York: WW Norton.

Spelman, Elizabeth V. 2002. *Repair: The Impulse to Restore in a Fragile World*. Boston, MA: Beacon.

Starks, Tricia. 2009. *The Body Soviet: Propaganda, Hygiene, and the Revolutionary State*. Madison: University of Wisconsin Press.

Stanley, Jo. 1970. Ballard Crashes. *Friends* 7: 4–5.

Stearns, Peter N. 1997. Stages of Consumerism: Recent Work on the Issue of Periodization. *Journal of Modern History* 69(Spring): 102–117.

Sterenberg, Matthew. 2013. *Mythic Thinking in Twentieth-Century Britain: Meaning for Modernity*. Basingstoke: Palgrave Macmillan.

Stewart, Susan. 1984. *On Longing*. Durham, NC: Duke University Press.

Strasser, Susan. 1999. *Waste and Want: A Social History of Trash*. New York: Metropolitan Books.

Stuart, Tristram. 2009. *Waste: Uncovering the Global Food Scandal*. New York: Penguin.

Tabbi, Joseph, and Rone Shavers, eds. 2007. *Paper Empire: William Gaddis and the World System*. Tuscaloosa: University of Alabama Press.

Tajiri, Yoshiki. 2007. *Samuel Beckett and the Prosthetic Body: The Organs and Senses in Modernism*. London: Palgrave Macmillan.

Taylor, Anya. 1977. Words, War and Meditation in Don DeLillo's *Endzone*. *International Fiction Review*, 68–70. http://journals.hil.unb.ca/index.php/IFR/article/viewFile/1322/14305. Accessed 12 Apr 2014.

Taylor, Michael R., and Guigone Rolland. 2002. *Giorgio de Chirico and the Myth of Ariadne*. London: Merrell in Association with the Philadelphia Museum of Art.

Temko, Christine. 2013. Regulation and Refuse Matter in Don DeLillo's *Underworld* and Eugene Marten's *Waste*. *Interdisciplinary Studies in Literature and Environment* 20(3): 494–512.

Tereszewski, Marcin. 2013. *The Aesthetics of Failure: Inexpressibility in Samuel Beckett's Fiction*. Cambridge Scholars: Newcastle Upon Tyne.

Thielemans, Johan. 1984. Art as Redemption of Trash. In *Recognition of William Gaddis*, edited by John Kuehl and Steven Moore, 135–146. Syracuse: Syracuse University Press.

Thompson, Michael. 1979. *Rubbish Theory: The Creation and Destruction of Value*. New York: Oxford University Press.

Tournier, Michel. *Gemini*. Trans. Ann Carter. Baltimore, MD: Johns Hopkins University Press, 1983 (1975).

Trauth, Kathleen M. et al. Expert Judgment on Markers to Deter Inadvertent Human Intrusion into the Waste Isolation Pilot Plant. Printed November 1993 by Sandia National Laboratories.

Trotter, David. 2000. *Cooking With Mud: The Idea of Mess in Nineteenth-Century Art and Fiction*. Oxford: Oxford University Press.

Vale, Vivian, and Andrea Juno. 1984. *Re/Search: J.G. Ballard, 8/9*. San Francisco, CA: Re/Search.

Veerbeck, Peter-Paul. 2005. *What Things Do: Philosophical Reflections on Technology, Agency, and Design*. University Park: Penn State University Press.

Viney, Will. 2007, 11 December. A Fierce and Wayward Beauty. *Ballardian*. http://www.ballardian.com/a-fierce-and-wayward-beauty-parts-1-2. Accessed 30 Oct 2015.

———. 2013. *Waste: A Philosophy of Things*. London: I.B. Tauris.

Waldman, Harriet. 1992. *Collage, Assemblage, and the Found Object*. London: Phaidon.

Waldman, Amy. 1999, 22 July. Bank Dips Its Toe in South Bronx; Commerce Gingerly Follows Housing in Ex Wasteland. *The New York Times*.

Wallace, David Foster. 1996. *Infinite Jest*. New York: Abacus.

Wallman, James. 2013. *Stuffocation: Living More with Less*. London: Cruz.

Watts, Harriet. 1980. *Chance: A Perspective on Dada*. Ann Arbor, Michigan: University Microfilms International.

Weart, Spencer. 2004. *The Discovery of Global Warming*. Cambridge: Harvard University Press.

Weber, Max. 1958. *The Protestant Ethic and the Spirit of Capitalism*. New York: Scribner.

Weintraub, Linda. 2012 [1922]. *To Life: Eco Art in Pursuit of a Sustainable Planet.* Berekely: University of California Press.

Whitaker, Jennifer Seymour. 1994. *Salvaging the Land of Plenty: Garbage and the American Dream.* New York: Harper Collins.

Whitely, Gillian. 2010. Rehabilitating Rubbish: Histories, Values, Aesthetics. In *Junk: Art and the Politics of Trash.* London: I.B. Tauris.

Williams, Rosalind. 1982. *Dream Worlds: Mass Consumption in Late Nineteenth-Century France.* Berkeley and Los Angeles: University of California Press.

Williams, Richard. 1998, January. Everything Under the Bomb: Interview with Don DeLillo. *The Guardian,* 10. http://www.guardian.co.uk/books/1998/jan/10/fiction.dondelillo. Accessed 10 Sep 2012.

Wingard, Jennifer. 2013. *Branded Bodies, Rhetoric and the Neoliberal Nation State.* New York and Plymouth: Lexington Books.

Winnicott, Derek. 1989 [1953]. *Playing and Reality.* New York: Routledge.

Woolf, Virginia. 2002. *A Haunted House, and Other Short Stories.* London: Mariner Books.

———. 2003 [1926]. *The Common Reader, Second Series.* London: Vintage.

Zimring, Carl A., and William L. Rathje, eds. 2012. *Encyclopedia of Consumption and Waste: The Social Science of Garbage.* London: Sage.

Zola, Emile. 2008 [1883]. *Ladies' Paradise.* Oxford: Oxford World Classics.

INDEX

© The Editor(s) (if applicable) and The Author(s) 2016   237
R. Dini, *Consumerism, Waste, and Re-Use in Twentieth-Century Fiction*,
DOI 10.1057/978-1-137-58165-5

tenements, 123, 124, 148
Theory of the Avant-Garde (Bürger), 31n55, 33, 63n2
The Unnameable (Beckett), 68, 80, 90, 92
"thingly turn,", 3
things
commodities and, 3, 4, 26, 27n4, 80, 127, 148, 157, 165, 187
waste and, 2, 4, 12, 14, 26, 30n43, 45, 69, 88, 101, 102, 127, 130, 131, 143, 182, 188, 209
Thing Theory, 3, 26, 27n3, 88, 96n23, 185
Thompson, Michael, 5, 27n8, 106, 157, 160
TIMWOODS, 6
totalitarianism
eradication of otherness and, 106
hygiene and, 107
waste and, 19
Transubstantiation, 115. *See also* Catholic Communion
trash, 5, 9, 15, 17, 22, 25, 28n11, 28n12, 57, 69, 76, 95n10, 103, 105, 106, 112, 128, 129, 136, 137, 138n11, 139n21, 148, 167, 168, 173, 187, 198, 199, 204, 210. *See also* discards; effluvia; excess; garbage; junk; remainders; remains; waste
Tristes Tropiques (Lévi-Strauss), 203
Trotter, David, 21, 22, 31n45, 61
Twin Towers, the, 164, 189. *See also* 9/11; Ground Zero; World Trade Center
"Two Figures" (de Chirico), 41, 42

U
"Ultimate City, The" (Ballard), 220
Ulysses (Joyce)
advertising and, 21

waste and, 10, 21, 30n43
uncanny, the, 14, 63, 85, 143, 204
Underworld (DeLillo), 144, 150–5, 158, 164, 165, 172–5, 177n26, 178n45, 186, 188
unemployment, 12, 13, 27n9, 29n23. *See also* employment/ unemployment; human waste; redundancy; work
urban disaster trilogy (Ballard), 2, 25, 100, 112–14, 137

V
V. (Pynchon), 100, 101, 138n1, 138n10
vaginal discharge. *See also* waste, biological
value
art and, 20, 26, 46, 50, 56, 62, 127, 130, 132, 168
capitalism and, 2, 16, 17, 34, 109, 133, 144, 146
commodities and, 3, 4
objects and, 9, 16, 17, 25, 34, 62, 70, 71, 77, 89, 101, 215
status and, 3, 4, 7, 17, 19, 58, 61, 68, 71, 75–7, 106–8, 115, 122, 215
usefulness and, 82
waste and, 2, 4, 14, 19, 25, 26, 45, 56–8, 68, 87, 89, 101, 103, 104, 116, 127, 130, 131, 215
work and, 34, 37, 52, 56
Vietnam War, 155
Villegle, Jacques, 71, 72, 74–6, 78
Viney, Will, 27n6, 30n43, 113, 140n31
Volcker Shock, 144

W
Waiting for Godot (Beckett), 72, 90
Waldman, Harriet, 63n3